THE FOREIGN OFFICE AND FINLAND 1938–1940

The Foreign Office and Finland 1938–1940 looks at the ways in which the Northern Department of the Foreign Office approached matters pertaining to Finland in the years 1938–1940, concentrating on the particular issues of the proposed refortification of the Åland Islands, Finnish rearmament and aid to Finland during the Winter War with the Soviet Union. At the beginning of this period, the Northern Department officials aimed at giving support to Finland while, at the same time, attempting to create an environment where Finland and the Soviet Union could reach agreement, thus keeping Finland out of the German sphere of influence. Their belief that the security interests of the USSR must be considered when dealing with Finland changed after the Soviet invasion of Finland at the end of November 1939. From this point on, the ability of the Northern Department officials to influence policy towards Finland declined, as the Cabinet became more interested in the situation. Nevertheless, Laurence Collier, the head of the department and his associates, continued to recommend particular forms of action, and their ideas were frequently at odds with what was being decided by the government. Their recommendations for military intervention against the USSR went far beyond what the government was prepared to consider.

Craig Gerrard is law librarian and legal researcher at Weightmans, a national law firm. He was awarded his PhD by the University of Leeds in 2001.

CASS CONTEMPORARY SECURITY STUDIES SERIES

THE FOREIGN OFFICE AND FINLAND 1938–1940

Diplomatic sideshow

Craig Gerrard

FRANK CASS
LONDON • NEW YORK

First published 2005
by Frank Cass
2 Park Square, Milton Park, Abingdon, Oxon OX14 4RN

Simultaneously published in the USA and Canada
by Frank Cass
711 Third Avenue, New York, NY 10017

Frank Cass is an imprint of the Taylor & Francis Group

Transferred to Digital Printing 2005

©2005 Craig Gerrard

Typeset in Times by Wearset Ltd, Boldon, Tyne and Wear

British Library Cataloguing in Publication Data
A catalogue record for this book is available from the British Library

Library of Congress Cataloging in Publication Data
Gerrard, Craig, 1960–
The Foreign Office and Finland, 1938–1940 : diplomatic sideshow /
Craig Gerrard.
p. cm.—(Cass contemporary security studies series)
Includes bibliographical references and index
1. Great Britain—Foreign relations—Finland. 2. Great
Britain–Foreign relations—1936–1945. 3. Finland–Foreign
relations—Great Britain. 4. Finland—Foreign relations—1917–1945.
I. Title. II. Series.

DA47.9.F5G47 2005

First issued in paperback 2012

ISBN13: 978-0-415-65243-8 (PBK)

ISBN13: 978-0-415-35003-7 (HBK)

CONTENTS

ACKNOWLEDGEMENTS

There are a lot of people I need to thank for the completion of this book and the PhD thesis which preceded it. I spent a lot of time in the Public Record Office and the staff there were always helpful and friendly. I also visited the Ulkoasiainministeriö Arkivisto in Helsinki and am particularly grateful to Petriina Chen who worked there at the time.

Being a librarian myself, I am very well disposed towards libraries and the people who work in them. There were many libraries which I used in the course of my research. The staff at the Brotherton Library at the University of Leeds should receive special thanks for all the help they gave me. The staff of the Sydney Jones library and the Law Faculty libraries at the University of Liverpool, of the various libraries of Liverpool John Moores University, of the library at Liverpool Hope University College, and of Liverpool City Libraries were also of immeasurable help to me. The work that they do to keep their institutions running smoothly and efficiently is constantly underrated. The staff at the Finnish Institute in Eagle Street, London, have also been very kind and helpful.

I became interested in history at a very young age, thanks to my parents buying me Ladybird books on famous historical figures such as William the Conqueror and Oliver Cromwell, and taking me on visits to castles, museums and other places of historical interest. This interest continued at school and there were two teachers at Bridgefield Comprehensive in Halewood, Merseyside, who helped to develop it, Mr Fisher and Mr Evans. A great deal of what they said has stayed with me and helped me in addressing my work. I was able to develop research skills to pursue historical enquiry thanks to the staff of the Library and Information School at Liverpool John Moores University. What I learned there has helped me in my paid employment as a librarian and researcher at a law firm and in my research which went towards my MA, my PhD and this book. My MA, which I completed as a part-time student at Liverpool Hope University College, was also a necessary step towards the creation of this book, giving me the confidence to go further and enrol for a PhD, which again I undertook on a part-time basis. John Davies and Dr Mike Hopkins were stimulating teachers and vital in encouraging me to continue my research. I completed my PhD at the School of Politics and Information Studies of the University of Leeds and would like to thank Dr Clive Jones for the help he gave me in submitting my PhD and to Ms Caroline Wise, the Administrative Officer for the School. Most of all I would like to thank Professor Caroline Kennedy-Pipe, now of the University of Sheffield, for being the best supervisor I could possibly have hoped for. Other academics that I need to thank for their comments and advice are Dr Paul Doerr of the University of Acadia, Canada, Professor Glyn Stone of the University of the West of England, Professor Jeffrey Richards of the University of Lancaster and Professor Patrick Salmon of the Foreign and Commonwealth Office. I am also grateful to Tom Snow for the help he gave me. I would also like to thank everybody at Frank Cass who has helped in the production of this book, and Susan Dunsmore who checked the manuscript and spotted my mistakes.

My work at Weightmans Solicitors has also been of benefit in undertaking the research for this book. Working in a legal environment has helped to stimulate me greatly and understand some of the legal issues which were involved in the relations between Great Britain and Finland. Conducting research at the same time as holding down a full-time job is not easy, but working in the environment that I did made it easier. I would like to thank all the partners and all the staff at Weightmans, past and present, particularly my colleagues in the Best Practice team, Laura Wilkin and Andrea Furmedge. I also need to thank Mark Forman, solicitor, for his legal advice.

My family have always been very important to me. I mentioned earlier that my parents first encouraged my interest in history and I could not have completed any of my education, let alone a PhD, without them. My twin brother, Grant, is as interested in history as I am and we talk about various historical topics as much as we do about football or rugby league. My sister, Kirsty, died in 1999, but would have loved to see this book. Finally, my wife Helen has been extremely supportive during all the years of mixing research with work, taking holidays to visit archives, and working on chapters of my thesis and book when we should have been out enjoying ourselves. Helen is an English teacher and knows more than enough to complete a doctorate in educational studies, something which I hope the publication of this book will encourage her to do. Maybe then I will be able to help her as much as she has helped me.

Craig Gerrard
Liverpool
September 2004

INTRODUCTION

The Second World War (1939–45) and the period leading up to it were a time of great characters, responsible for events of incalculable importance. The decisions made by these people, Churchill, Stalin, and Hitler among them, shaped the course which world events took, the effects of which are still being felt today. Moreover, their actions, and indeed, perhaps most importantly, their image, still exert a strong hold on the popular imagination decades after their death. Churchillian literature shows no sign of abating, and his victory in the 'Great Britons' contest of 2003 has installed him even more firmly as Great Britain's leading political hero, as well as being identified as Britain's most potent historical myth.[1] Stalin, or the adjective derived from his name, is now used derogatively by the public when referring to any severe and repressive measure, from traffic wardens to bleak housing estates. It seems that a whole industry has grown up around television documentaries about Hitler. These leaders, and their immediate associates, played a critical part in the outbreak and outcome of the war. The decisions taken and the formulation of policy below this level will always hold less immediate attraction to the public, or even to historians. A.J.P. Taylor's remark that a diplomatic history of Britain's role in the early Cold War period was 'at best ... a competent précis of "what one clerk said to another clerk" during a period when great events were happening a long way from Whitehall'[2] was made with the intention of reducing the 'clerks' to the role of Rosencrantz and Guildenstern in *Hamlet*. If this assessment were true, then there would be little or no value in the hundreds, if not thousands, of works on diplomatic history, including this one. The 'clerks', having no effect on or input into the great events happening in the world would be no more than a distraction, possibly an amusing one, but probably an unnecessary one.

This book owes a great deal to those previous works in which clerks engaged in conversations with each other, and naturally places a greater importance on their actions. Rather than Rosencrantz and Guildenstern, these clerks can, at the very least, be seen as the girl in Thompson and Heneker's sublime 'Thing-ummy-bob'.[3] This is the most basic defence of a

1

study of their roles. In reality, the clerks could be influential in the construction of many policies. This book is concerned with the policy of the Northern Department of the Foreign Office towards Finland; in other words, it is a study of a small section of a single government department towards a very small country at a time when the world's attention was occupied with other matters. Put another way, it is the story of how a small department conducted policy in an area which was of complete indifference to the rest of government, and how they attempted to influence policy once the rest of government had decided that this area might, after all, have some significance.

Finland forms the main focus for examining the perspectives and actions of Northern Department officials, but clearly the diplomats concerned were conscious of the developing political situation in Europe and the effect that the policies that they advocated would have in Berlin and in Moscow. Viewed in this manner, the first five chapters of the book deal with the approach of the Second World War and the different entanglements that the European nations found themselves in once hostilities had started. Of course, events involving Finland may seem very insignificant when considering the origins of the war itself, but the officials charged with formulating policy towards Finland and the Baltic area had to attempt to further British interests against a background of a war that seemed inevitable. Britain and Finland enjoyed friendly relations but the possible Soviet alliance in the forthcoming war with Germany, which so many in the Northern Department coveted, was the main stumbling block when it came to convincing Finland to resist the temptation of entering into the German orbit of influence. The problems of pursuing incompatible policies with the intention of securing a perfect outcome are illustrated in these opening chapters.

The second half of the book details the changes in Northern Department thinking once the Soviet Union had invaded Finland with a view to installing a pro-Soviet government there. It was at this point that Northern Department influence in formulating policy towards Finland decreased because the invasion turned Finland from a country of only very peripheral interest to one of salient importance in the eyes of the British Cabinet. From 30 November 1939 onwards, British policy towards Finland was governed by the Cabinet and the influence of the Northern Department decreased commensurately. This did not mean that the Department ceased to have any importance and it certainly did not mean that radical alternatives to government policy were not advocated. The closing chapters demonstrate clearly how Laurence Collier and Fitzroy Maclean, the two leading members of the Northern Department, diverged in outlook from their superiors. The narrator in Robert Frost's poem, 'The Road Less Travelled', concluded that once a path is taken and 'way leads on to way', then no return is possible, yet the choice of paths was nevertheless there initially. Collier and Maclean advocated a different path to the one which ultimately 'made all the difference', and their perspectives, especially given the respect with which Collier is regarded by historians for his pre-war disdain for appeasement and Maclean's post-war fame, are surely worthy of attention.

Every historical narrative must have a starting point. There were, of course, many antecedents to the events with which this particular story begins. However, the remilitarisation of the Åland Islands has been chosen because it represented an attempt to interfere with the strategic balance in the Baltic region and was of vital interest to both Germany and the Soviet Union at a time when international relations appeared to be deteriorating so fast that war, at some point in the near future, was a distinct likelihood. The impact that the plans could have on these states was something that the diplomats at the Northern Department felt unable to ignore. Furthermore, as the initiator of the archipelago's demilitarised status in 1856, and as a guarantor of the reaffirmed status following the League of Nations' decision in 1921, Britain had an obligation to monitor matters in the area. The decision by the Finns and the Swedes to begin military preparations on the islands was taken because of the fear of war and the need to protect their own integrity should it come to that. War did break out, and Finland, at least, was unable to avoid becoming a victim of the momentum that all wars bring with them. The book ends with the termination of the Finno-Soviet 'Winter War', and the acknowledgement within the Northern Department and the Foreign Office that, whatever policies Britain pursued towards Finland, they could never be an important element in the future conduct of Britain's war with Germany or in Britain's foreign policy towards the USSR.

British and French policy towards Finland at the time of the Winter War has not been the most investigated aspect of the Second World War period, but major work on the topic has been produced and comprehensively documented by Max Jakobson[4] and Jukka Nevakivi.[5] Jakobson's work is still essential reading, despite its publication before the opening of the British archives, while Nevakivi has benefited from access to documentary materials. Nevakivi's work is mainly concerned with the decisions made at the highest political levels, and while he acknowledges the contribution of Laurence Collier and his associates in the early part of the book, their presence is not felt in his later chapters. Nevakivi deals expertly with the policies pursued by the Prime Minister, the Foreign Secretary and his leading adviser, Alexander Cadogan. In contrast, this present study is more concerned with the arguments which were taking place, and, indeed, the policy which was being formulated, further down the line. The PhD theses by Patrick Salmon[6] and Paul Doerr[7] both influenced the writing of this present work but, again, the focus of the present work differs from that of Salmon and Doerr. Salmon's concern is with British policy towards the Nordic countries as a whole, not just Finland, while Doerr's examination of the Northern Department is concerned with its relationship with and attitude to the Soviet Union – a subject of some concern to the present book but certainly not identical.

Policies pursued and policies recommended or suggested are all a part of this book. It is hoped that it can convey both the influence of a section of the Foreign Office at a time when the attention of the government was diverted elsewhere, and the limits of that influence when the government eventually did become involved, towards a small country, at a time of deep international crisis.

1

1938: BRITISH POLICY, THE ÅLAND ISLANDS AND FINNISH REARMAMENT

This chapter examines the British response to plans by the Finnish Government and military to fortify the Åland Islands, which lay in the Gulf of Bothnia between Finland and Sweden, and also looks at the British attempts at involvement in the Finnish rearmament programme. On both issues, diplomats working at the Northern Department of the Foreign Office in London aimed to hold or contain German influence and penetration into the northern Baltic area. As will be shown, in the case of the Åland Islands, the means of achieving this goal changed from opposition to refortification to qualified support for the Finnish proposals. At the same time that the British diplomats were pursuing this aim by attempting to convince the Finns that Britain was a better friend than Germany, the British were aware of the problems posed by what might be termed the Soviet dimension and the mutual suspicions which divided Finland and the Soviet Union. This chapter underlines the importance which the Northern Department attached to allaying Soviet fears, and preventing the expansion of German interests in the Baltic. Due to the competing interests of Finland and the USSR, this was not an easy matter, and this chapter illuminates the problems which the Northern Department had to deal with in pursuing this idea.

By the beginning of 1938, it was clear to British policy-makers that Europe was in the middle of a period of extreme tension and danger, with the distinct possibility that war would be the result. Of greatest concern was the fact that Germany had expanded its military influence into the Rhineland and Austria. These were regions which were of natural interest to Germany on ethnic, linguistic and historical grounds. Yet Hitler's actions left open the possibility that territorial demands could be made elsewhere in Europe. The diplomats in the Northern Department were aware that the Baltic was not immune to German penetration and hoped to prevent Britain's political influence and strategic position in the region from deteriorating.

The German *Anschluss* with Austria, continuing Italian involvement in the Spanish Civil War and the widening theatre of Japanese aggression in the Far East, provided sufficient material for more than a few sleepless nights among members of the British Government and policy-making elite during 1938. The disturbing scenario of encroachment by foreign powers into territory which Britain regarded as within its legitimate sphere of influence in Europe, the Mediterranean and the China Sea was enough to contemplate without assigning the status of immediate and pressing concern to areas outside the limits where Britain could expect to influence events directly. However, lack of proximity to the vital areas of British interest did not mean that states falling into the latter category were dismissed from consideration without comment or consultation, and low priority did not mean no priority. This notion forms the basis for this chapter: how was British policy towards Finland formulated at a time when major events were being decided around the world? To what extent were British and Finnish interests deemed to coincide? Where did Britain perceive Finland's sympathies to lie and how was the prospect of Nordic cooperation viewed? In what ways did London expect to influence Finnish matters? These are questions which matter for four reasons: first, their answers provide some kind of forerunner to the Winter War months of November 1939–March 1940 when Finland and the Nordic area as a whole did attain a position of prominence in British decision-making circles. Second, they introduce and illustrate the problems which arose in the attempt to upgrade a low priority area into an area of high priority (a status which Finland acquired during the Winter War). Third, they demonstrate the desire of the Northern Department to prevent Finland falling into Germany's sphere of influence. Finally, any major revisions of policy which Finland attempted to undertake would inevitably lead to a reaction from the Soviet Union, whom the Northern Department did not wish to offend.

British perception of Finland's relations with the Soviet Union

The two issues in Finnish politics which most interested the British in the late 1930s were those of rearmament and the status of the Åland Islands. These two areas overlapped. Both areas were tied into domains of more general concern in central and northern Europe as a whole. Discussion in policy-making circles (and quite often it got no further than discussion) and decisions implemented, were made against the twin spectres of Nazi Germany and Soviet Russia as both these states had an interest in Finland. Until 1918 Finland had been a Grand Duchy of the Tsar's Empire, while Germany had intervened in the Finnish Civil War in March 1918, helping to crush communist insurgents and drive the remnants of the Russian armed forces back to their homeland. The Treaty of Tartu (Dorpat) in 1920 ended hostilities between Finland and their former masters, in which

British torpedo boats operating from Finnish waters had attacked Kronstadt. The Treaty gave Finland control of the far northern Petsamo area and thus access to the Arctic but the confirmation of Karelia's status as part of the USSR provided a source of potential conflict which was only eased in summer 1922 when a frontier peace agreement was signed. Karelia was viewed by many Finns as belonging to Finland, and the first Finnish Government had even attempted military action to bring the territory under its jurisdiction. The Treaty defused some of the tension surrounding Karelia. On the surface, relations between Finland and the Soviet Union were relatively calm for the next 17 years.[1] However, despite a non-aggression pact signed between Finland and the USSR in 1932, suspicions remained on both sides of the border. Finland feared that Moscow entertained revanchist claims to its territory, while the Soviet Government, even at this stage, worried about the proximity of Leningrad to the Finnish border and the danger that Peter the Great's capital city would face if Finland were allied to any hostile power. This assessment was not unduly unjustified. The British Minister in Helsinki, Thomas Snow, observed 'a hatred and distrust' of the Soviet Union to be a characteristic of 'Finnish national sentiment' and expressed concern that this feeling could lead Finland to side with Germany in a war in which Britain was allied with the Soviet Union.[2] In addition, many ethnic Finns were to be found in the Soviet Republic of Karelia, and the Kremlin was aware of the desire of some in Finland to have them brought under their own sovereignty.

The uneasy relationship between Finland and Moscow posed problems as the international situation deteriorated during the 1930s. By 1938, the threat of a new war in Europe was no longer the figment of a disturbed imagination. The Third German Reich, under Hitler's guidance, was dismantling the onerous terms of the Treaty of Versailles bit by bit, to the detriment of the geopolitical stability which had existed since 1919. The Soviet Union, encouraged by the success of the first five-year economic plan and concerned by German expansion which threatened to end on the borders of the Ukraine, had begun moves which aimed to bring Finland within its security sphere. In addition, Spain's civil war, with its unsettling influence in the Mediterranean, dragged on. Europe was in its most unstable position for two decades. This was the daunting background in which the British diplomats and politicians concerned with Finland worked.

In general, diplomatic work can be eased by having a sympathetic partner to work with. It is not unreasonable to expect two nations with favourable views of each other to enjoy good relations and for the work of a great power to be made easier when a small state expresses a welcoming attitude. The presence of conciliatory and compatible perspectives ought to facilitate policies of common interest, or at least of benefit to the stronger power, being undertaken. It would, therefore, be short-sighted to consider British policy carried out in respect to developments in Finland, particularly regarding rearmament and the Ålands, without taking the general view which each nation entertained of the other into consideration.

Britain and the new Finnish Government

The 1937 election had produced a satisfactory result so far as Britain was concerned. The suspected German sympathies of Pehr Evind Svinhufvud, Finland's first head of state, had been replaced in the presidential office by the more moderate tendencies of Kyosti Kallio. The new President installed the Liberal A.K. Cajander as Prime Minister, who in turn brought fellow Liberal Rudolf Holsti, a noted Anglophile, into his Cabinet as Foreign Minister. Cajander also gave Cabinet representation to Social Democrats, ending the 'political quarantine' which had been imposed on them since the end of the civil war.[3] The incorporation of Social Democrats into the government was intended to heal divisions which had existed since the end of the civil war, and also send a message to Moscow that the new government was not dogmatically anti-socialist. Indeed, Holsti, the Foreign Minister, had lost no time in attempting to improve relations with Moscow. All this provided grounds for satisfaction in the Northern Department.

This seemed to present some cause for optimism in Britain regarding future Anglo-Finnish relations as a similarly positive outlook could be applied to the commercial area. By the mid-to-late 1930s trade between Finland and the United Kingdom was in a healthy state. Some 44 per cent of Finnish exports went to Britain, making the UK Finland's biggest market by far. At the same time Germany accounted for 12 per cent of Finnish exports and the Soviet Union only 1 per cent. It was particularly gratifying that Britain stood so far ahead of Germany. Furthermore, Finnish goods (principally mechanical and chemical pulp, timber and other wood-based products) maintained high export levels and good profit margins throughout the Depression decade. Transactions in the other direction were not quite so spectacular, but Finland's table of imports was headed by Britain with 19 per cent of the market, just ahead of Germany's 17 per cent.[4]

The conduct of Britain's regular business relations with Finland was handled by the Northern Department of the Foreign Office, with matters only rarely reaching Cabinet level, or even the Foreign Secretary. Laurence Collier headed the department; he was an opponent of appeasement and critical of some of the less democratic tendencies in Finland, notably the semi-fascist Lapua movement of the early 1930s,[5] and he suspected that the Finnish armed forces were inclined to lean towards Germany. Nonetheless, he had great sympathy for the Finns, an emotion which was to be evident in the difficult years which lay ahead.[6] His fears concerning

Germany had led him to conclude, as early as 1936, that Finland should be encouraged to establish closer ties with the Scandinavian nations, as a means of safeguarding its territorial integrity against any encroachment by its powerful neighbours, both Germany and the Soviet Union.[7]

The beginning of the Åland Islands debate

It was a question of sovereignty, or rather the rights of a sovereign nation to alter the status of territory under its control, which arose at the beginning of 1938 and tested British wisdom until the eve of war. The Åland Islands, lying in the Gulf of Bothnia between Finland and Sweden, had been awarded to Finland by a decision of the Council of the League of Nations in 1921, despite the fact that the islands were populated by Swedish speakers. At the same time, the League Council recommended 'the conclusion of an international convention to demilitarise and neutralise the archipelago'.[8] When the Convention was signed in October 1921, the signatory powers – Sweden, Finland, Estonia, Latvia, Poland, Germany, Denmark, Great Britain, France and Italy – reaffirmed an 1856 agreement on the demilitarisation of the Ålands, signed by Britain, France and Russia. The successor state to the latter, the USSR, lacking a government which was internationally recognised, was not asked to sign at the time, and indeed refused to do so when given the opportunity in subsequent years.[9] The question of how to respond to proposals to change the status of the islands regarding fortification was one which never interested the British Cabinet and the issue was never discussed at Cabinet level.[10] Presumably, it was regarded as an issue of only peripheral interest, which the Cabinet did not need to waste its time on. This was despite it being an issue which involved the interests of the two greatest powers on the Continent, Germany and the USSR. The Cabinet's indifference meant that the Foreign Office, specifically its Northern Department, was entirely responsible for a matter regarded as being of considerable importance to the security interests of the Soviet Union.

The closing days of 1937 saw press stories in both Finland and Sweden calling for the refortification of the Åland Islands. *Ajan Sunta,* the organ of the Patriotic People's Party,[11] Finland's semi-fascist party, led the way, referring to an article by a Dr Grussner in a German periodical claiming that such a step would represent the best guarantee of peace in the region. *Aftonbladet,* a Swedish newspaper with suspected Nazi affiliations, went further and reported that a group of Finnish and German officers had landed on the islands and inspected the dismantled forts. Within a fortnight this paper began to agitate for the Swedish Government to bring pressure on Finland to take steps towards establishing a military presence on the Ålands. More seriously, the Swedish newspaper *Stockholms-Tidningen,* believed to have strong contacts with the Swedish Foreign

Ministry, began to cautiously advocate refortification.[12] This newspaper interest lacked any official confirmation. In fact, General Oesch, the Chief of the Finnish General Staff, claimed that no plans were under consideration and that while a visit to the islands had taken place, it had only been made with the intention of increasing topographical knowledge and the party had included Captain Moore, the British Naval Adviser to Finland.[13]

The presence of a British representative undermined suggestions that the Finnish armed forces were acting with the connivance of the German authorities. Yet, despite this disclaimer from the military and the silence of the two Nordic governments on the matter, covert talks had indeed been instigated at foreign minister level in October 1937, when Finland's Rudolf Holsti had discussed the subject with his Swedish opposite number, Rickard Sandler. The correspondence which the rumours stirred up within the Northern Department was therefore not based on a hypothetical thesis.

British diplomatic response to the refortification news

However, in ignorance of such collusion, the Northern Department and the British Minister in Helsinki could only discuss their options in terms of possibilities. Thomas Snow believed that, in the event of heightened tensions in the Baltic region, and without a Nordic military presence, the Ålands would be occupied by the Soviet Union, an act which could lead to interference with Germany's iron ore shipments from Sweden ('a question which ... seems to be something like an obsession with the German military authorities').[14] He did not make clear whether he thought such Soviet expansion desirable. The alternative was, however, occupation of the islands by the Germans. Collier expressed the view that the overriding political consideration regarding Finnish moves to fortify the Åland Islands was that throughout Europe it would be seen as a move undertaken at German instigation. This alone was an argument for Britain to oppose refortification but he also felt that 'it is not desirable to release the German Government of anxiety regarding their supplies of vital raw material – such as Swedish iron – if they went to war'. As a signatory to the 1921 Convention, Britain was in a position to veto any proposed change to the status quo.[15] The only explanation for his comment that the islands would pose a greater threat to German interests without the presence of Finnish troops is that he believed that the chances of collaboration between Germans and Finns were reasonably high. This was an attitude which he would shortly reconsider.

For the next few weeks, the Finnish and Swedish authorities maintained their silence on the issue of refortification, but rumours of the possible change in the military status of the Åland Islands, far from being a talking shop confined to diplomats and Nordic newspapers, managed to find its way into the British Parliament. The Liberal MP, Sir Geoffrey Mander, raised the matter in the House of Commons on 15 March. He advised talks with the other signatories to the 1921 Convention with a view to the rigid application of the non-fortification terms. This ought to have been done, he reasoned, in consequence of the pressure that the German Government was applying in favour of fortification. When he was assured by Under-Secretary of State for Foreign Affairs, R.A. ('Rab') Butler that the Finnish Government would scrupulously respect the Convention terms, Mander told the House that he had 'reason to believe that this is another attempt at power politics on the part of Germany'.[16] In the wake of this statement, Georg Gripenberg, the Finnish Minister in London, called at the Foreign Office to enquire if 'there was anything behind' Mander's question, with its inference that Finland was at the beck and call of Germany. R.H. Hadow, First Secretary at the Northern Department, assured the Finnish Minister that Mander had been given no official briefing. Gripenberg, satisfied with this, told Hadow that his country considered itself bound by the Convention and did not wish to 'stir up a hornet's nest' by taking any precipitate actions.[17]

Thomas Snow and support for refortification

On 23 March, Snow wrote to Collier, begging to disagree with the Head of the Northern Department's assessment that fortification would ease German worries in the Baltic. On the contrary, Snow believed that the *Anschluss* had changed the situation; a move to restore military capability to the Ålands would give the appearance of reinsurance against Germany as much as against the Soviet Union. He also conjectured that remilitarisation would have the effect of increasing rather than lessening German worries in the Baltic, presumably because it might give the Swedes sufficient feeling of security to sever the iron ore supplies to Germany in time of war. As a parting shot, he pointed to Britain's status as 'the only power other than the Soviet Union to oppose Finnish aspirations on the Ålands'.[18] The inference was that such identification with Moscow was not something which would be viewed with equanimity in Helsinki.

A few days later, Collier wrote back, explaining to Snow that the information which Gripenberg had supplied to Hadow had suggested no inclination to arm the islands and that, therefore, the Minister should leave the matter alone unless he were to receive serious reports of activity, or intended activity, in connection with the Ålands.[19]

No such instructions were communicated to the British Legation at Stockholm, where the Minister, Sir Edmund Monson, was still interested in the treatment accorded to the islands by the Swedish press. Mainstream newspapers were now calling for a revision to the Convention and one, *Dagens-Nyheter,* had published a summary of a pamphlet written by

L.J. Sansamo, a member of the Finnish General Staff, advocating fortification by Finland alone. The paper's editorial commented that Sansamo and his supporters were hoping that the Swedish Government would sound out the British Government on the subject. In response, the Northern Department wondered why the Swedish Government was doing nothing to dispel the assumptions of the press, which had no basis in the policy of either the Swedish or Finnish governments.[20]

Snow had taken note of his instructions to ignore speculation unless he came across anything tangible, so it must be presumed that he felt some satisfaction when informing London of a conversation between Wing Commander Frederick West, air attaché at the British Legation, and Colonel Melander, Chief of the Military Intelligence Department of the Finnish General Staff. Melander told West that refortification would be aimed at Germany and their iron ore supply route and not the 'hereditary enemy', the USSR. When West asked whether it would be natural to expect some sort of protest from Germany if this were the case, Melander had abruptly dropped the subject.[21] This would suggest that Melander had neither the conviction nor authority to back up his claim and had done it in order to persuade the British to back refortification in principle.

However interesting the above despatch may have seemed, it provided no official confirmation of formal planning regarding the Åland Islands, and any actions remained purely hypothetical. Snow's next correspondence changed this. On 18 April, Snow contacted the Northern Department with the news that Finland's Foreign Minister, Rudolf Holsti, had told him that he would be discussing changes to the 1921 Convention with his Swedish counterpart, Rickard Sandler, at their next meeting. Snow had replied, according to his instructions, that the British Government did not wish to see Russo-Finnish relations ruined by the Åland question. To Collier he said that the assumption that refortification would be in the German interest was no longer applicable since Holsti was committed to better relations with the Soviet Union and would never deliberately further German interests. Collier remained to be convinced. He referred to Gripenberg's denials and also raised the fears of the Estonian Government, who were worried that any change to the status of the Ålands could bring an 'unpredictable' response from Moscow.[22] Collier's scepticism was apparent in a Northern Department memo on the possible attitude of the Soviet Union, the Baltic States, Scandinavia and Finland to an attack by Germany on Czechoslovakia, which made the assessment that Finland (along with Latvia and Estonia) harboured no illusions regarding German ambitions but were sufficiently anti-Russian to gravitate towards the German camp. It was predicted that if the Åland Islands were to be fortified, the defences would be aimed against the Soviet Union.[23]

On 27 April, Snow telegraphed London with the news that Holsti's meeting with Sandler was being delayed on the insistence of C.G. Mannerheim, the hero of Finland's civil war, the country's first regent, and a very influential figure, that Moscow must not be consulted on the matter. Holsti deplored Mannerheim's views, especially as the Soviet Minister in Stockholm, Alexandra Kollontai, had told the Swedish Government that Moscow was interested in the Åland question. Snow hoped that the Finns would not put any barriers in the way of consulting Moscow, and wished to represent to the parties to the 1921 Convention that changing circumstances demanded that their original guarantee should be substituted for individual undertakings to respect neutrality, leaving Finland and Sweden free to construct the necessary military works. Rather optimistically, he believed that the Soviet Union would have no objection to a scheme which would, in his view, most seriously affect Germany. As non-signatories in 1921, the Russians stood to be excluded from Holsti's plan as well as that of Mannerheim, but the third legal adviser at the Foreign Office, G.M. Fitzmaurice, in a long minute, argued forcefully that the 1921 Convention merely reaffirmed the terms of Treaty of 1856, which Russia had signed, thus giving the present Soviet state grounds for participation in any discussions.

Collier's position on refortification

Armed with the legalities and the knowledge of Finnish desire to reinstall fortifications in the Ålands, Collier set out tentative recommendations for British policy: first, it might be advisable to oppose fortification 'but not on our own account'; second, if the Finns were to consult Britain, they would have to consult the USSR as well; third, nobody other than signatories need be consulted. Having laid this out, he proceeded to address a letter to the Service Ministries, asking for their views on whether remilitarisation would, or would not, be to the strategic advantage of the United Kingdom. Snow was notified accordingly.[24] When Snow approached Holsti on 12 May, the Finnish Foreign Minister expressed doubt as to whether Russian consent was legally necessary but agreed that they would be informed of developments, in line with the wishes of the Swedish Government. Asked if the Soviet Government would be formally consulted, Holsti replied that 'consult' was too strong a word.[25] Although Holsti had committed himself to an extent less than the Northern Department might have hoped, it was certainly more than they feared, and satisfaction could be garnered from the moderate position from which Finnish policy appeared to be being steered.

Moscow's position on refortification

One indication of how the Soviet Government felt on the matter, and proof that Collier was correct in believing that Russian agreement was a *sine qua non* for a smooth ride in changing the military status of the Ålands, came in articles published in *Pravda* and *Moscow News* in mid-June. The latter was particularly vitriolic in its condemnation of what it assumed were Finland's plans. It warned that fortification would make Germany 'mistress of the Baltic' and that Berlin was being assisted in this process by 'Finnish militarists' who were acting on orders from the German Government.[26] This was, no doubt, overstating the case, but Chilston, the British Ambassador in Moscow, informed the Northern Department that the Soviet Government were 'a good deal perturbed at the [Finnish] proposal'. Hadow's comments on this message revealed his predictable belief that Mannerheim and his advisers wished to fortify the islands against the USSR. He also contended that Soviet strength, and the threat of its being used, were driving the nations bordering it towards Germany. Collier did not contest the fact that German influence seemed to be on the increase but, contrary to Hadow, he identified Soviet weakness, rather than strength, of being the cause. In any case, he saw no reason to 'doubt that the Germans want the islands fortified'.[27]

At that moment, the future of the Åland Islands remained unclear. So, for that matter, did British policy. The Northern Department favoured a balancing act. Collier's recommendations provided some guidelines but his query to the War Office (see p. 13), the Admiralty and the Air Ministry had been referred to the Chiefs of Staff Committee of the Committee of Imperial Defence. In the period before their considered reply (which took five months), the Northern Department could act with no certainty for fear of contradicting Britain's strategic requirements.[28] This did not prevent comment or reaction, as will be discussed below. In the meantime, another matter, important to both Britain and Finland, and not unrelated to Finland's Åland question, began to attract attention, that of Finnish rearmament.

Britain and the issue of Finnish rearmament

The policy of the Northern Department relating to Finnish rearmament, like the policy concerning the Ålands, was formulated with other countries in mind, namely, Germany and the USSR. Despite some internal debate, it was important from the British perspective that Finland remained as well disposed as possible towards Britain in order that it would be responsive to London's wishes. This meant attempting to manoeuvre Finnish policy-makers away from German influence, and creating an atmosphere in which the Soviet Union would not feel threatened by, or suspicious of, Finnish defence policy. The aims were remarkably similar to the British policy over the Åland Islands.

The notion of rearmament inevitably led to a number of competing concerns for the Northern Department: what was necessary over what was important; what was desirable over what was affordable; what was efficient over what was realistic; and this was not a uniquely Finnish problem in the late 1930s. The two great Western democracies, Britain and France, faced their own dilemmas. The Treasury and Prime Minister insisted on fiscal stability in Britain, while allowing for a rearmament programme which recognised the limits to which British defence spending could be extended,[29] and economic and industrial troubles hindered the rearmament programme in France. Germany had decided to build up its military capability significantly. The Soviet Union's capacity for producing hardware had increased, but the purges of the military in the mid and late 1930s had eliminated many of those most proficient at using it.

The Finnish Government, in recognition of an increasingly threatening and dangerous world, began to face its own problems following an investigation by the Department of War Economy at the end of 1937, when an appropriation to the value of 2911 million marks was proposed for the purchase of armaments, equipment and related products such as raw material, industrial products and buildings. This amount was not, however, commensurate with Finland's budgetary capabilities. It was unlikely that the country could afford to put so much money into this particular channel at a time of economic troubles with Finland trying to cope with the effects of the global depression. The public of a democratic country were unlikely to be happy at the prospect of a drop in availability of consumer goods, owing to the transfer of industrial plant to arms manufacture. Nevertheless, the sum of 2710 million marks for a programme to be carried out over seven years was accepted by the Eduskunta, Finland's parliament, in February 1938.[30]

In terms of the major events which were happening in Europe, and indeed around the world at this time, the Finnish question made only a very tiny splash. Nevertheless, the questions relating to the Åland Islands and Finnish rearmament were of significance in the wider context of European relations as far as the Northern Department was concerned. The question of providing the materials for Finnish rearmament was treated largely as a political matter by the Northern Department. Whether Finnish needs could or could not be met was something which had to be agreed by the War Department, the Air Ministry, and the Admiralty. The different perspectives of the diplomats at the Northern Department, on the one hand, and the practical concerns of the military representatives, on the other, were to be an invariably irreconcilable problem over the next few months. The requirements of Britain's own forces were the priority for the Service Ministries, and the fear at the Northern Department that British influence in Finland should not suffer, was not at the forefront of their minds.

Finland, although it did not rank very highly in terms of the priority Britain gave to foreign countries for the export of warlike materials, did rank above its Scandinavian neighbours. In 1937, it had been placed 11th in a priority list of 20 foreign countries for British arms exports. This was such a well-kept secret that Lord Chatfield, the Minister for the Co-ordination of Defence, was unaware of it. When the Department of Overseas Trade approached the Foreign Office with a suggestion that Britain help Finland by meeting their need for certain defence requirements, they admitted 'the low position of Finland in the general order of priority' and the difficulty which obtaining munitions for export would entail, but Collier decided that it would be worth asking the Chief of the Finnish General Staff to reveal specific Finnish requests when he visited Britain in the near future.[31] The Board of Trade doubted whether Britain could supply enough material to satisfy the Finnish Government's 'basic requirements' programme at the present time but thought it would be useful to ascertain what Finland might require for future reference. The Board had considered the possibility that Finland's proposed expenditure in the arms field might just afford the means to redress Britain's adverse balance of trade with Finland,[32] which as illustrated above (p. 8), operated much to the advantage of the Finns. Britain was buying more from Finland than it was selling to it.

Two communications from Snow gave a pointer to the motives which inspired British diplomats to seek opportunities to meet Finnish defence requirements. On 11 July, he made a proposal, which was endorsed by Collier, that he enquire of the Finnish Government what kinds of arms they intended to buy abroad and where they expected to buy them. A week later, he reported a conversation he had had with General Valve of the Finnish Navy, who was apparently anxious that as great a proportion as possible of orders should be placed with the UK but was concerned that his country might find them rather too expensive.[33] It was believed at the Northern Department that meeting Finland's defence requirements would be good for diplomatic reasons. A failure to do so would, in all probability, drive the Finns towards Germany, hence Snow's interest in ascertaining requirements.

Hopes of keeping Finland out of a dependence on Germany, which could turn into a political embrace, were given a slight boost when Snow met Colonel Olenius of the Finnish military on 13 September. The Colonel was convinced that his Defence Ministry would do all in its power to place orders with Britain, but asked that British firms should not solicit for contracts prior to an invitation to tender. The Commercial Secretary at the Legation, Eric Lingeman, exploiting the difference between advising and soliciting, recommended that the Finnish military would find it worthwhile to purchase cartridge cups from Imperial Chemical Industries (ICI), a British company. This suggestion was followed up immediately by the Finns, who approached ICI for the cups plus a consignment of howitzers. Unfortunately, ICI turned the offer down, owing to their inability to supply such goods in the quantities desired. In the light of Lingeman's recommendation this incapacity was a little embarrassing. Snow was very unhappy when the news reached him, fearing the effect it would have on the Finns' view of British efficiency, and lamenting the probability that it would give Britain the label of a useless source of supply.[34]

The possibility of Finnish patronage being awarded to Germany as a result of Britain's inability to meet requirements was increased further when it was discovered that the defence authorities were considering an approach to the Germans with a view to purchasing 17 aeroplanes on floats, capable of landing and taking off from water. The Bristol Aeroplane Company, the British firm most likely to meet aeronautical orders for exports, did not manufacture any planes of this type. Indeed, it had not even experimented with such a design, owing to the 'preoccupation with RAF orders'. Snow, informing the Northern Department of what he saw as a 'sad' situation went on 'to draw special attention to this position, which is all the more regrettable in that it will afford Germany the opportunity, for which it has been looking, without success up to date, of obtaining a foothold in the Finnish Air-Force'.[35] In response, B.E. Gage, a Northern Department official, suggested that

> while recognising the urgency of our own requirements I suggest that the political importance of keeping these supplies out of German hands is worth an enquiry of the Department of Transport and Air Ministry as to whether any exception can be made in these . . . cases.

Following up this suggestion, Gage was able to extract an assurance from the Air Ministry that the Bristol company was now in direct communication with the Finnish Air Department.[36] The affair of the seaplanes was to be resolved happily for the British, thanks to the efforts of Wing Commander Frederick West, Air Attaché at the British Legation in Helsinki. Following Snow's anxious communication to London, West had visited General Lundqvist, head of the Finnish Air force, and learned that the General would prefer to buy machines from the Bristol company and even construct planes to a Dutch design in Finland itself, than take business to Germany.[37] Lundqvist was not lying. The Germans approached the Finnish Air Ministry with a very low price for their hydroplanes but Lundqvist managed to push it even lower. Unwilling to take this kind of bargaining any further, the Germans refused to comply with Lundqvist's request and, on 6 October, withdrew their offer, leaving the path clear for the Finns to instigate alternative plans.

Snow had no doubt that this satisfying turn of events was due entirely to the work of West and believed that Lundqvist had acted as he had as a parting gift to West, who was about to leave the Legation staff. Collier expressed his gratitude and admiration for West, and even Lord Halifax was able to tear himself away from more pressing concerns to render thanks to the Wing Commander.[38] He had indeed performed admirable work in preventing German manufacturers gaining an advantage in Finland, and helped to satisfy the primary objective of the Northern Department in the Nordic area, which was to keep German influence at bay. British interest in Finnish rearmament was political, and to a lesser extent economic, rather than military. Finland was never considered as a potential ally to be drawn into a defensive arrangement – it was hoped that the Finns would not commit themselves to such grouping. The Finnish Government had always insisted that it occupied a position of neutrality and the British hoped to ensure that this would always be the case. The important thing for Britain was to prevent Finland from slipping into the German orbit, and matters appeared to be modestly working out towards this end.

The Northern Department and support for the principle of refortification of the Ålands

Meanwhile, further developments in the Åland saga had steered the Northern Department towards support for the principle of refortification. This change in thinking was initially occasioned by concern for a particular individual rather than a volte face on the diplomatic, political and strategic consequences of the Finns' projected policy. Holsti, during a conversation on the last day of May 1938, had given Snow reason to believe that his position as Foreign Minister was under threat from pro-German elements within Finland and Snow conveyed these fears back to London. Collier shared these apprehensions and minuted that 'we should do all that we can both in the Åland question and generally to make things easy for Dr Holsti', as he was 'the best friend we have' in Finland.[39] Alfred Duff Cooper, the First Lord of the Admiralty, shortly before his resignation, was to utter, quite unsolicited, similar views. This affair will be discussed later in this chapter (p. 20). The intention of the Finnish Foreign Minister to at least let the Soviet Union know what plans were being made was clearly preferable to what the General Staff appeared to want. On 10 June, Hadow circulated a memo, explaining the views of General Oesch (and, it was thought, General Mannerheim as well) who had affirmed Finland's right to trade with Germany and who expressed optimism regarding the army's ability to contain the Red Army, providing Poland and Romania were engaged simultaneously.[40] This was the view of the military rather than the government, which meant that the preservation of Holsti's more moderate and realistic views within the Finnish Cabinet was all the more desirable. Oesch's views also showed how attractive the prospect of an efficient German supplier could be to the Finns.

Britain's official position was expressed in terms of the Soviet Union's right to consultation and whether refortification would affect British strategic interest in any way. Collier informed Chilston, the Ambassador in

Moscow that he was of the opinion that 'any proposals are to be depre-
cated which are likely to be regarded, particularly in the Soviet Union, as
put forward at German instigation and in German interests',[41] but Collier,
for reasons detailed above, met Holsti on 12 July in an attempt to find a
position which Britain and Finland would find equally amenable. Holsti
told Collier that Finland and Sweden had agreed on a plan of action, that
the only country which would be detrimentally affected by remilitarisation
was Germany and that he hoped that it would be possible for Britain to
approach the Soviet Union, to convince them that they should not worry
and thus give consent to the plan. Later, when Collier considered this
question, he weighed up the problems which had been posed. To bolster
Holsti's position, an attempt to secure Russian co-operation needed to be
made and if, as seemed likely, the Åland question was going to be released
to the international public, this method seemed 'the one least likely to
cause trouble'. If Moscow refused to grant consent, then Finland and
Sweden should be persuaded to 'leave the matter in abeyance'. In any
case, if Britain declined to get involved in the manner requested, Holsti's
'already precarious position' would be further endangered and the
problem would not go away but would only be raised in a way less suitable
to British interests.[42] It is interesting to note that during the Anglo-Franco-
Soviet negotiations in Spring 1939 Molotov contended that British
involvement would satisfy the Finns regarding the need for protection in a
similar way to how Holsti thought British intercession would placate
Moscow over the Ålands.

However, this position was not universally endorsed within the Northern Department. As was demonstrated in minutes on the 'General Survey
of material resources and industry and their bearing upon national war
potential' produced by the Industrial Intelligence Centre (ITC), the
Northern Department had a high degree of scepticism towards any Finnish
stance on neutrality. A.S. Halford, a Northern Department clerk, interpreted the statistics supplied by the IIC as showing that due to the reserves
of copper, nickel and other materials held by Finland, it would be unlikely
that neutrality could be preserved in the event of war. If the proposed
Åland fortification went ahead, Germany would supply the materials
necessary to the task, thus cancelling out the work needed to prevent them
establishing a foothold. Collier disagreed, contending that Sweden would
provide the material in order to gain the consent of the Soviet Union. The
pessimistic Hadow suggested that Finland's lack of war industries and
effective supply line meant that their exports and resources should be considered as part of Germany's. Collier was far more confident than his subordinate, or even than he himself had been earlier in the year and
answered Hadow's criticism by saying that neutrality was a viable option
for Finland as a result of its friendship with Sweden. The positions of the
two men were not so far apart as they seemed. Halford and Hadow feared

a Finnish connection with Germany. Collier did too, but believed that this would only be a possibility if the USSR, feeling threatened by the prospect of militarisation in the Baltic, protested loudly enough to drive Finland into the German camp. If Russia were consulted every step of the way and assured that it would be Germany which would be affected adversely, the contingency would probably never arise.

Duff Cooper's correspondence, referred to earlier, arrived in the last week of August during his Baltic visit. In Duff Cooper's opinion, British consent to refortification ought to be given because if the islands were left unprotected in time of war, Germany could easily seize them to protect 'supplies from the north' and also because it would strengthen the position of the 'pro-British' Holsti. While Collier could not complain about the general thrust of Duff Cooper's argument, he did record legitimate reservations about precipitately airing this view publicly, worrying that if this were to be done 'the Soviet Government will not be accommodating'. Collier consequently briefed the Foreign Secretary, Lord Halifax, to this effect. He duly informed Duff Cooper of these fears and recommended that he refrain from making any public comment on the matter.[43]

Despite his own doubts, Collier's word prevailed and the Northern Department settled on a policy which accepted refortification, providing the Chiefs of Staff agreed and that Finland's Åland policy did not antagonise Moscow. In the end, no formal request for the kind of British intervention outlined above was made but this did not prevent the odd comment being made on the matter. Hadow, for one, thought that the second objective of keeping Moscow happy might be hard to realise. In early September he minuted his conviction that Mannerheim and the Finnish military were 'on the German side if Russia tries to reach the Baltic', presumably referring to the areas of the Baltic outside Soviet territorial waters. He also felt that Swedish 'neutrality and ability to trade with Germany in iron ore would continue'. *Stockholms Tidningen,* a Swedish newspaper, had reported that Finland would soon fortify Lagkar and Koker, the southernmost islands in the Åland group, a move which would help the Germans in any wartime race for the Ålands with the Soviet Union. In any case, Hadow doubted that Finland would wait for Soviet consent as Sweden now seemed to 'connive at fortification'.[44] This was not an unsupported conjecture. Erik Boheman, the Secretary of the Swedish Foreign Ministry, had told the British Minister, Edmund Monson, that the security of the Ålands was now of 'vital interest' for Sweden and that it would help Finland in the event of attack. Perhaps it was because Boheman saw Germany as the principal threat to the security of the Baltic area, or perhaps it was an attempt to win the support of Monson, but the Secretary General told the Briton that Germany was engaged in efforts to separate Finland from its Swedish neighbours, and was planning an occupation of the Ålands itself.[45]

Predictably, Hadow was not convinced by Boheman's reasoning. On receiving Monson's information from Stockholm, he contacted Sir Robert Vansittart, the Permanent Under-Secretary for Foreign Affairs, to apprise him of the news from Sweden. After relating Boheman's argument, he declared his own view that the Swedish plan was much more likely to benefit Germany than the USSR. His own information suggested that the Finnish military would be more inclined to use the defences against encroachment from the direction of Leningrad than Kiel. The iron ore route was vital and to protect it Germany would presumably hope to become 'master of the Baltic',[46] an assessment remarkably similar to that made by *Moscow News* earlier. Intelligence from Estonia also intimated that an affirmative German response was likely to be matched by an equally hostile one from Moscow.[47]

On 19 September, Hadow circulated a memo on 'Possible opposition to a German attack on Czechoslovakia by the Soviet Union, Poland, Roumania, the Baltic States and Finland'. In it he expressed his opinion that while Sweden genuinely hoped that fortification of the Åland Islands would be a means of preventing either Germany or Russia 'seizing the key to the Gulf of Bothnia', the Finnish attitude, personified by Mannerheim, saw the Soviet Union as the only danger and would be prepared to give covert assistance to Germany in the event of a European conflict in return for the promise of German help if the Soviet Union attacked Finnish territory.[48]

Hadow received further confirmation of his suspicions through Lieutenant-Colonel N.C.B. Brownjohn, a War Office official, with experience in Finland's Baltic neighbour, Estonia. Like the Estonians, the Finns hated the Russians, he declared, and while they would remain neutral in the event of a general European conflict if they could, they would welcome any assistance from Germany against an anticipated Russian attack. If such a war were to break out (and on 27 September, the date of this communication, it seemed a real possibility) and were to see Britain and the USSR fighting as allies, all possible pressure would have to be exerted on the Kremlin against taking any action which 'would drive Finland and Estonia into the German camp'. He feared that an alliance with the Soviet Union would do more harm than good 'by antagonising our potential friends'.[49] Quite what military use these 'potential friends' would have been is not something which the Colonel made explicit. Hadow minuted the following comments two days after Chamberlain's successful Munich visit had averted war over Czechoslovakia. This war scare had, he noted, shown the prevalent fear of Moscow which existed in the Baltic countries. This fact would have to be borne in mind if the next crisis was to bring calls for an alliance to be signed with the USSR. 'It is essential,' he emphasised, 'that Great Britain should not appear to further Soviet policy ... in the Baltic.'[50] This would seem to be an argument against protecting Soviet sensibilities over the Åland Islands, and deprecating (though not in so many words) attempts to involve Moscow in the refortification process. Why he thought it so essential to avoid alienating the Finns among others, when he thought they were certain to support German ambitions, is not at all clear. Snow also thought that a British alliance with the USSR would not be welcomed in Helsinki and that a 'stiff attitude towards Great Britain' was the best that could be hoped for.[51]

These fears of a closer relationship with the Soviet Union were lifted from an unexpected quarter on 28 September. R.A. Butler, the Under-Secretary of State at the Foreign Office, who, in common with Neville Chamberlain the Prime Minister whom he faithfully served, and who was as deprecatory of the 'benefits' of a Soviet alliance as his master, relayed some hopeful news from Geneva. He was spending time with the British delegation as matters began to come to a head over the border in Munich. Both the Swedish and Finnish Foreign Ministers had called to see him, he related, and had told him of their plans to militarise the southernmost islands to create a 'defensive belt' in the Baltic. This in itself would have created little interest in the Northern Department – they had, after all, heard it all before – but the news that Maxim Litvinov, the Soviet Commissar for Foreign Affairs, had reacted favourably to the scheme was worth thinking about. If true, it was something to relieve Collier's mind, but it did nothing to dispel Hadow's pessimism. Hadow doubted the veracity of the story. If the Finns were to fortify the Ålands with Soviet acquiescence, then presumably they would be used to deny Germany the supply of iron ore if a Russo-German war broke out. The influence of Mannerheim would see to it that this could never happen and that as long as he remained an informal 'Chief', then refortification could only serve Germany.[52] It turned out that Hadow was correct in maintaining a sceptical attitude: Sandler, the Swedish Foreign Minister, confessed in November that Litvinov had expressed no opinion during their conversation at Geneva.[53] Any optimism that Collier may have had was dissipated when the Soviet newspaper *Izvestiya* ran an article attacking the proposed militarisation of the islands and referring to a plot hatched between the 'Finnish fascists and German geopoliticians'. The Northern Department Chief sadly minuted that Holsti's hope that the Russians were 'coming round' seemed to be based on a false premise, as indeed was the information regarding Litvinov.[54]

Still, if Collier in London and Holsti in Helsinki had little to cheer about, the Soviet attitude had apparently done little to dissuade others in Finland from implementing their plan. The Czechoslovakia crisis in September, when it appeared as if war might break out between Germany, on the one side, and Great Britain and France, on the other, had, allegedly, convinced members of the government and the military that an unfortified archipelago would leave them dangerously exposed in time of war. There also seemed to be some satisfaction in the fact that the Munich conference had sidelined the Russians. Mussolini was being given the credit for this satisfying (in Finnish eyes) turn of events and Mannerheim had sent Il Duce his personal congratulations.[55] If nothing else, now was not the moment when Britain was about to drive Finland into a German embrace by a flirtation with Moscow.

The Chiefs of Staff's Report on the Åland Islands

The Chiefs of Staff's report, which the Northern Department had been anticipating since May, arrived on 21 October. The Chiefs concluded that 'in certain circumstances, fortification of the Åland Islands might have a favourable though distant repercussion on British strategic interests' and in no case could it 'react unfavourably on them'. The reasons given differed very little from arguments later taken up by Chamberlain's War Cabinet. These were that in the event of war with Germany, the Royal Navy would attempt to block Germany's supply of Swedish iron ore *en route* from the Norwegian port of Narvik, leaving the Germans completely dependent on the Baltic route starting at the eastern Swedish port of Luleå for the precious metal. If it appeared that the Soviet Union were to ally with Britain, Germany would likely seize the Ålands to forestall a Russian occupation and to keep the Baltic sea lanes open. If the islands were protected by the Finnish military, Germany could swiftly find the Luleå route severed by Russian naval operations. Munch-Petersen has argued that 'two unexpressed assumptions [lay] behind this reasoning'. These were that the Soviet Union had no chance of reaching the Ålands before Germany and that the Red Navy could wreak some degree of havoc in the event of the Germans failing to achieve this goal.[56] In addition, it could also be suggested that Britain's military planners ignored the possibility that Finland, having set up defences on the islands, might feel better disposed towards Berlin than Moscow. It was a question that the Foreign Office was unable to ignore in the arguments over refortification and rearmament. G.M. Fitzmaurice, the legal adviser, was the first to take issue with the specifics of the report. On 1 November, he argued that Germany had no need to physically seize the Ålands, merely keep them out of hostile (Soviet) hands and the Finns were just as good as the Germans in this respect. However, if the islands were left unfortified, then there was 'just a chance' that the Russians could reach them first. Taking this possibility into consideration, he felt that the Chiefs of Staff's conclusion that fortification 'can in no sense be unfavourable to our interests' was not proven beyond a doubt. The respective attitudes of the German and Russian governments seemed to confirm his argument, which ran as follows:

The Germans, as might be expected, are in favour of fortification, for fortification can in no case turn out to their disadvantage. The Russians, on the other hand, are against it and for the same reason. They perceive that fortification can only be to their disadvantage and cannot be to Germany's disadvantage. If the islands are left unfortified ... [the Soviet Union] may be able to seize them, while if the Germans should seize them this does not add substantially to the security which Germany would achieve if the Russians were kept out by the fact of Finnish fortification.[57]

In this case, Fitzmaurice contended, British interests would best be served by the preservation of the status quo and any scheme which sought to back refortification would need to be approached with great caution. By way of support, Fitzmaurice referred to the minute on the same paper by B.E. Gage of the Northern Department, which had also urged that the Chiefs' conclusions could not be unthinkingly acted upon.[58] Gage felt that the fact that the Soviet Union appeared to be bitterly opposed to fortification and the probability of a total reduction of British influence over Moscow following the Munich conference meant that Dr Holsti's hopes of British mediation with the USSR regarding fortification could not be realised easily. Collier and Laurence Oliphant, his immediate superior, both took note of Gage's short minute and particularly Fitzmaurice's longer assessment, but a higher authority poured scorn on such thinking.

Alexander Cadogan, the newly appointed Permanent Under-Secretary at the Foreign Office, minuted a rejoinder to the concerns of his subordinates saying that Erik Boheman of the Swedish Foreign Office had told him that the Swedish and Finnish governments were just about to present their plan to the guarantor powers (which included Germany) and the Council of the League of Nations (which included Russia). When asked about the likely Russian attitude, Boheman had replied that he could not see them causing any trouble. The clear implication was that unconditional support should be given by Britain to the Nordic wishes, as Cadogan was unwilling to accept the notion that Finland could show partiality to Germany. His willingness to accept the Chiefs of Staff's premises regarding the denial of Germany's iron ore by means of Finnish fortification, on the other hand, was very evident. Undeterred by this comment from above, Fitzmaurice composed an even longer minute. He explained more explicitly his belief that fortification of the islands, whether by Germany or Finland, would mean the denial of the same to the Russians, a state of affairs which could only suit Germany. Without a strategic naval base in the Gulf of Finland, the Red Navy would be unable to interfere with the German iron ore supply in any way. However, if they were able to reach the Ålands first, in the event of a European war breaking out, then their chances for effective naval control over the Baltic would be very high and

their likely less than 'scrupulous ... methods' (for instance, targetting ships in Swedish territorial waters) would help them in consolidating this state of affairs. Given the proximity to the Åland Islands which the Red Navy achieved during the tense days of the Munich crisis, which will be touched on later (pp. 26–27), Fitzmaurice's hopes of the Russians winning the race to the islands do not seem particularly far-fetched. Faced with Fitzmaurice's persistence, Cadogan was honest enough to admit that his own suggestions may have been 'amateurish', and the legal adviser's points were sent to the Chiefs of Staff for further consideration.[59]

Fitzmaurice's minute had the effect of reawakening some of the misgivings which the Northern Department had entertained about Finland conforming to German wishes. These had previously manifested themselves over the fears for Holsti's position. When Holsti did fall, in the middle of November, the initial fear was that German influence was responsible but calmer reflection revealed that Eljas Erkko, Holsti's replacement, had more in common with his predecessor than had been feared.

There was little change, therefore, in the Finnish corner. The same could be said of British policy. The Chiefs of Staff replied to Fitzmaurice's points in the middle of December, seeing 'no reason to depart from the views expressed in their earlier report'. The Northern Department, despite reservations, accepted the military opinion and the refortification of the Åland Islands became a cause compatible with British interests.[60] The next Finnish move was awaited. The Northern Department was in a position where it could react to developments but could not push its own views onto the Finns.

Finnish objections to an article by the RIIA

The Northern Department was moving towards accommodating Finland's position regarding refortification, but elements in Finland expressed concern over what they saw as misguided views on the part of the British. In May 1938, an odd incident had arisen which had threatened to cause a slight rift between Britain and Finland. The leading articles in *Helsingin Sanomat,* the most popular Finnish newspaper, had, on 12 and 13 May, been devoted to an attack on the Royal Institute of International Affairs (RIIA) *Survey of International Affairs* yearbook for 1936. The authors complained that Arnold Toynbee of the RIIA had represented Finland as a dangerous country, desirous of national expansion at Russian expense, and which was indulging in schemes to obtain German aid in the pursuit of this end. The yearbook had, they contended, conveyed an impression that the writer had used information from hostile sources, adding ominously, 'even if one must suppose he had access to British official information'.

On hearing this news, the Northern Department disparaged 'ill-informed foreigners' who believed that the RIIA was an organ of the

Foreign Office. Collier contacted Gripenberg to explain the true position, that His Majesty's Government were not responsible for the RIIA and that the author (who was not Toynbee) had not been given access to British official information. The Minister acknowledged this explanation and had in fact approached Toynbee, who had personally reassured him that the articles did not represent official British thinking. Collier then asked Snow to contact *Helsingin Sanomat* to explain the situation to the editor. Rather than go directly to the newspaper, Snow conveyed the information to Erkko to pass on. In reply he received a rather abrupt letter from Erkko, giving thanks for the explanation but regretting that the likes of Professor Toynbee should fall prey to German and Russian propaganda.[61] The yearbook had in fact contained two articles which dealt briefly with Finland. The first, in the introduction, did indeed conform to the claims of the Finnish press, but the second, while detailing the temptations which could face the Finns, went on to describe how the country under Kallio's Presidency and Holsti's foreign ministership was determined on improving relations with Moscow and also with London and Paris. This had not been picked up by the newspaper, nor had the RIIA's title page self-description of its own unofficial and non-political status.[62]

The affair caused only minor embarrassment to the British (outside the Northern Department, it remained unknown) but was a reminder of the sensitivities of the Finns, particularly for a government which purported to be breaking with recent traditions regarding the USSR. These sensitivities were heightened by the tense situation emanating from central Europe as the summer months moved on. In early September, Finnish Prime Minister A.K. Cajander made a speech calling for the 'extension of Finland's natural connexion (*sic*) with the great western democracies' and expressing the need to fortify the Åland Islands for the purpose of defence. He spoke of his hope that the Nordic nations would be able to preserve their neutrality during any conflict. Doubtless he was sincere in this, and his feelings towards Britain and France were probably broadcast to allay the fears that the Soviet Union almost certainly entertained about German influence in Finland. In response, Hadow gloomily scrawled a minute on the report that if war did break out, Kallio would be an early casualty, with Mannerheim probably taking over and then extending benevolent neutrality towards Germany.[63]

Soviet moves in the Baltic at the time of the Munich Conference

In late September, as Europe seemed to be counting down towards war, and with the eyes which would soon be fixed on Munich still gazing at Prague, the Finns were given a hint that their theoretical neutrality might not long survive a breakdown of peace on the Continent. Reports of the

alleged movements of the Soviet Baltic Fleet towards the Åland Islands, and disturbances on the frontier were rife in Helsinki, though they lacked official confirmation. However, on 28 September, the day before Chamberlain's historic meeting with Hitler, the Red Navy was indeed observed steaming towards Hankö, west of Helsinki. The next day, after the news from Munich had reached them, it was seen sailing back to its base. In relating this news to Halifax, Snow urged the Foreign Secretary to impress upon the Soviet Government that anything resembling a provocation towards Finland could be exploited by the Germans. Snow had been told by Holsti (during his days in office) that Germany, in circumstances such as these, would be likely to offer assistance against the Russian threat. In the end, the rather low key show of strength by the Russians in the Baltic seemed to have caused some disappointment in the German Legation in Helsinki (although it did show that it would not be impossible for the Russians to pursue an adventurous policy in the region). It did not quite tally with their scare stories of how a European war would be the catalyst for a Soviet invasion.[64]

Fears of German propaganda in Finland

Snow's report had outlined the nature of German propaganda in Finland, and how it was playing on the traditional fear of Russia. It was not just Snow who was concerned about German propaganda. Gripenberg told Collier of the fear that haunted Cajander of a probable German economic and cultural drive and his hope that Britain might try to establish a more prominent position. A visit to Finland by the British fleet would be good for both countries. Alfred Duff Cooper's visit had been appreciated but his resignation as First Lord of the Admiralty, following the Munich conference, had led to the assumption by Germans and some Finns that his interest in Finland would count against it with Chamberlain and his present colleagues. Collier had heard similar talk. He told Gripenberg that Snow had been told that the German Legation expected his recall because of his friendship with Duff Cooper. The Germans presumably hoped that these rumours would undermine Finnish confidence in Britain and would lead them to look at the Reich as a more reliable partner. They were also offering the Finns, at least in non-government circles, a lot more than the British could. According to Gripenberg, a group of 'prominent Finns' had been told while on a visit to Berlin, not only by Nazi leaders but also at the Wilhelmstrasse 'that developments were now impending which would make it worth Finland's while to stand well with Germany, as she would then be able to take Eastern Karelia and any other parts of the USSR she may wish to claim'.[65]

The Yartsev Plan

Such comments would have caused no surprise in Moscow. In April 1938, Boris Yartsev, Second Secretary of the Soviet Legation in Helsinki, acting on orders which came directly from the Kremlin rather than his immediate superiors, contacted Holsti with an unprecedented offer. Yartsev told Holsti that the plans of aggression which the Germans held against Russia would involve an attack through Finland, as a means to encircle Leningrad. If Germany were allowed to carry out these operations unopposed, then the Red Army would not wait at its own borders but would advance as far as possible into Finland to meet the enemy. If Finland were to oppose the landings, then Russia would be prepared to extend every possible assistance. In addition, he felt that the Finns should be prepared to cede the island of Suursaari in the Gulf of Finland to the Soviet Government.[66] The talks initiated by Yartsev were to drag on for a year without any tangible agreement being reached. The threat that Moscow believed Germany posed to Finland and the alleged promises which the Germans had been making were not taken by the British as something which would induce the Finns to automatically jump to the Nazi whip. Captain N.C. Moore, British naval adviser in Helsinki, believed that in the event of a war between Germany and the West, Finnish policy would be, first, to stay neutral as long as possible, second, to protest but to do nothing more if any portion of its territory were to be occupied by German forces, and, third, to resist to the last man if any attempt were made by Russia to occupy Finnish territory. Collier was slightly more optimistic, believing that the second point of Moore's analysis needed qualification – if the Åland Islands were attacked after Finland and Sweden had reached agreement about its defences, it would be impossible for them to do nothing. Even so, it was implied that the Russians were viewed in Finland as representing a greater threat.[67]

This perception held little currency at the Northern Department. While attempts at political subversion were thought possible, military attacks in the Nordic area were deemed unlikely. A memo by Colonel Vale, military attaché in Latvia, found its way to the Northern Department and offered the consideration that without exceptional weather conditions of little snow and hard frost, the Soviet forces would find the conquest of Finland a very difficult task. Collier was satisfied with this information. He had met Vale a few weeks earlier, while the Colonel had been on leave, and had been informed that stories of Soviet preparations for invasion had no foundation whatsoever. Their fortifications on the Finnish border were defensive in character and rumours of offensive action could usually be traced to German sources.[68]

As far as the Northern Department was concerned, Germany was the greater threat to Finland, in the sense that it was more likely to beguile the

Finns with supplies of war and other material. It represented competition to British interests in a way that it was inconceivable to imagine the Russians fulfilling, and this was the arena in which the contest for Finnish allegiance took place. Finland was never seen as a potential military ally in Britain, and Northern Department policy regarding the fortification of the Åland Islands, rearmament and general public relations was conducted with a view to keeping Finland away from Germany, yet encouraging it to avoid antagonising Moscow. Within a few months this policy had been modified and the British began to follow a line, in order to smooth negotiations with the Soviet Union, which, if followed through, would have compromised Finland's independent status, and left them with the avenue to Berlin as the most attractive on offer. Ironically, Germany, like Britain, would have been satisfied with a guarantee of Finnish neutrality. Helsinki would have liked the Soviet Union to recognise its desired status but the Kremlin wanted Finland to entrust its security to Moscow. Anything else would be seen as a security threat.[69] This incompatibility regarding Finland's position meant that, sooner or later, British aims in the region would be frustrated and Finnish neutrality would be violated.

The officials at the Northern Department were aware that the prospects for a lasting peace in Europe were deteriorating. In their policy towards Finland in 1938, they attempted to minimise German influence in the northern Baltic area. If Finland did not find support forthcoming from Britain, then it might be forced to turn to Germany. Fear of the Soviet Union was a constant presence in Helsinki and the policy which the Northern Department followed in 1938 attempted to satisfy the sensitivities of the Finnish and Soviet governments without allowing Germany to expand its influence and improve its political and strategic position.

2

1939: ATTEMPTS TO SOLVE THE ÅLAND ISLANDS PROBLEM

This chapter examines how the question of the Åland Islands was dealt with by members of the Northern Department of the Foreign Office and other British representatives, such as Thomas Snow, the Minister in Helsinki. The islands were seen as being an issue which could play a part in drawing up alignments at a time when the threat of war was growing across Europe. British policy was to agree to remilitarisation of the Ålands, providing the consent of all the signatories to the 1921 Convention was given, and with the extra proviso that the Soviet Union, a non-signatory, be consulted. The possibility of the islands regaining a military status had emerged in 1938, although no official statement of such intention had been made by the Finnish Government. The Northern Department, as demonstrated in the previous chapter, had maintained a cautious policy towards any changes, being anxious to satisfy Finnish wishes without provoking the Soviet Union. This chapter looks at developments following the formal announcement in early 1939 by the Finnish Government, in partnership with the Government of Sweden, of plans for refortification, when the need for approval from interested parties became imperative. For a while it appeared as if German consent would be withheld, thus damaging Germany's reputation in Finland and paving the way for what it was hoped in London would be a reconciliation between Finland and the Soviet Union. Interestingly, Germany's legal right to veto the proposals was brushed under the carpet. In 1938, the legal rights of the Soviet Union had been upheld by the Northern Department, despite being more tenuous than Germany's. It was further hoped that if Finnish and Soviet differences could be reconciled, then negotiations between Britain and the USSR would be helped. Unfortunately for the British, German consent was eventually given, while the Soviet Union constantly deferred giving a firm decision. Even when the matter reached the League of Nations Council, a decision was not reached, although hope still existed that a compromise between Helsinki and Moscow could be negotiated. During this time, Northern Department officials in general, and Laurence Collier in particular, were clear in their desire to see the Soviet Union included in negotiations. This was not the state of affairs in Munich on 29 September. The Northern Department's willingness to address the question of Soviet anxieties in the Baltic, with a view to isolating Germany in that region, have largely been ignored in accounts of the last few months of peace in Europe. This chapter reveals the year's developments regarding the Åland Islands and illustrates how the Northern Department's goals were frustrated.

Far from being a final rearrangement of the borders of Europe, Germany's annexation of the Sudetenland accelerated the demand for further territorial changes, principally by the Third Reich. At the Munich conference, which had led to the Czechoslovak Government being forced to accede their German-speaking areas to Hitler, the Soviet Union had been excluded from the decision-making process completely. This pleased some people in high office in Britain at the time. The British Prime Minister, Neville Chamberlain, had no confidence in the military capabilities of the Red Army and believed that, as an ally, the USSR could prove to be a great liability, not least because many European nations who were threatened by Hitler were no less suspicious of Stalin's intentions. Any accommodation with Moscow could drive these states into the arms of Germany. Views similar to Chamberlain's were held at the Foreign Office, as will be demonstrated, although there was no desire in the Northern Department to ignore Russian sensibilities completely.

The question of the Åland Islands went straight to the heart of the dilemma which the Northern Department faced and had no easy solutions. Foreign Office staff believed that if the Finns were denied support for their project for the remilitarisation of part of their own territory, then an inclination towards Germany, already suspected in the Finnish military, might occur in political circles as well. Equally, however, if Finland was given too much encouragement, then the Soviet Government, prone to seeing conspiracies and ulterior motives behind any action, could well interpret the Finnish plan, and British support for it, as being due to German instigation or at least connivance. The dilemma was further complicated by the lack of consensus in the Foreign Office as to which situation on the islands would best serve British interests. It seemed that the one constant requirement was that the Soviet Union be consulted on all projected changes to the islands' status, as this was deemed necessary to fulfil the demands of international law. Moscow's involvement in the matter was thought desirable, in some quarters, in view of the worsening situation in Europe. The Chiefs of Staff's report (see pp. 23–25) had declared that fortification could not be detrimental to British interests, but doubts had arisen within the Northern Department as to the accuracy of the forecast. These misgivings were to act as a brake preventing the Northern Department wholeheartedly committing itself to the approval of the Nordic plans. When approval was given, it was granted with little enthusiasm and with the condition that the USSR be consulted.

Opinion at the Foreign Office

Munich and its aftermath had made a big impression on Foreign Office personnel as a whole. An examination of what senior officials were thinking at this time helps to put the views of Collier, the most important British official so far as matters concerning Finland were concerned, in context. Collier was among the contributors to a series of papers submitted to the Cabinet in November 1938 under the collective heading 'Possible future course of British policy'.[1] His co-contributors included William Strang, head of the Central Department, Frank Ashton-Gwatkin, an economic specialist, and Gladwyn Jebb, who was currently serving as private secretary to Alexander Cadogan, the Permanent Under-Secretary at the Foreign Office. Strang, a rarity at the Foreign Office in that he was a product of the grammar school system rather than an alumnus of one of the major public schools, headed the most prestigious department at the Foreign Office. While advocating the strengthening of British defences in order to withstand a future German onslaught, he argued for a policy of delimitation, defending British interests in the Mediterranean and the Near East as zones of 'first importance to us', while writing off 'Central and South-eastern Europe' to German political and economic hegemony. Northern Europe failed to gain a mention in his assessment,[2] but he expressed a desire to see France break off its treaty obligations to Poland and, by implication, Russia.[3] To all intents and purposes, this was advocating a recognition of a German sphere of influence in the Baltic. Gladwyn Jebb went further by recommending that France denounce its pact with the Soviet Union with the 'unavowed' intention, 'reminiscent of Machiavelli' of indicating that Germany could always seek expansion in the Ukraine. The Soviet Union, in his opinion, would be a wholly unreliable and untrustworthy ally. Although he did call for a strengthening of Britain's defences, he did not want it to go so far as to place a strain on the economy, thus advocating a line which would not 'jar on the known sensibilities of the controllers of British foreign policy'.[4] He undoubtedly had Neville Chamberlain in mind. Alexander Cadogan, the Permanent Under-Secretary of the Foreign Office, agreed with these ideas. In general, he doubted the possibility of 'peace in our time' and envisioned a time when the British would find themselves 'back in the old lawless Europe'.[5] Collier took a much more idealistic line, arguing that immediate 'British interests' should not be the sole determining factor in the decision to intervene in European affairs. It was his paper which 'expressed most emphatically a disapproving judgement of the whole trend of recent British policy'.[6] These interests ought to take in moral as well as territorial considerations, in his view, a position which, if followed in practice, gave Finland the same importance as Poland, Romania or Greece.[7] Significantly he also advocated a *modus vivendi* with the USSR.[8] Unlike figures such as Winston

Churchill, Collier was part of the policy-making elite and the arguments he presented in this paper and later, especially in relation to Finland, came from a genuine position of responsibility. In assessing the importance of the papers, Canadian historian Donald Lammers contended that they made very little difference to government planning, and argued that the authors would have been taken aback if the guarantees of March 1939 to Poland and Romania had been predicted in November 1938.[9] In a completely separate memorandum, composed four days before Christmas Day in 1938, Collier warned that since the Munich conference, the evidence of Germany's intention to expand had grown. With reference to Finland, he pointed to the protests made by the German Minister in Helsinki, von Blücher, against a speech made by A.K. Cajander, the Finnish Prime Minister, in which he had advocated the expansion of trade with Britain and an increase in the use of English and French in schools. Collier also identified the Finnish IKL Party, a group with known fascist sympathies, as being subsidised by the German Government.[10] Collier's views on the European situation at this time are important in understanding his insistence that Finland consult the Soviet Union before announcing any change to the status of the Åland Islands. If this were done and agreement were reached, then the chances of preventing German hegemony in the Baltic would be greater.

The Swedish and Finnish plan for the remilitarisation of the Ålands

The Swedish-Finnish plan for the remilitarisation of the Ålands, which had been common knowledge in the diplomatic chambers of Europe for some time, was officially announced on 7 January. The plan involved 'the concession to Finland of the right to take all kinds of military measures of a defensive character within the southernmost part of the neutralised zone' and authorised the Finns to take certain measures of a defensive character in the remainder of the islands.[11] *The Times* reported the agreement two days later, noting that the delegations which would be set up by the two governments would 'notify' the USSR. Collier was unhappy with the assumptions which lay behind *The Times* piece. The paper seemed to think that 'plain sailing' could be expected from now on and that the agreement only needed the approval of the Finnish and Swedish governments, followed by the consent of the League of Nations. This reasoning ignored the fact that it was the British view that the Soviet Union 'must be consulted and not merely notified and that their consent is by no means a foregone conclusion'.[12]

Reaction to the plan

On the same day, Alexander Cadogan, Permanent Under-Secretary at the Foreign Office, held a meeting with M. Prytz, the Swedish Minister in

33

London, to be informed that both his government and that of Finland would now approach His Majesty's Government (HMG) as one of the signatories of the Convention, with a view to obtaining its approval for the change sought to the status of the islands. Prytz was sure that the Germans would have no objections and added that he believed the agreement of the Soviet Union was likely. After considering the memo which the Minister left with him, detailing the full terms of the Finno-Swedish agreement, Cadogan sent instructions to Sir E. Monson, the British representative in Stockholm, instructing him to make clear to the Swedish Government that the Soviet Union had a legal right to be consulted. He went on to say that HMG would raise no objections if the Soviet Union and the Convention's signatories were happy with the agreement. As the Finns sought to be released from the restrictions of the Convention, all parties would need to give their approval. If the Finns or Swedes were to give the impression that British approval would be given regardless of the rights of the Russians, a 'politically undesirable' message would be received by the Kremlin.[13]

Collier received some mildly encouraging news from Snow on 17 January. The Minister in Finland had spoken to Foreign Minister Erkko about the proposals and had been assured that as soon as they had been approved by the two parliaments, they would be presented to the signatory powers. When Snow repeated the consistent wish of HMG that the USSR be consulted, Erkko replied that Holsti had mentioned the matter to Litvinov, the Soviet Commissar for Foreign Affairs, while in Geneva, and Litvinov had, apparently, raised no objection, simply saying that he would bring the question to the attention of his government. Later in the conversation, Erkko said that the Soviet Union would be informed of the modifications and would be asked to give their support in the League Council. They would be informed in their capacity of members of the Council and as signatories of the 1856 treaty, but as they did not sign the Convention in 1921 they would not be formally asked for their consent to the new arrangement.[14]

The news which Erkko had reported from Geneva found some confirmation in a despatch from Under-Secretary of State R.A. Butler, who was with the UK delegation at the League of Nations. Butler wrote that the Finns and Swedes were hoping that the matter would come before the League Council in May. They were optimistic that their plans would obtain the consent of all the signatories and did not seem to think that Moscow would create any difficulties. Collier noted hopefully that it did seem as though the Soviet Government, as well as the signatories, would be consulted. However, Soviet suspicion could be expected, as it was the Finnish General Staff, rather than their Swedish counterparts, who were the prime movers and they were notorious for their susceptibility to German influence. If nothing else though, the Russians would be given a say at the Council meeting, due to their presence on this body. Fitzmaurice, third legal adviser at the Foreign Office, commented that in his opinion, reference to the Council was not really necessary, since the matter depended entirely on the Conventions of 1856 and 1921, and the plan would remain illegal until *all* interested parties (including the Soviet Union) gave their assent. This, according to Fitzmaurice, would be the best line for Britain to take, rather than to say that British approval was dependent on the attitude of the Soviet Union[15] although there did not seem to be too much difference between the two approaches in reality. Collier decided that the line holding that all interested parties must grant assent was the best one to take and consequently informed Gripenberg, the Finnish Minister and Prytz that HMG saw no objection in principle to the proposals on the understanding which they had maintained all along, that the other parties in general, and the Soviet Union in particular, be consulted.[16]

Russian sensitivities

A chance to sound out Soviet opinion arrived when Halifax met the Anglophile Soviet Ambassador, Ivan Maisky, for talks on 27 January. Halifax told Maisky that the British government had no objection in principle to the Nordic proposals. For his part, the Ambassador informed the Foreign Secretary of the misgivings his government entertained on the matter. The Åland Islands were of great significance to his country, he explained, pointing out the Russian fear that no fortifications which the Finns could install would be able to prevent Germany from seizing the islands in the event of war. If the Germans succeeded in this task, they would inherit a ready-made system of fortifications, upon which they could improve and use to establish a dominant position in the Gulf of Finland. On the other hand, if the islands were to retain their present unfortified status, then the Germans would find it much harder to hold onto them in a war. The Ambassador's comments contained traces of Fitzmaurice's reasoning following the Chiefs of Staff's report (although the legal adviser had felt that the Soviet Union could win the race for the islands) but raised some doubts in the Northern Department. Daniel Lascelles, First Secretary at the department, expressed worry that the seizure of the Ålands by the Russians would lead to Finland taking Germany's side in a war, whereas their capture by Germany would not have the opposite effect. Collier, however, held a much more optimistic opinion, minuting that the Finns would resist any attempt at invasion and that if they suffered casualties they would regard it as a *casus belli*.[17] The difficulty lay in convincing the Soviet Union, who had a far more urgent interest in Baltic developments than Britain, that this was the case. Gripenberg had assured Collier in mid-February that a German violation of any Finnish territory would lead to a state of war between Finland and Germany, but no official guarantee by the government of Finland had been given to this effect. If this was the key to Soviet acquiescence, as Collier believed,[18] then its implementation would not only lead to the realisation of the proposals but would initiate better relations generally between Finland and the USSR, and would remove obstacles in the way of a closer understanding between London and Moscow. Unfortunately, Gripenberg aside, there were no such signs that such a declaration on the part of the Finnish Government was imminent.

Collier could at least feel reasonably comfortable in the knowledge that the Finno-Swedish proposals had been publicly declared. The matter had been fixed firmly enough to be discussed in Parliament. On 15 February, Wilfred Roberts, Liberal MP for Cumberland North, and Sir Robert Gower, Conservative MP for Gillingham, raised questions in the House of Commons requesting information on the government's attitude towards fortification of the Ålands, and whether the likely response of other interested parties, including the Soviet Union, had been determined. In reply, Under-Secretary Butler stated the British position, but conceded that the views of other governments were unknown to him at that moment.[19]

The German position

The following week, some indication of German thought was gained when Freiherr von Welk of the German Embassy called at the Foreign Office and held a conversation with B.E. Gage of the Northern Department. He asked Gage whether British assent was conditional on the concurrence of the Soviet Union or merely on their concurrence being sought. Gage replied that it was the latter, but for fortification to fulfil the requirements of legality, Soviet concurrence should be obtained. In any case, the matter would come before the Council where the legality of any action taken without the consent of the Soviet Government would be discussed. Von Welk then informed Gage that his country were certain to give consent but doubted that the Russians would do likewise.[20]

This assessment did not particularly tally with reports coming from Helsinki. The German Minister, von Blücher, an aristocratic non-Nazi with known Finnish sympathies, had complained at the Finnish Foreign Ministry of unfriendliness shown towards his country. Foreign Minister Erkko answered that Germany had not replied to the Finnish request for approval of their proposals, while Britain and France had wasted little time giving their views. Snow attributed the dilatory attitude of the Germans as being due to difficulty in avoiding the League of Nations, a body which Germany had left years earlier, but Erkko 'did not exclude the view that the proposals might be proving less attractive' to Berlin than might have appeared at first sight. Collier saw in such a scenario a consummation devoutly to be wished for, as a refusal by Germany to consent to the plans would lose it the sympathy of the Finnish General Staff. He did, however, expect the Germans to grant their approval eventually.[21] By witholding assent, the Germans, as signatories of the 1921 Convention, would have placed a veto on the Finnish plans. Collier's comment, therefore, would suggest that his main interest was in precluding any possible growth in Germany's sphere of influence, rather than a desire to see the Finns bolster their defences *per se*. Alternatively, it might suggest that he was prepared to overlook legal objections to fortification provided they came from Germany.

In fact, German support for fortification had never been as solid as British personnel had assumed. Von Blücher, the German Minister in Helsinki, had advised his government as early as November 1938 that fortification of the islands would not necessarily be in Germany's interests. The Swedish Government and military, he contended, had no belief in a Russian threat and saw the proposals as a safeguard against German aggression. While the Finnish officer corps were well disposed towards Germany, the government and the centre and leftist parties which supported it were inclined to adopt the Swedish attitude. If the German Government were to be approached by the two Nordic governments for their approval, they would be faced with what would amount to a demand for 'our consent to a fortification of the Åland Islands *against Germany*' (von Blücher's emphasis).[22] Fear for the consequences for their country if the Finns were to be appeased in this matter was not confined to von Blücher. On January 20, less than a fortnight after the formal Finno-Swedish announcement of their plans, an official in the German Economic Policy Department minuted his opinion on the likely significance which a group of fortified islands in the Gulf of Bothnia would assume. The Germans, quite naturally, were as aware of the importance of iron ore shipments from Sweden as were the British. A strong military base on the route from Luleå, Sweden, to Germany could easily disrupt the traffic, which was so vital for German industry. If fortified, the Swedes would be more likely to succumb to British pressure to cut off German supplies, in the knowledge that the newly built fortifications would present an obstacle to any retaliation by the Reich.[23] It was this notion of Swedish participation which was mainly responsible for German anxieties. Sweden had no legal right to station troops on the island. After all, it was only one of a number of signatories to the Convention, all of whom had the same rights and responsibilities as the Swedes. A conference in the Wilhelmstrasse on January 17 discussed the Åland problem with barely a mention of Finland. It was agreed that the Swedish presence on the islands could have dire consequences for the iron ore supply and that the Swedish Government would have to provide guarantees for its future. However, the most frightening prospect was that of a Soviet seizure. As the paper's author,

Lieutenant Commander Neubauer, concluded, the most important thing, as far as the Germans were concerned, was for the Ålands to 'remain neutralized and the powers defending the islands [to] remain neutral'.[24] The dilemma which the Germans had to face, therefore, was that unarmed neutrality could lead to Soviet occupation, while Swedish involvement in a military presence could keep the Russians out but could possibly be turned against Germany.

An important factor in restraining the Germans from informing the Finns of their intentions was the lack of public response from the Soviet Union. It could be assumed that the reply from Moscow would not be in favour of disrupting the status quo in the Baltic, but there was no certainty. In these conditions, rumours took on an exaggerated level of importance. In early February, von Blücher contacted the Wilhelmstrasse with a new story about Russian attitudes towards the Ålands. Erkko had, he wrote with some assurance, informed him that Maisky in London and Suritz in Paris had told the foreign ministers in the respective capitals that a secret agreement regarding the islands was in force between Finland and Germany. This provided Finland with the licence to fortify the islands and, in an emergency, put the fortifications at Germany's disposal.[25] As no record of such speculation by the Russians can be found in the Foreign Office archives, there is some reason to doubt von Blücher's information. Maisky, as related above, had expressed concern about the implications for his country's security if the Finnish plan were to be implemented, but had not gone so far as to suggest that the Finnish and German governments were acting in collusion for the purpose of Baltic domination.

The opinions at the Northern Department regarding the Finnish plans

The uncertainty over the German reply did not obscure the fact that Russian intentions remained similarly oblique. No definite answer regarding the fortification proposals had come from Moscow but there seemed no real grounds for optimism. Collier's suggestion that Finland supply the Soviet Union with an official guarantee had not been taken up by the Finns but it seemed that the Russians shared his way of thinking. In mid-March, Litvinov asked Erkko to receive M. Stein, a former Soviet Minister in Finland who had more lately served as Ambassador in Rome. When Erkko and Stein met, the Russian wasted no time in raising the matter of a guarantee. As his government could not be sure of the Finnish attitude in wartime, it would be desirable for the Government of Finland to make concessions to the Soviet Union over the Baltic islands of Lauanssarri and Seiskari, preferably transferring them to direct Soviet rule. Even with the offer of exchanging 'Russian Carelia' for this territory, Erkko refused. He told Snow that he feared that the USSR was intent on taking these islands and the Ålands at some point, perhaps before the outbreak of any hostilities. This assessment garnered a mixed response in the Northern Department. Lascelles welcomed the idea of the Russians gaining 'a forward line', as it would enable them to sever Germany's iron ore link from Sweden. He did concede, however, that while Russian domination of the entrance to the Gulf of Bothnia would be good news for Britain, it certainly would not be so for Finland. Collier expressed concern that if the Russians took control of any Finnish territory unilaterally, Finland would move closer to Germany 'more than neutralising any advantage' for Britain. If, on the other hand, the Finns asked the British to approach Moscow, advising them to drop the idea, then some good might come of it. The Soviet desire for a joint 'anti-aggression' declaration (aimed against Germany) could be used to dissuade them from the pursuit of actions which would drive the Finns into the German camp. If Moscow then asked for guarantees of Finnish neutrality, he argued that 'we would be in a strong position for pressing the Finnish Government to take measures which would make it impossible for their neutrality to be compromised by the pro-German elements in the Finnish General Staff'. He realistically concluded, however, that London was not in a strong position to bring effective pressure to bear on the Russians.[26] Munich had seen to that and the names of Chamberlain and Halifax carried far more weight than that of Collier in the Kremlin.

Snow was also worried about the possibly disastrous results of the Soviet Union seizing the two islands without any German provocation. Germany would be handed 'an excuse if not justification for intervention here on the lines it pleases'. Lascelles noted that the Northern Department was aware of the potentially calamitous consequences but argued that there was nothing to suggest that violent action was a genuine possibility: 'The Soviet Government, with all their faults, are not given to such methods', a naïve assessment in view of what was to happen later. Snow was informed of this view and told that no action would be taken unless the Finnish Government made a direct approach.[27]

News from Moscow indicated that the Soviet Government viewed the concession of the two islands as crucial to future developments in the Baltic. The British Ambassador, Sir William Seeds, reported his understanding that Litvinov felt that his government had no objections in principle to the remilitarisation of the Ålands but could only give an official answer when 'negotiations for a guarantee (in other words, those regarding Lauanssarri and Seiskari) were concluded in Helsinki'. On hearing news of this linkage, Lascelles commented that while these negotiations 'savoured of blackmail', they did confirm his impression that there was no immediate danger of the Soviet Union resorting to force.[28]

In early April, Wing Commander Johnson met with Colonel Melander, the Chief of Intelligence at the Finnish General Staff. The meeting took place within a week of Germany occupying what had been left of Czecho-Slovakia after Munich and revealing themselves to be, beyond a doubt, the most aggressive and expansionist state in Europe. In view of this situation, Melander told Johnson that although his country hoped to stay neutral, any state attempting to seize Finnish territory would be treated as an enemy. The absence of a reply from Berlin regarding the Ålands question may also have played some part in determining Melander's assertive attitude. It seemed that von Blücher felt that his country would withhold consent. On hearing this, Lascelles commented that German confidence in a benevolent Finland was not as strong as it had been.[29]

Attempts to mollify the USSR

Given the seemingly ambiguous position of the German Government, the hope for a positive response from the Soviet Union became more urgent. Lascelles retained his conviction that the intentions of the Soviet Government were 'to keep out of trouble as long as possible and to avoid all initiative'. This particular comment came as a response to information supplied by a 'high ranking Estonian politician' that the USSR would give consent, provided the defences installed were strong enough to survive any attack.[30] The cautious optimism which the Northern Department extended to Russian intentions was, however, not shared in Helsinki, in either British or Finnish circles. Snow was unconvinced by the Northern Department argument that the Soviet Union would not resort to force, as it did not correlate with the intelligence which Erkko had communicated to him. The Foreign Minister had received 'sure information that Russia would seize the islands in the case of hostilities'.[31] Although Snow thought that Finland would resist any aggression, he was certain that the first choice of enemy would be the Soviet Union. He then proffered advice which he had given before,[32] that the Foreign Office should make all possible efforts to dissuade Moscow from taking 'provocative action'. Given that Finland's preferred enemy was the USSR, making efforts to prevent the possibility of any 'prior action' by the Russians seemed to make sense. Snow seemingly believed he had played his own small part in this effort following his lunch with the Soviet Minister Dereviansky and the English historian E.H. Carr, a noted Soviet specialist and former Foreign Office official who had played a part in determining the Foreign Office outlook at the time of the Finnish Civil War of 1918. Snow had been asked by his Russian counterpart what he expected the Finns to do in the event of a German-Soviet war and in reply he had stated that Finland would treat the first power to violate its territorial integrity as an enemy. After considering Snow's communication, Lascelles decided that the Minister was right to urge restraint on Moscow but for somewhat different reasons. He felt that elements of the Finnish General Staff would like any excuse to move closer to Germany, and believed that they had recently been in touch with their German counterparts. Snow was accordingly instructed to inform Erkko that nothing could provoke Soviet aggression more than these 'confabulations'.[33]

In contrast to the view that Britain took a lethargic and apathetic, if not hostile, line with the Soviet Union at this time,[34] at Northern Department level at least, a much more favourable attitude towards Moscow could be observed. The orthodox interpretations that British proposals regarding the USSR lacked imagination can be challenged by an examination of the correspondence between the Northern Department and Snow. Quite clearly, Germany was viewed as the enemy, with Russia being seen as a possible ally whose ability to disrupt Germany's iron ore supply was a great attraction. The problem was that Moscow was lacking the opportunity to improve relations with Finland. Snow, who despite his suspicions of Russian intentions, was far from being anti-Soviet at this time, lamented the dilatoriness of the Soviet Union regarding a reply on the Åland question, 'thus depriving themselves of a golden opportunity of creating a favourable impression ... at Germany's expense'. Gage felt the same way, noting also that a favourable Soviet reply would help facilitate an Anglo-Soviet accord in any discussions.[35] Writing this minute mere days after the ill-fated Moscow talks were suggested, Gage unknowingly identified a major stumbling block, which would obstruct progress.

A glimmer of hope regarding the seizure of their 'golden opportunity' by Moscow arose when, on 21 April, the Soviet Minister in Helsinki, Dereviansky, informed the British Legation staff that his government's consent was dependent on their receiving a guarantee that the Åland Islands would be used exclusively for the defence of Finland and Sweden against aggression. This stance suggested that the Soviet object was to guarantee that the Ålands would not be used by Germany to prevent vessels from operating in the Gulf of Bothnia against German shipping. Lascelles commented that it would be difficult for the Finns to refuse such a proposal, assuming of course that it was made.[36]

German agreement to the plan

Any optimistic thoughts that the Soviet Union could exploit the hesitation of Germany were squashed on 25 April, when von Blücher, the German representative in Helsinki, informed Erkko of his government's consent to refortification.[37] The news of the seeming change in the German Government's attitude was picked up on in the War Office some three weeks later by Colonel Barker Benfield. He told Frank Roberts of the Foreign Office about the despatch sent to him by Lieutenant-Colonel Vale, military attaché in Latvia. Vale had contended that since Germany had appeared to be withholding consent to fortification only a few weeks earlier, the change of mind must be due to the signing of non-aggression pacts by Finland and Sweden. Benfield doubted this logic, as both of those states had turned down the German offer of a pact.[38] Collier, however, found the contention plausible, commenting that even if Germany had not got the pacts, other motives, such as the need to avoid antagonising Finland, would surely have played a part.[39] A further blow came when Finnish-Soviet negotiations over Seiskari and Lauanssari broke down. Snow pointed out, once again, the dangers of precipitate Soviet action which he thought might be imminent. Armed with this information and advice, Lascelles composed a memorandum stating that so far no such message had been conveyed to the Soviet Government because: (a) there seemed no likelihood of a Soviet attack; (b) the Finns had not approached His Majesty's Government to undertake an intercession of this kind, although Snow had warned that they would be unlikely to, as many high-ranking Finns would be glad of the excuse of Soviet provocation in order to side with Germany; and (c) Ambassador Seeds believed that a direct request of this nature would be poorly received by the Soviet Government who were, in his view, apt to believe 'that any counsels of moderation on our part are but a prelude to a successful action by Germany'. With reference to the second point, Lascelles thought that, in British interests, the Finns would have to be saved from themselves. The third point was, he thought, anticipating the outcome of the still-to-be-arranged Moscow talks, likely to 'become even more cogent if, as seems probable, we fall out with the Russians over the question of general co-operation against aggression'. Even so, the chance to give advice should, he thought, be taken. If Moscow were to be warned in this way, the Finns ought to be cautioned to avoid any contact with the German General Staff as any intimacy would be likely to increase Soviet suspicions and provoke an attack. A telegram was sent to Seeds on 27 April, recommending that the Ambassador sound Litvinov, the Commissar for Foreign Affairs and a staunch advocate of collective security against the German threat, on the subject.[40]

The League of Nations debate on the Ålands

Of course, the Northern Department and other British officials were not the only people in the world to discuss the issue of the Åland Islands. The very fact that the 1921 Convention had been agreed as a result of deliberations by the League of Nations meant that it was an international issue. The Northern Department officials had made constant reference to the necessity of securing the agreement of all the signatories to the Convention, and, in addition, that of the Soviet Union. For this reason international talks on the matter were essential, and, therefore, in May attention turned to Geneva where the Åland question was to be debated at the League of Nations session in the middle of the month.

As a final piece of advice before the session commenced, Snow warned the Northern Department of the 'painful impression' which would be created if the British delegation were to raise legal difficulties.[41] However, the briefing drafted for the delegation by B.E. Gage of the Northern Department stipulated that all legal requirements would have to be complied with. If this were to be done, then the UK delegation should advocate that the Council approve the proposal. If not, it would be necessary to press for postponement until the replies of all parties concerned had been received.[42] There can be little doubt that he was referring to the Soviet Union. This represented an acknowledgement of the desirability of pacifying the USSR or a feeling that to preserve the status quo might be in the interests of both London and Moscow.

The hopes of balancing the possibly conflicting aspirations of both Finland and the Soviet Union received a jolt when Ivan Maisky, the Soviet Ambassador in London and serving President of the League Council at Geneva, requested a postponement of the Åland debate on behalf of his government. Moscow deemed it necessary to call for an adjournment, as the Finns had not complied with requests which the Russians had made for details of the proposed fortification. Maisky's next step was to call on R.A. Butler, who headed the British delegation on 24 May. After expressing appreciation for a House of Commons debate, which had taken place the previous Friday, he asked Butler to use his influence to call off proceedings. He warned that if a vote were to be called, then the Soviet Union would vote against the proposal. Maisky went on to say that if the vote were carried against Soviet opposition, then a 'painful' impression would be given and 'a future agreement by way of diplomatic exchanges rendered much less likely'. Butler left Maisky with a non-committal answer but harboured a feeling that Moscow wanted the question postponed until such time as it could involve itself in the fortification work, alongside Finland and Sweden.[43]

Butler then conversed with M. Charveriat, his French equivalent, to plan future moves. They agreed to work with the Rapporteur appointed to examine the question, to try and come up with a resolution which met the Russian wish. 'In view of the negotiations which were proceeding on greater international issues', this was eminently enticing.[44] It would seem that the hope had arisen that an accommodation with Moscow over a comparatively minor issue would facilitate a benevolent Soviet attitude in the negotiations for an alliance which were taking place in the Soviet capital at that time.

On the same day, Snow made an exhortation for Britain to lean to the Finnish side, if a choice between Finland and the USSR had to be made. The British position in Finland had already deteriorated as a result of the Anglo-Soviet conversations elsewhere and to support the Soviet call for adjournment would have serious repercussions for the British in Helsinki.

The Russians, he argued, had no need to fear a German occupation of the Åland Islands with Finnish connivance, as any attempt at invasion would be resisted and the Germans would baulk at the prospect of a costly undertaking. From a British perspective, fortification would enable Finland to maintain neutrality and would deter a German occupation aimed at neutralising the Soviet Baltic fleet. Conversely, Soviet opposition to fortification created an impression of Russian aggression and would give Germany a 'cheap pretext' for forestalling these designs. In addition, it would deprive Finland of the material means of resisting Germany, depriving themselves of any reasonable grounds for complaint if Finland failed to resist and, more importantly, would deny Finland the means of resisting aggression at the very moment when the Kremlin themselves were proclaiming their readiness to defend Finland. If His Majesty's Government were to associate themselves with Russian opposition, they would lay themselves open to these criticisms also.[45] Lord Halifax agreed and on 25 May, Butler was instructed to vote against postponement in the event of no compromise being reached.

This possibility seemed more than likely. The Finnish delegate at Geneva had approached his Soviet opposite number with an assurance that his government were committed to neutrality. The Soviet delegate replied that his government were worried that Finland's assurances of defending itself were akin to those made by Czecho-Slovakia in March, which had consisted of a tale of sound and fury signifying only an unopposed German occupation. For this reason, the Soviet Union wanted military details and also the right to assist Finland actively in the defence of the islands, a line of argument not unrelated to the conversations and bargaining occurring between the Russians and British elsewhere.[46]

In the event, no vote at all was necessary. The Rapporteur proposed a compromise 'that while the question would not be postponed', his report would make no recommendation and would merely state that 'all signatories had approved the Plan'.[47] The Finns and Swedes were prepared to accept this solution, and an open clash between themselves and the USSR, with the unpleasant implications for both Finno-Soviet and Anglo-Soviet relations which such a quarrel could have entailed, was avoided. On 27 May, the report was submitted, with no requirement for a Council decision. Information which Collier picked up from the Swedish Foreign Minister Sandler, however, suggested that work on fortifications would now proceed, without Soviet, or indeed international, approval.[48]

Finland's decision to refortify the islands and the Northern Department's reaction

Collier's belief that the islands would now be fortified in any case informed his reply to a request from Snow, asking for permission to sound

Erkko as to the intentions of his government. Snow had also mentioned a query which the Finnish defence minister had lodged at the Legation, prior to the Geneva talks, asking if Britain could supply guns and motor torpedo boats for the defence of the Åland Islands. As the Finns had almost certainly decided their next move, Collier told Snow that there was no reason why British firms shouldn't profit from the decision.[49] In view of the problems which British companies were encountering in attempting to raise their production to meet Finnish defence needs, it is hard to believe that this was a hope born out of a great deal of confidence. Even at this stage, however, after Britain had decided to overlook Soviet objections at Geneva and was willing to give approval to immediate fortification, some elements in Finland insisted that British support lay behind the Soviet request for adjournment, citing messages from Berlin to this effect and an article from the *Manchester Guardian* of 29 May. In fact, while the latter article had said that it would not be surprising if the British Government changed its mind over the Åland issue, this had amounted to only one sentence and the story had no government authority. Collier complained that the Finnish Government knew exactly what the British attitude in Geneva had been and should have let this be known in responsible circles, i.e. the press. One sentence was hardly worth attracting attention to when negotiations with the Russians were approaching a 'critical stage'.[50]

On 14 June, a Finnish delegation left for Moscow to deliver a draft note advising the Russians of the strategic objectives of fortifying the Åland Islands. The visit was not a successful one, the Russians being unimpressed by Finnish claims that their plan would protect shipping in the Gulf of Bothnia. Lascelles was similarly sceptical about the Finnish avowal. He doubted that they could prevent Germany establishing some control in the area and that wartime shipping between Finland and Sweden would not be safeguarded.[51] Snow believed that the easiest explanation for the negative Soviet attitude was that they hoped to be able to seize the Ålands themselves, a possibility which some Foreign Office officials had earlier declared would not be detrimental to British interests. The Minister in Helsinki, however, was not of this opinion. If Soviet forces were to occupy the Åland Islands, while sharing an alliance with Great Britain, the result would be 'a deplorable start for hostilities ... on the basis of a common antipathy to aggression'. An 'unbearable stress' would be placed on Britain's 'moral case' and support in the United States would be lost.[52] Snow went on to say that the Finns were now willing to trade the two islands of Lauanssari and Seiskari for territory along the White Sea. Lascelles found this piece of information encouraging, minuting that a less intransigent stance was all to the good. Collier assessed the situation rather more pessimistically. He doubted that there would be time for a bargain 'before the crisis is on us – in which case we may well be faced with the disastrous situation foreshadowed [by Snow]'.[53]

Collier was right about the imminence of a crisis but wrong in believing that it would resemble that outlined by Snow. On 24 August, the German Foreign Minister, Joachim von Ribbentrop, in a dramatic visit to Moscow, concluded a non-aggression pact with Soviet Commissar for Foreign Affairs, Vyacheslav Molotov. This meant that by the time the Northern Department was able to consider Snow's message from Helsinki that the Finnish Government was now ready '[to go] ahead with the work' on fortifying the Åland Islands, the question had ceased to have any importance for Britain. Lascelles noted that the Soviet-German pact had changed things enormously: the Soviet Union would no longer hope to use the Ålands to intercept iron ore traffic. He could also have said that its fear of being attacked by Germany via these islands had disappeared. Lascelles, obviously feeling let down by the Russians, then complained that 'even before the pact they had the nerve to demand that *we* should station a large naval contingent in the Baltic', a reference to Soviet demands during the Moscow negotiations regarding an Anglo-French-Soviet pact. Lascelles' disappointment was all too apparent, yet this statement could also be interpreted as a suggestion that the Baltic should have been the natural place for the Soviet fleet to dominate. Nonetheless, he conceded that the question of the Åland Islands had now lost its importance for Britain. The official attitude in favour of fortification had always been subject to doubts whether the Soviet Union could help British interests more if the islands were left undefended. Now that these doubts had been removed, any steps taken by Finland and Sweden to protect themselves against what could be joint pressure by the USSR and Germany could be welcomed wholeheartedly.[54] Sweden would not be involved, and indeed the islands would not be fortified, but dangerous days for both Finland and Britain were about to begin. Britain could no longer expect to wield influence of any kind in the Baltic, except through its soon-to-be-overwhelmed ally Poland, but the central question which had been vexing the Northern Department throughout the whole saga of Åland remilitarisation – how to integrate Finnish integrity with an accommodation with the Soviet Union and thus defeat German ambitions in the Baltic – had not disappeared.

3

1939: THE PROBLEMS OF REARMAMENT

The inadequacies of Britain's defence mechanisms were not as apparent through 1939 as they were shown to be in May 1940, but a study of how the Northern Department reacted to requests for military equipment from Finland at the time show what a poor position Britain's defence policy was in. Chapter 1 showed the frustrations of Northern Department officials when trying to convince the War Office and Air Ministry to accept Finnish orders for military equipment placed in the UK during 1938. In 1939, with the fear of war increasing, these same problems remained and took on even greater urgency. This chapter examines the manner in which Finnish requirements were handled by the British authorities and the conflict of priorities between the diplomats of the Northern Department, who stressed the necessity of meeting Finnish orders and entertaining senior Finnish personnel, and the officials of the service departments, who had their own concerns about Britain's immediate military, as opposed to political, needs. The concern of the Northern Department regarding Finland was to attempt to keep the Helsinki government away from engaging in close ties with the government of the Third Reich. They argued that by providing Finland with the material which it requested and by accommodating the wishes of Finnish military personnel to visit Britain, the Finnish Government would feel less inclined to turn towards Germany for help. Their problem was that in attempting to meet this goal through the provision of military assistance to Finland, the suspicions of the Soviet Union were likely to be aroused. It would have been to Moscow's benefit to have the number of potential enemies reduced, and the weaning away of Finland from German influence was designed to realise this aim. The attempt to achieve a settlement over the Åland Islands which met Finnish aspirations and conciliated Soviet security fears was thus tied in, for the Northern Department, with the efforts to meet Finnish defence requirements. If Moscow trusted Finland, then it would be more likely to understand the British strategy of weaning it away from Germany through rearmament. The Soviet Union figures only indirectly in this chapter, but, as a potential ally against

Germany and a potential enemy of Finland, it played a part in Northern Department calculations.

Rearmament in Britain

An understanding of how the process of Finnish rearmament was viewed in Britain can only be arrived at by a prior realisation of the state of Britain's own rearmament programme in the months after Munich. Any moves towards rearmament in the United Kingdom at this time were hampered by the Treasury's insistence on a prudent fiscal policy. The Chancellor, Sir John Simon, a Liberal by party affiliation but a staunch supporter of Chamberlain, feared that if a war involving Britain broke out, then gold reserves would be exhausted within a terrifyingly short time and that the diversion of economic and industrial activities from peaceful enterprise to war preparation would lead to a decline of exports in peace time.[1] Investing in war materials which were economically unproductive and which might never be called upon was not an attractive prospect for Simon. He preferred to balance the budget and keep the cost of rearmament down to a level acceptable to his perception of Britain's economic capacity. So seemingly successful was he at this that he was attacked by one Air Marshal who accused him of being determined 'to preserve enough money in Britain to pay an indemnity after Britain has been defeated'.[2]

Simon's opposition notwithstanding, Britain's rearmament effort did begin to make progress during 1939, although the results were not always spectacular. Pressure from Leslie Hore-Belisha, Secretary of State at the War Office, led to a doubling of the size of the Territorial Army but at the cost of diverting material away from the main field force,[3] a move which hardly convinced Hitler that the British Army was in any position to destroy his plans for a *Mitteleuropa*. The Royal Navy's plans for the re-establishment of a two power standard were abandoned for reasons of expense. On the bright side, the Air Ministry's plans for expanding the Royal Air Force in terms of fighters, bombers and anti-aircraft guns were approved by the Cabinet despite the opposition of Simon. Priority was given to fighter aircraft, the establishment of radar systems to detect imminent enemy attack, and a ground to air control system.[4] This decision was to prove crucial during the Battle of Britain, but in 1939 it looked as though Britain was preparing for defensive actions rather than a strategy of taking the war to the enemy.

German 'adventurism'

Many states were frightened of German power after Munich. What was left of Czechoslovakia had good reason to be when, on 15 March, Hitler's forces turned Bohemia and Moravia into a German protectorate, and at the same time established an 'independent' Slovakia. Lithuania felt the full force of German pressure six days later, feeling compelled to hand over the predominantly German-speaking Memel area of the country. Hitler's desire to reunite the currently disparate sections of Prussia and bring the free city of Danzig under the jurisdiction of the Reich was to lead to an Anglo-French guarantee to Poland at the end of March.

In contrast, Finland had no fears of trouble from the south. Unlike Memel or Danzig, Finland was not the source of German irredentist claims, although the absence of historical German interests had not saved the rump state of Czecho-Slovakia. Finland and Germany had traditionally shared good relations and trade between the two states was healthy, although Germany lagged behind Britain in this respect. The Finns were not facing the future with great confidence, however. While it was believed in Helsinki that no aggressive ultimatums were likely to come from Germany, the same optimistic disposition was not held towards their giant eastern neighbour, the USSR. The Finns did indeed have good reason for not expecting goodwill to emanate from the direction of Moscow. In November 1936, Andrei Zhdanov, a high profile figure in the Soviet hierarchy, had made a speech to the Soviet Congress which had received international coverage. In it he gave warning to the states bordering the USSR not to allow themselves to drift into the Nazi camp. Finland in particular was singled out and told of the fatal consequences that would ensue from any 'adventurism' on its part.[5] Relations between Helsinki and Moscow had improved by 1938, but the lack of enthusiasm given to the September 1938 initiative of Boris Yartsev, an official at the Soviet Legation in Helsinki, for a military and economic assistance pact between their two nations (see Chapter 1) and the lack of progress towards a mutually acceptable programme for the remilitarisation of the Åland Islands were instrumental in cooling relations in the latter quarter of 1938 and the opening months of 1939.[6] Churchill's comment that 'Finland and the three Baltic States did not know whether it was German aggression or Soviet rescue that they dreaded more',[7] is misleading. German threat was not an issue for Finland or the three small states across the Baltic, but fear of Soviet penetration was. The paralysis in British (and French) policy which Churchill attributed to the 'hideous choice' (between Germany and Russia) facing the Finns and others was more accurately caused by the Allied disinclination to give the Soviet Union *carte blanche* in the Baltic region. The choices facing Finland regarding Germany and the Soviet Union and the policies followed by the Anglo-French allies towards Finland in their discussions with the Soviet Government will be discussed more fully in the next chapter.

British policy and Finland

Finland's position vis-à-vis Germany and the Soviet Union meant that British policy had to be conducted in a different manner to that which it operated towards states such as Poland and Greece, who justifiably felt anxious about Axis intentions. The problem was that any support given to Finland could have the effect of straining relations between London and Moscow. As will be demonstrated, it was felt by Laurence Collier and other officials that enough military aid should be given to Finland to create a positive impression of Britain in Helsinki, while attempting to subdue Soviet suspicions of what the weapons would be used for. If Finland was clearly separated from German influence, then this goal would be easier to achieve. For this reason, Collier and Snow were convinced that Britain should attempt to meet Finnish defence requirements. Although Finland was suspected of possessing a pro-German military staff, influential Finnish officers, notably the Anglophile General Lundqvist of the Air Force, had been persuaded by the air attaché at the British Legation, Wing Commander 'Freddie' West, to place orders for defence equipment with British firms Bristol, Vickers and ICI in 1938. The inability of the latter two firms to supply the Finns with cartridge cups and howitzers had led Snow to despair of the impression of British inefficiency which was likely to be conveyed and the probability of the Finns labelling Britain as a useless source of supply. Wing Commander West had also managed to persuade Lundqvist to keep faith with the Bristol Aeroplane Company, despite this firm not even manufacturing the type of seaplane which the Finnish defence establishment required. West returned to Britain in October 1938 and his place was taken by Wing Commander J. Johnson. He was to prove as indefatigable a fighter for British interests as his predecessor. One of his first tasks was to reassure Lundqvist over the non-appearance of certain items which had been ordered from Bristol. Lundqvist told Johnson that he had completed arrangements for the purchase of a licence to build Dutch-designed Fokker T.8.W.(a) seaplanes using Bristol Mercury engines. The outstanding parts could, he thought, affect those plans adversely – after all, if Bristol couldn't meet Finnish needs in peace time, what would happen in war? He urged that action be taken to remedy this position as delays could be used by certain elements in Finland 'as a reason for trading elsewhere in the future, particularly as in this case Finland definitely considered the purchase of German seaplanes before finally deciding on the Fokker-Bristol combination'.[8]

The Finnish Minister of Defence had expressed his dissatisfaction at this state of affairs to Lundqvist, leading Snow to conjecture that the company's position with the Finnish Air Force would be jeopardised if it failed to fulfil its contract.[9] The seeming tardiness of the Bristol Company to meet its orders contrasted sharply with the customer service supplied by

Germany and the United States. When Johnson drew the preponderance of German and American machinery and lathes at a Tampere aircraft factory to Lundqvist's attention, the General replied that this was because they could deliver in six months rather than eighteen months. Lundqvist also revealed the pressure he had come under, while on a visit to Berlin, to buy more Air Force equipment in Germany. He had replied that although he admired German efficiency and organisation, it would be impossible to switch orders when 'England always buys more produce from us than we buy from her'. Northern Department official, B.E. Gage minuted at this point that 'it is not pleasurable to read that purchases from us are made on the grounds of expediency rather than efficiency'.[10]

Snow in Helsinki had decried the efficiency, or lack of it, demonstrated by Vickers Armstrong and ICI the previous September when these two companies had been unable to supply shell cases and field howitzers for the Finnish army. His fears that Britain would be viewed in Finnish circles as a useless source of supply appeared to be borne out when M. Von Knorring of the Finnish Ministry for Foreign Affairs told Eric Lingeman, Commercial Secretary at the British Legation, that not only could a Belgian company actually supply the equipment, they could do it at a cheaper rate than their British counterparts. The Belgian offer had then been undercut, unfortunately by the Germans. An order for anti-aircraft shell cases which Vickers had hoped to get was also placed with German manufacturers, at a price 25 per cent below the Vickers' quotation. Even though the blow was softened by an order being given to Messrs de Jersey (the local agents for British companies) for flame tracer ammunition, despite being allegedly 20 per cent higher than their German competitors, Gage still felt justified in commenting that the position was 'not ... very satisfactory'.[11]

Opposition from the War Office

Unfortunately for the Legation staff at Helsinki, the shortcomings of British firms were not the only obstacle in the way of providing a satisfactory service to the Finnish defence establishment. Following a mid-February enquiry placed through de Jersey for heavy tanks from Vickers, the Foreign Office made enquiries at the War Office on the availability of the latest models.[12] When the reply from the War Office arrived, it was somewhat disappointing. No tanks of the type required by the Finns could be released, although Vickers Armstrong had been given permission to supply different models providing no interference with War Department contracts was involved. This was not as hopeful as it appeared. After British requirements had been met, outstanding orders from Turkey and Greece for tanks of this type would have to be met, and the War Office was emphatic that these states should take precedence over Finland.[13]

The War Office was similarly obstructive over the flame tracer bullets which had been ordered from ICI, despite being priced 20 per cent higher than their German equivalent. On hearing of the agreement, Colonel Harding of the War Office told ICI that they must not agree to any foreign deliveries of this type of ammunition before April 1939 and that deliveries could only be made after that date if the British military's own require- ment of 25 million rounds had been met, which would effectively mean March 1940 at the earliest. This was clearly a poor way to treat the Finns who, in their own interests, could have placed the order elsewhere. Instead, the political gesture, which the order could justifiably be inter- preted as, was not being met in a reciprocal fashion.

Despite feeling let down, the Finns apparently understood the dif- ficulties and as the treaty contained a *force majeure* clause, they were willing to vary the terms materially.[14] Unfortunately, the War Office was not prepared to see the terms varied and explained to Collier that ICI had been far too optimistic concerning its ability to supply the ammunition. The company had been asked to supply two different types of flame tracer bullet – three million rounds of 7.62 mm and one million rounds of .303". The second category could possibly be delivered by September but the former could not be sent until March 1940 at the earliest. Harding promised to see if the matter could be reconsidered but thought that any modifications were almost certainly out of the question. Gage, who was showing a particular interest in this issue, explained the political reasons for accommodating the Finns and the desirability that the order should not be placed in Germany. One million rounds out of a total of 25 million did not seem much, he reasoned, and could surely be spared. Moreover, the Finns were prepared to accept the *force majeure* clause in the contract, and this demonstration of goodwill ought not to be ridden over.[15] However, it was the responsibility of Harding and the War Office to privil- ege military needs over political considerations. Harding replied that after a thorough examination of the question at the War Office, it had been decided that the conditions for export could not possibly be modified. On present forecasts ICI would not even be able to supply the War Depart- ment requirements of 25 million rounds and could not possibly supply the Finns before 1940. He admitted that this was unfortunate but argued that even if allowances were made for political considerations, the Northern Department would have to agree that the requirements of the British forces, the Dominions, the colonies and the Egyptian government should take precedence over Finland. Gage did not agree but conceded that it was useless to take the matter further. Perhaps surprisingly, in a demon- stration of what Gage called 'very goodwill towards us on Finland's part', the Finns kept their order with ICI.[16] The War Office viewed this outcome as justifying its stance but the disappointing conclusion from the Finnish perspective would have given ammunition to those people in Helsinki wishing to trade with a more efficient supplier in Germany, although the Nazi-Soviet pact of August was to preclude this consummation.

The differing perspectives of the Northern Department, who wanted to assist the process of Finnish rearmament in order to bolster political ties, and the War Office, who were adamant that Britain's immediate interests be secured in case of war, meant that an agreement between them was unlikely. A limited number of possibly obsolete tanks and relatively small supplies of ammunition were not sufficient to prevent Finland from being overrun in the event of a determined attack by one of its powerful neighbours, yet, as the diplomats would have it, it could act as a means of securing British political influence in Helsinki. The War Office was not blind to these arguments, but as Finland was not considered an area of vital strategic interest, it viewed any attempt at arming Finland at the expense of the metropolis and the Empire as misguided.[17]

Opposition from the Air Ministry

The Northern Department's problems with the service ministries were not limited to the War Office. During the month of May a problem arose with the Air Ministry. Unlike the dispute with the War Office it did not involve the sale of material but did question the importance of Finland to Britain. In the first week of May, the Northern Department received a despatch from Wing Commander Johnson recommending that an invitation be extended to General Lundqvist to visit the United Kingdom and inspect the development of aircraft production. Johnson reminded the department that Lundqvist had generally shown pro-British tendencies during his period of control of the Finnish Air force and had been responsible for placing orders with the Bristol company. However, delays in the delivery of parts were exposing him to criticism from officers of the General Staff who wished to prevent further orders. The Germans, it seemed, were trying to capitalise on this, but if Lundqvist 'were to visit England, he could not fail to be impressed with the progress of rearmament and aircraft production'.[18] As plane and engine orders were due to be placed in the summer, no time should be lost in issuing the invitation. Johnson's despatch met with general agreement in the Northern Department. Collier and Gage expressed approval, the latter commenting that 'our interest in Finland is surely very much to the point'. More importantly, the Secretary of State for Foreign Affairs, Lord Halifax, was in agreement and it was on his instruction that Collier wrote to Sir Kingsley Wood, the Secretary of State at the Air Ministry, expressing the hope that an invitation could be issued at the earliest opportunity.[19]

The reply from the Air Ministry on 12 June was disappointing. It was felt that no invitation could be extended at the present time due to visits by representatives from Turkey, Romania and Poland. Wood promised that his ministry would contact the Northern Department in the second week of July when the visitors had been dealt with. Far from being concerned at the 'ostentatious' invitation which it was now known that the commander of the Luftwaffe, Hermann Göring, had given to Lundqvist, Major Boyle of the Air Ministry contended that it would be better if Lundqvist went to Germany first.[20] This was not the feeling at the Foreign Office where marginal comments regretted the 'indecision of the Air Ministry' which meant that 'the Germans have got in first'.[21]

Sir Lancelot Oliphant, Permanent Assistant Secretary at the Foreign Office, with responsibility for the Northern Department, consequently wrote to Air Chief Marshal Sir Cyril Newall on 28 June, reminding him of Johnson's recommendation and stressing the political benefits. From this perspective, he argued, the idea of a visit by Lundqvist was an excellent one and he hoped that it would still be possible to issue an invitation. He appreciated the complications raised by the already arranged visits by Turks, Romanians and Poles but felt uneasy at the prospect of a delay of a fortnight or more before anything could be done. He then gave warning of the consequences of a delayed invitation:

> Major-General Lundqvist is a good friend of this country but there are limits to all international friendships and it would not be safe to assume that his sentiments will always remain the same if we give the impression of doing little to encourage them. He has recently had an invitation from the Germans who will do their best to persuade him that it is in the interests of his country to have not only German technical advice but also German machines: nor is such persuasion lacking in Finland itself. In fact, the situation is such that we shall need all the friends we can make or keep.

He continued by expressing the hope that Newall could issue an invitation for Lundqvist to come in perhaps the second week of July.[22]

On 7 July Oliphant received a reply from Newall. The Air Chief Marshal explained that Lundqvist could not be invited at the time which the Northern Department thought appropriate because the staff of the Air Ministry were too busy with their Polish, Turkish and Romanian visitors, whose countries 'are of real importance to us in war'. In any case, issuing an invitation so soon after Lundqvist received one from Germany would only create the impression that Britain was in a state of anxiety when it came to competing with the Germans. The best time to invite a Finnish guest, in his opinion, would be September, as this would coincide with large-scale army manoeuvres. Oliphant wrote back, pleading the political benefits of an immediate invitation but it was in vain and Newall acted upon his own suggestion.[23] As the manoeuvres across Europe in September were on a larger scale than Newall seemed to anticipate, the visit was fated not to be. While the Northern Department and larger Foreign Office had a good case for their largely political arguments, the Air Ministry could hardly be blamed for taking the line that it did. Poland and Romania were protected by British guarantee and it was hoped that Turkey would also enter the Allies' defensive system. On the other hand, Finland had no guarantee from Britain and did not want one on the conditions which were currently on offer, specifically that the USSR would also act as a guarantor power. The only guarantees which Finland was prepared to accept were unilateral ones from Britain and France which would, in Finnish eyes at least, be directed against the Soviet Union rather than Germany. At a time when negotiations were under way towards an Anglo-French-Soviet pact, this was clearly unacceptable.

At the same time as the debate over whether Lundqvist could be invited to Britain was going on, negotiations for equipment for the Finnish Air Force were also under way. For the purpose of experimental work, the Finns wished to purchase Taurus aeroplane engines from Britain. It was Wing Commander Johnson's opinion that if the Finns were satisfied with the engine, then they would be likely to place large orders for it.[24] The Finns, however, were adamant on the need for a quick promise of delivery, no later than 31 May, as the decision on aircraft policy would be taken on 1 June. Ominously, the Germans had already made an offer of fighter aircraft.[25] Fortunately, Major Boyle gave permission for the Finns to test the engine.

When Johnson next met with Lundqvist, in the first days of June, to discuss requirements, the good news regarding the Taurus engines was tempered by the reality that their manufacture and delivery could not take place until 1940. General Mannerheim, the *éminence grise* of the Finnish military, had thus advised that their immediate needs would have to be met by overseas purchase. When Lundqvist said that Germany had boasted of its ability to supply a delivery of Messerschmitts immediately, Johnson retorted that if they could do that, then the planes could not be very good. Lundqvist then asked the Wing Commander to find out how quickly 30 Spitfires could be delivered. Johnson duly despatched this enquiry, along with his opinion that Mannerheim was justly doubtful of his country's ability to produce a modern fighter and had wisely decided to look abroad. Collier, for one, doubted that Britain was the right place to look, commenting ironically that the Air Ministry hadn't even been able to supply a plane to take General Kirke on his visit to Finland.[26]

Johnson received a reply directly from the Air Ministry in mid-July. Not surprisingly, it said that no Spitfires could be sold to Finland owing to commitments from the usual customers, Poland, Romania and Turkey. Lundqvist had expected this answer and told Johnson that Finland couldn't afford them in any case, although he hinted at the importance which his country attached to defensive weapons when he added that Mannerheim was extremely nervous about the European situation.[27]

Despite these setbacks, it seemed for a brief time in early August that Finnish confidence in the British ability to provide aeronautical supplies would be boosted when the Air Ministry decided that the Bristol Aeroplane Co. could deliver a Taurus engine to Finland by October 1939, and not some time in 1940 as had previously been thought.[28] However, this gesture wasn't enough. On 16 August, Lundqvist informed Johnson that his Air Force would be purchasing planes from the United States. This was unfortunate for the loss it occasioned for Britain's market share in Finland, but it was admitted by Snow that, from a political perspective, it was preferable for Finnish orders to be placed across the Atlantic rather than across the Baltic.[29]

The Admiralty caused less disappointment in Finnish (and Northern Department) quarters than the other service ministries, mainly because less orders were placed through them. The Admiralty had approved an order for the Vespers Co. of Portsmouth to supply the Finnish forces with four motor torpedo boats, but it had been given before Neville Chamberlain's declaration of war on Germany on 3 September. Obviously conscious of the likelihood that Britain's capacity to supply had been adversely affected by its newly acquired belligerent status, and presumably aware of the unreliability of British firms and service ministries in time of peace, the Finnish General Valve made enquiries with Captain N.C. Moore, the British Naval Adviser in Helsinki, on 9 September as to what would happen to their order. The argument in the Northern Department regarding political benefits was no longer being used by its members. Lascelles minuted that the question of the motor torpedo boats was one for the Admiralty but it was very unlikely, in view of British requirements, that the Finns could be satisfied, making no mention of the harm such a stance could have on Anglo-Finnish relations.[30]

The notion was still retained by the leading British personnel in Helsinki, however. Captain Moore felt that the fulfilment of orders for the motor torpedo boats plus the delivery of an order for six tanks, outstanding since 1936, would create goodwill towards Britain among the Finns, although the execution of an order three years after it was placed would hardly be deserving of congratulations. Snow agreed, stating that the position of His Majesty's Government required strengthening as a powerful faction in Finland looked to Germany as their best source of supply.[31] At this time, the additional protocol to the Nazi-Soviet pact of August was still secret and Snow could not know that Hitler and Ribbentrop had quite happily consigned Finland to the USSR's sphere of influence, thus declining the opportunity to act as any sort of arsenal for the Finns. In a marginal comment, Lascelles, argued that a 'more aggressive Soviet line' meant that a greater importance should now be attached to meeting orders. Being made on 22 September, Lascelles' comment was no doubt influenced by the Soviet occupation of eastern Poland five days earlier. Collier was probably bearing the same question in mind when he noticed that 'this provides us with the opportunity to take up the whole question of help for Finland'.[32] Collier's attitude may seem surprising, given his insistence over the Åland Islands that the Soviet Union must be consulted and that the interest in his department for Finnish rearmament was political and had operated under the assumption that Finland should be kept away from Germany. It was now clear that any weapons that Finland acquired would now most probably be used against the USSR, when Collier had formerly hoped for a reconciliation between the two states at Germany's expense. His motives, however, were at this stage more complex than being merely the need to arm a small state against an aggressive neighbour and were consistent with the stand he had hitherto taken.

The effect of the Nazi-Soviet pact

On 3 September Germany became an enemy of Britain in fact as well as theory. The Nazi-Soviet pact changed the situation in northern Europe significantly. The pact had not caused London to break relations with Moscow but the fact that the Soviet Union could now be ruled out as an ally and would possibly act as a benevolent neutral in Germany's favour meant that the importance of Finland was about to be raised, not just in Northern Department eyes, but in those of British policy-makers in general. When war between Finland and Russia broke out at the end of November, it was to prove difficult for British politicians to divorce its implications from the conflict in which they themselves were engaged in.

The USSR has largely been excluded from this chapter. This is not because it was viewed as peripheral or irrelevant. On the contrary, the Finnish Government and military were only too aware of the dangers that could emerge from across their eastern border. As far as the Northern Department and Snow were concerned at this stage, however, the Soviet Union's presence was only felt indirectly on the matter of Finnish rearmament. The officials at the Northern Department were not arguing that Finland needed weapons to protect itself from Germany, rather that by meeting Finnish requirements, the British authorities could help to prevent Finland from moving into Germany's security circle. These political considerations were at the root of the disagreements with the service ministries, who were concerned with strategic matters and believed, furthermore, that Britain was in no position to supply peripheral states with materials which could be needed for the defence of the Empire. Any weapons that the Finns could procure, from Britain or anywhere else, were unlikely to be used to help the British Government uphold its obligations to Poland or other guaranteed states. The only direction from which the Finnish Government could see a military threat emanating was Moscow, and any strengthening of its own defences would be designed to meet this threat. This may seem, *prima facie,* to suggest that the Northern Department hoped to indulge these Finnish designs, but an examination of their arguments shows that their real motive was to keep Finland as far away from German influence as possible, an outcome which would bring the unstated benefit of reducing possible adversaries for the Soviet Union in the event of a German-Soviet war. In retrospect, it would seem that the success of this policy was dependent upon two conditions. First, that the arguments of the Northern Department were accepted, with the service ministries proving able to accommodate these proposals, and, second, that Germany was unable to conclude a pact with the USSR. Neither of these conditions were to be met. Ironically, the arguments of both the Northern Department and the service ministries acknowledged the likelihood of war with Germany. Collier and his associates, plus the British Legation staff in Helsinki, thought that in this contingency Germany should be allowed the least possible influence. Their recommendations were more anti-German than pro-Finnish and, in their view, if British influence increased in Finland, the chances of breaking down barriers which were preventing the establishment of an alliance between the Western powers and the Soviet Union would increase. These must have seemed very specious arguments to the military experts who, very plausibly, thought that war materials were in scarce enough supply without wasting them on states whose survival was not material to Britain's own. When Britain finally declared war on Germany on 3 September, the arguments of the service ministries became even more pertinent. The question of meeting Finnish defence needs did not disappear, but Finland began to seem further away. The manner in which Finnish requirements were handled is the subject of a later chapter.

Directly, over the Åland Islands, and indirectly, over rearmament, the Northern Department showed an awareness of Soviet concerns. While delaying face-to-face confrontation with the Soviet Government in the spring and summer of 1939, British negotiators had to maintain a similar consciousness of Finnish interests and attempt to find some common ground which the Finns and Russians could share. The next chapter will discuss the attempts by British officials during these months to bring about an agreement which would satisfy the security requirements of Finland, the Soviet Union, and Great Britain.

4

BRITAIN, THE USSR AND THE QUESTION OF FINLAND

When Britain and France declared war on Germany on 3 September 1939, they acted in fulfilment of the terms of the guarantee which had been provided to Poland the previous March. Other states in Europe – Romania, Greece and Turkey among them – had been given similar Anglo-French pledges of allied assistance. Finland, however, received no such guarantee from Britain, France, or, indeed, any other power, although Britain was asked by the Soviet Government during the Moscow talks to include Finland within the states it guaranteed against aggression. This chapter demonstrates the problems which were thrown up by this request. Finnish reluctance to accept an unwanted guarantee from the USSR, with Britain and France as additional signatories, was to prove a major stumbling block when the Allies attempted to engage Moscow in an alliance agreement aimed against Germany in the spring and summer months of 1939. The many obstacles to a successful conclusion of the talks have been well discussed, debated and disputed over the years but it is the Finnish aspect to the so-called Moscow negotiations involving the Western powers and the Soviet Union, rather than the talks as a holistic entity which will be considered in this chapter. The chapter also investigates the problems which British negotiators faced in attempting to reconcile Finnish *amour propre* with Soviet security demands. The difference in interpretation of the Soviet Union by the Northern Department as opposed to other elements of the British policy-making establishment is something which is highlighted when looking at the Finnish angle, which was of some importance to Collier and his colleagues. Neville Chamberlain had confided to his diary on 26 March that he felt a 'profound distrust of Russia', doubting its military capabilities, distrusting its motives which seemed 'to be concerned only with getting everyone else by the ears' and focusing on the suspicion felt by small states which bordered the USSR, including Finland.[1] While Neville Chamberlain and the Cabinet's Foreign Policy Committee debated the pros and cons of effecting an alliance with Soviet Russia, Laurence Collier never doubted that an association with the Soviet Union was a desirable objective. Indeed, Collier's understanding of the necessity of

59

allaying Russian doubts, and of the need to avoid any situation whereby Moscow felt its security threatened has been demonstrated earlier in this study. Although uninvolved with the face-to-face discussions in Moscow, Collier attempted to do all he could to make the talks successful. It has become an almost accepted tenet of British historiography that while influential people such as Churchill were urging that an agreement with Moscow be reached, those people actually charged with the implementation of policy were never too keen on this option. This chapter demonstrates how the policy of Collier, a senior official at the Foreign Office, towards Finland, adhered to this aim, and that the desire for an alliance with the USSR was held by British policy-makers, that is to say Collier, and not just opposition figures such as Churchill and Eden.

The Anglo-Franco-Soviet negotiations, held in Moscow during the spring and summer of 1939, are an essential ingredient in accounts of the origins of the Second World War. However, this chapter is not concerned with the implications of the talks or indeed with their results. Instead, this chapter centres around a hitherto unexplored area – that of the Finnish dimension: the way in which Finland proved to be a significant matter for discussion and the way in which the Northern Department and Snow, in particular, assessed and dealt with the consequences. The Finnish aspect, if we can call it that, has been noted in many commentaries but no detailed examination of the Northern Department papers relating to the Finnish angle of the discussions has been presented. While Paul Doerr's thesis on the Northern Department and the Soviet Union in the 1930s does indeed examine the negotiations conducted at the level of Halifax and Seeds, Finnish considerations are generally overlooked.[2] This may be explained by the fact that the negotiations with Moscow were not actually in the hands of the Northern Department. It is accurate to say that the Moscow negotiations and tensions they caused within Finland have indeed received comprehensive treatment by Finnish historians. It must also be pointed out that on the whole they have relied on Finnish sources. No detailed examination of the British views on Finland during this time has been made. Because the purpose of the talks in Moscow was to effect an alliance against Germany, the Central Department was the department of the Foreign Office responsible, but they did refer papers to the Northern Department when their advice was required. Indeed, it was to the Northern Department that the Finnish Minister in London, Georg Gripenberg, most frequently turned.

The Northern Department and Snow attempted to guide opinion and policy, not only in Britain but also in Finland, and this chapter looks at how this was attempted against a background of impending war, unrelieved suspicions between the Finnish and Soviet Governments, and a British Government which seemed unable to make any progress in its negotiations for an anti-German alliance.

The guarantee to Poland

Neville Chamberlain had hoped that Hitler would stand by the promises he had made at Munich but these hopes were dashed on 15 March when German forces marched into the remains of Czecho-Slovakia, establishing a protectorate over Bohemia and Moravia and declaring Slovakia to be an 'independent' state. Hitler's ambitions became even clearer a week later when Lithuania transferred the Memel district of its territory to the Reich's jurisdiction after receiving an uncompromising ultimatum from Berlin. Doubts over whether Hitler was 'a misunderstood nationalist' or 'a maniac bent on world domination' were receding by the day and Chamberlain could no longer believe in Hitler's words.[3]

On 31 March 1939, a guarantee was given by Britain to protect Poland's independence. This placed Germany in the position of facing a potential war on two fronts and it satisfied Chamberlain that it would deter Hitler from further action.[4] Despite the Prime Minister's optimistic outlook, talks between British and Soviet representatives took place between March and August with a view to allying the two powers into a formal coalition aimed against Hitler. At the same time, unrelated talks had got underway in Geneva over the question of the refortification of the Åland Islands. During this debate on the Åland Islands in May (see Chapter 2) both Thomas Snow and Under-Secretary of State for Foreign Affairs, R.A. Butler, had drawn attention to these negotiations and the negative impact on both Anglo-Finnish and Anglo-Soviet relations which they could occasion. They were aware that failure to meet Soviet requirements over the Åland Islands would not further progress towards a general agreement with Moscow, and that consequently the talks in Geneva impacted on those in Moscow. The Moscow talks constituted an important diplomatic affair, while the Åland debate at the League of Nations was much more of a sideshow, but the issues of Finno-Soviet mistrust were evident at both. Finland was a major issue during the Moscow talks and the Finnish profile expanded so much as to become visible to luminaries such as Lord Halifax and Sir William Seeds, the British Ambassador in Moscow. This meant that from spring 1939 onwards, policy towards Finland, which had previously been the prerogative of the Northern Department, was suddenly the concern of the higher echelons of the Foreign Office.

When the Munich conference decided the fate of Czechoslovakia in September 1938, it had been hoped in Britain that Germany was now a satiated state and that there would be no need to forge an alliance against it. March 1939 was to prove such assessments hopelessly inaccurate, with the aforementioned German advances into Bohemia, Moravia and Memel. The 'golden age' of peace which Sir Samuel Hoare had forecast only a day before the German invasion of Czecho-Slovakia now looked as if it could only be achieved after a violent interlude. It was towards the end of March that tentative suggestions for co-operation, from both British and Soviet sides, began. Four days after the occupation of the remaining Czech lands, Maxim Litvinov, the Soviet Commissar for Foreign Affairs, suggested to Sir William Seeds that a conference be held between Britain, the USSR, France, Poland and Romania to discuss how they might co-ordinate action to deal with the German threat.[5] This idea was rejected by the British Cabinet but the principle of co-operation was kept alive. The British Government proposed a declaration of warning be made to Germany by Britain, France, Poland and the USSR. This proposal was delivered to the respective governments on 20 March.[6] This was not what Moscow ideally wanted but the process of negotiations between the Western powers and the Soviet Union had begun. This process was to culminate in Moscow's rejection of the Allies in favour of a pact with Germany.

The objections of the 'border states' towards British collaboration with the Soviet Union

One of the most serious problems to bedevil the negotiations was the objection to any involvement of the Soviet Union by other countries, notably Poland and Romania, which received guarantees from Britain and France on 31 March and 13 April respectively. The difficulties created by the attitudes of these governments towards the USSR have been well documented,[7] but little has been written about the similar complaints vocalised by the Finnish Government or British policy towards them. The Finns were never happy about a British association with the USSR and had actually anticipated western approaches which were made to Moscow. On 22 March, Snow, in a despatch taken by the Central Department, warned the Foreign Office of a 'very considerable cooling off in sympathy' which had resulted from rumours that His Majesty's Government was considering an alliance with the Soviet Union. The fact that Britain had no comparable treaty to that existing between France and the Soviet Union, he argued, 'was one of the main props ... of Finnish sympathy for the Western Powers'.[8] The Minister did not say so but could have argued in support of his argument that this sympathy for Britain could have acted as a counter-balance to the support for Germany which was alleged by some at the Northern Department to be strong in certain Finnish quarters (see Chapter 1). Snow went on to say that he had been pushing the line that closer relations between Britain and Russia would be a further guarantee of Finland's position vis-à-vis the USSR, and that the Finnish Foreign Minister, Eljas Erkko, believed that rapprochement between Britain and Russia was a better prospect than a Russo-German rapprochement. Sadly, Snow doubted that either of these contentions carried any conviction and felt 'distressed at the position which seems to be developing' in reference to the negative view of the USSR.[9]

D.W. Lascelles' immediate comment that 'these unfortunate reactions are not confined to Finland'[10] was all too accurate. Polish, Romanian, Dominion and Roman Catholic opinion all seemed set against any close Western collaboration with Moscow.[11] These observations, plus his own evaluation of 'the completely unreliable nature of the Soviet government', notwithstanding, Lascelles argued that German aggression in central and eastern Europe had left Britain with little choice other than to involve the USSR. The Northern Department drafted a reply for Cadogan to send to Snow. It sympathised with his difficult position and reassured him that his anxieties would not be overlooked in deciding future policy.[12] It was not only Snow who found the situation awkward. Collier viewed the task of finding a way to calm Finland's fears that Britain would not leave it to the mercy of the Russians with some trepidation. He could not see how the problem could be addressed. If nothing were done, then the danger of pro-German elements in Finland gaining the upper hand 'with incalculable consequences for the strategic situation' would be magnified.[13] The key to the problem was a recognition by both Finland and the Soviet Union of compatible and mutual aims: to restrict German influence in the Baltic region. Collier was working towards this aim in insisting on consultation with the USSR over the Åland Islands, but also attempting to meet the needs of the Finnish military with the intention of detaching the Finns from Germany. Unfortunately for Collier, it was the fear of Soviet, rather than German, expansion which was responsible for apprehension within the Finnish Government, and led to the fear of Finnish collusion with Germany. These factors led to a Soviet unwillingness to compromise.

The decision to enter into talks with Moscow

The events of late March and early April, however, gave no cause to disturb Snow. Poland was given a firm guarantee by the British and French governments on 31 March, but no further approaches were made to Moscow until 14 April. A Cabinet meeting of the previous day had decided 'to discuss Russia'.[14] After consideration, the Cabinet resolved to instruct Seeds to approach Litvinov with the intention of determining whether the Soviet Union would render assistance to any European neighbour which found itself the victim of German aggression.[15]

Seeds was an experienced diplomat who had all but retired from diplomatic life. As a young man he had spent time in imperial Russia and had maintained a fascination with all things Russian. When the chance of an ambassadorial post in Moscow arose, he had accepted it with great satisfaction. One of his first acts after arrival in the Soviet capital had been to warn the Foreign Office in a widely circulated despatch on 21 March that Moscow would like to see Germany and the West destroy themselves in a costly war, which left the Soviet Union untouched and as the leading power on the Continent. By the time he received his instructions about determining the likelihood of Moscow assisting any neighbour which might fall victim to German aggression, he believed this eventuality to be less likely, but one which could arise if the Soviet Union was not tied to a Western security group. More alarmingly, he saw the 'possible danger' of Hitler bribing Stalin with promises of Soviet rule over parts of Poland, Bessarabia and the Baltic States.[16] This is exactly what came to pass, but in the meantime Seeds felt vindicated enough in his fear when Litvinov rejected the British suggestion which Seeds had conveyed as being wholly inadequate and responded with a proposal of his own.[17]

Moscow's ideas for a system of guarantees

During his time in office, Litvinov, the People's Commissar for Foreign Affairs, had cultivated an image as a proponent of collective security in Europe. He had been able to operate in the sphere of foreign policy without the interference of Stalin, who 'had little experience of the outside world' and seemed prepared, at least until the aftermath of the Munich conference, to leave foreign policy to Litvinov.[18] The conclusion of the Munich crisis had seen the Soviet Union excluded from the drawing up of the new map of Europe and marked a major defeat for the collective security policy. Nevertheless, Litvinov retained his position. However, his policy of collective security had metamorphosed into a call for a straight alliance between Britain, France and the USSR, which he presented to Seeds on 17 April. It was envisaged that this alliance would act as a guarantee against aggression aimed at the USSR or any of the eastern European states bordering it between the Baltic and the Black Sea.[19]

The reaction of Finland to Anglo-Soviet talks

The fact that many of these countries may not have wanted a guarantee from an alliance involving the USSR was not a matter which seemed to bother Litvinov. Russia had no common border with Germany and consequently any German attack would have to be made through the border states. As was explained in Chapter 1, this fear had lain behind the proposals put forward to the Finnish Foreign Ministry during the so-called Yartsev initiative by the Soviet Union the previous year. Boris Yartsev, a relatively low-ranking official at the Soviet Legation in Helsinki, had approached the Finnish Foreign Ministry in the spring of 1938, expressing a fear that Finland could be used by German forces as a jumping-off board for an attack on the USSR. This threat, he explained, could not be viewed with equanimity in Moscow, and if German forces were to land in Finland, then the Red Army would not wait for them to reach the Russian border before engaging with them. In addition, he called for the island of Suursaari in the Gulf of Finland to be ceded to the Soviet Union for the purposes of converting it into an armed fortress. In return, he conceded that Finland could fortify the Åland Islands but only under Soviet supervision.[20] The conversations initiated by Yartsev ended without any change to the status quo but the Soviet Government made another attempt at persuading the Finnish Government to cede territory in March 1939. This time the Soviet diplomat Boris Stein pursued conversations with Erkko with the aim of securing a Soviet lease over the islands of Suursaari, Lauansaari and Seiskaari. By way of pressuring the Finns at this point, Moscow broke off the Soviet-Finnish trade negotiations.[21] When these talks ended without achieving the Soviet aim, Stein made clear that his government would not give up its demand for Gulf of Finland islands as they were of such importance to Russian security.[22] The proposals which Litvinov presented to Seeds were, therefore, consistent with previous Soviet policy, and, if they had been party to them, would not have surprised the Finnish Government, although they had no official confirmation of the discussions.

The content of these tentative discussions remained secret but rumours were rife. The German news service bureau arranged for a message to reach the Finnish press, saying that the British contingent at the Moscow negotiations had agreed to give the Soviet Union a free hand in Finland. Snow attempted to reassure Erkko, who had confronted the British Minister over the story on 25 April, saying that he had no information to suggest that Finland had been mentioned in the talks.[23] The Germans seemed to be working hard at spreading rumours. As well as suggesting that the British and Russians were conspiring to devour Finland, they began to 'sedulously' spread stories in Berlin that Finland was about to join the Anti-Comintern Pact, the loose ideological grouping established between Germany, Italy and Japan which aimed at defeating the forces of communism. Gripenberg called on Collier on 25 April to assure him that his government would take no such step. However, it feared German pressure and was anxious to say 'both to Germans and ... the pro-German sections of Finnish public opinion' that no departure from its neutral position was necessary. Although Collier told Gripenberg, after consultation with the Central Department, which was handling negotiations with Moscow, that nothing was contemplated which would 'protect' Finland against its will,[24] the prospect of falling prey to the Soviet Union was, unfortunately, a fear which the Germans could exploit. Erkko demonstrated these very fears when he warned Snow on 25 April of the 'political capital' which Germany could make from the reports of Britain acceding to Soviet plans for the Baltic. He suggested that the Germans were likely to come forward with their own offers to Finland.[25]

Yet the Soviet Government had not mentioned Finland by name and Snow was technically correct in informing the nervous Erkko that Finland had not been a topic of conversation between British and Soviet negotiators. Strang and Collier were equally 'truthful' when attempting to allay the fears of Gripenberg on 25 April.[26]

However, given the Soviet stance over the Åland Islands and previous approaches to the Finnish Government and the territories which the Russians intended to include in their plan, it can be taken as almost certain that Moscow was interested in enforcing a guarantee on Finland. In a Cabinet minute, Alexander Cadogan, Permanent Under-Secretary at the Foreign Office, summarised the problems which faced British policy-makers: 'We have to balance the advantage of a paper commitment by Russia to join in a war on our side against the disadvantage of associating ourselves openly with Russia.'[27] The disadvantages to which he referred were exemplified by the haste in which Erkko and Gripenberg sought the truth behind rumours which they feared presaged a dreadful consummation.

Roosevelt's appeal to Hitler and its effect in Europe

While these talks were continuing and the possibility of war showed no sign of receding, an intervention of a kind arrived from across the Atlantic Ocean. On 15 April, US President Franklin Roosevelt issued an appeal to Hitler (and Mussolini) to work towards peace in Europe. He urged as a first step that the two dictators should give an understanding not to attack any state on a list of 31 countries in Europe and the Middle East. Finland, probably for no particular reason, was first on the list.[28] Some commentators have argued that Roosevelt was only fooling himself if he thought that such a toothless intervention would have any effect in persuading Europe's leading dictators to desist from taking any action on which they had already decided. Indeed, his message has deservedly been derided over the years, with D.C. Watt's castigation of its 'disordered priorities' and 'easy rhetoric' summing up its feebleness.[29] The response Roosevelt's message brought from Hitler was contained in a speech made on 28 April in which the German dictator announced that the governments of all the states enumerated by Roosevelt had declared that they saw no danger of a German attack.[30] The next day the German Government went further. Joachim von Ribbentrop, the German Foreign Minister, summoned the representatives of the Nordic and Baltic states in Berlin to the Wilhelmstrasse to propose the conclusion of bilateral pacts of non-aggression.[31] This proposal confirmed the worst fears of Collier that Finland was easy prey for German opportunism. The German démarche also had the effect of sowing uncertainty regarding the already unclear British position with the Soviet Union. This part of the story is covered well in most standard histories of the origins of the Second World War, but aside from some (certainly not all) of these studies mentioning Finland's eventual rejection of Ribbentrop's offer, the interaction between the British and Finnish sides over this incident has been completely ignored. The outcome of Roosevelt's intervention and Ribbentrop's proposal was an increase in the problems which the Northern Department had to face.

The German offer to Finland and other Baltic States

Things were made difficult because Erkko, knowing that the British were hoping that his government would reject Ribbentrop's offer, began to tie in the German offer with the outcome of the Anglo-French-Soviet discussions. He informed Snow, in the second week of May, that the Finnish reply to Germany depended on two conditions. The first was that Finland should receive no guarantee of any kind from the Soviet Union. If this could be agreed, then Finland could reply in the negative to Germany. If, however, a pact between the Russians and the Western Allies materialised, Erkko thought that internal pressure would lead to an acceptance of the German offer. At the same time that Snow was being addressed by Erkko, Lord Halifax was coincidentally hearing the same message from Gripenberg. Halifax assured Gripenberg that the Soviet idea of guaranteeing all states 'from the Baltic to the Black Sea' had been taken in London to refer to Poland, the Baltic States and Romania. Finland, he affirmed, had not been mentioned at all, and, in any case, HMG had rejected the Russian plan.[32]

The second condition attached by Erkko, and repeated in London by Gripenberg, was that Moscow should allow a speedy and satisfactory settlement of the Åland question. Snow noted Erkko's point but was not in a position to tell him the likely response of HMG. Collier spoke with Gripenberg after the Finn's meeting with Halifax and told him that the problem of a possible Soviet veto over the Åland Islands would have to be addressed when it arose. He was more forthcoming with his colleagues in the Northern Department, arguing that if the Soviet Government did object to the fortification of the Åland Islands, then it would be difficult for HMG, in view of its previous stance, to follow the 'presumably illegal course of overriding the Soviet veto'. G.M. Fitzmaurice, the third legal adviser at the Foreign Office, claimed that from a legal perspective, ways could be found to support the Finnish perspective without obtaining Soviet consent.

Collier's point was political rather than legal, however he tried to disguise it, and his comment made in the same minute that the possible Finnish pact with Germany provides 'additional reason for trying to bring the Soviet Government into line' substantiates this interpretation.[33] He was again pursuing the line that if the suspicions that existed between the USSR and Finland could be broken down, then the obstacles which stood in the way of an agreement between Britain and the Soviet Union could be lessened, if not removed. At times, however, he could not disguise his frustration at what he saw as Finnish intransigence. After Erkko asked Snow on 12 May to ensure that HMG made it plain to the Soviet Government that they interpreted the Soviet proposals as excluding Finland, Collier erupted in anger. The Finns were being 'rather unreasonable' he argued. They had been told that Britain had not accepted the Soviet proposal and to 'expect us to raise this point with the Soviet government ... at a time when we have already incurred Soviet suspicions owing to our attitude towards the Soviet proposals is surely a bit much'.[34] It would be unfair to suggest that Collier was in favour of jettisoning Finnish interests in order to secure a working agreement with Moscow, but his comments revealed an intuition that maintaining Finnish goodwill unquestioningly would not be viewed with great equanimity in the Kremlin.

Finland's reaction to the German offer of a pact

The fear of Finland entering into a non-aggression pact with Germany disappeared on 16 May when the Finnish Minister in Berlin received instructions to reject Ribbentrop's offer.[35] The decision had not, apparently, been taken lightly. Erkko displayed great anxiety that the responsibility to reject the German offer had been thrust upon him and rumours abounded of differing opinions within the Finnish army. The Commander-in-Chief, General Osterman, had argued forcefully and vociferously against the rejection of the pact offer, and Erkko had only managed to carry his point thanks to the support he received from General Oesch, the Chief of the General Staff. The stance of the latter came as a surprise to Collier who revealed that he had previously thought of Oesch as being pro-German.[36] He was later informed by Snow that the General's change of heart had come about as a result of his shock at Germany's occupation of Czechoslovakia.[37]

Of all the Nordic countries, only Denmark reacted positively to the German proposal and entered into a non-aggression pact with Germany. The complete worthlessness of the pact that the Danes had entered into was demonstrated when Hitler ordered the occupation of their country some 12 months later. More significantly, as far as Soviet suspicions in the Baltic were concerned, were the agreements by Estonia and Latvia to conclude pacts of non-aggression with Germany. The fact that Hitler was later willing to sacrifice the independence of the Baltic States to the USSR, despite the conclusion of the pacts, again shows the insignificance which Hitler attached to these signatures.

The appointment of Molotov as Commissar for Foreign Affairs

The relatively good news for the Northern Department of the Finnish 'snub' to Germany had to be set against developments in Moscow. On 3

May, Maxim Litvinov was dismissed by Stalin as Commissar for Foreign Affairs and replaced by Vyacheslav Molotov. The significance of the replacement of the proponent of collective security by a loyal and long-standing follower of Stalin has formed an ongoing topic for debate[38] but the implications for Finland were clear. On 15 May, Molotov summoned Seeds to tell him that the Soviet Government had rejected the latest Western proposals which had in fact been only a slight amendment to their submission of a month earlier, and repeated the Soviet demands. This time, however, Finland was mentioned by name. This inclusion was seen as 'significant' by Cadogan, who argued that it meant that the issue of Finland would have to be taken up with the Soviet Union in connection with Anglo-Soviet relations in the face of aggression.[39] Snow and the British Ministers in Latvia and Estonia were immediately informed that the Soviet Union wished to include Finland within the guarantee.[40]

Seeds confronted Molotov with an argument against the inclusion of Finland in a security arrangement. He informed the Commissar that Britain associated Finland with the Scandinavian rather than the Baltic States. For this reason, the British Government preferred that Finland maintain its neutrality on the same lines as Norway and Sweden (who had remained outside the 1914–1918 conflict) and believed that 'this could be assured if Finland were not reminded of certain unpleasant historical associations with Russia'. In reply, Molotov declared that his government regarded Finland as a Baltic rather than a Scandinavian nation and suggested that if Britain and France were to openly associate with the Soviet Union, then Finnish suspicions would be weakened.[41] There was some force in Molotov's argument but it relied on the Finnish Government trusting Britain enough to balance future Soviet influence in Finland. The delays and problems which had characterised the British effort to aid Finland's rearmament had not helped to create such a feeling. The arguments which Collier and his colleagues had presented to the service ministries (discussed in Chapters 1 and 3) now appeared even stronger. The difficulties in securing an agreement with Moscow were correspondingly greater. Halifax acknowledged this when he told the Cabinet that the governments of Finland and the Baltic States were unwilling to receive any sort of guarantee from the Soviet Union. However, he hoped that these problems could be surmounted and thought that an agreement ought to be reached as soon as possible.[42] He knew as well as anyone how difficult these problems were. Gripenberg had told him on 10 May that Finland wanted to maintain a strict neutrality and that any guarantee would not be compatible with this. Halifax had assured him that even were Finland to be mentioned by name (which it hadn't been at that point), the British Government would not agree to the proposal.[43]

The Chiefs of Staff's views on a Soviet alliance

An aide-mémoire presented to the Cabinet by the Chiefs of Staff Committee on 16 May agreed with Halifax that an agreement between the Western powers and the USSR was a necessary measure to prevent further German aggression and expansion. However, they believed that a German attack on the Soviet Union via Finland or the Baltic States was unlikely. If Germany did attack and occupy these small nations, then it was possible that the USSR would declare war, but refuse to move outside its own frontiers. In these circumstances, Britain and France would bear the brunt of the war so 'from a strictly military point of view, we should refuse to guarantee any of the Baltic States'.[44]

Snow's opposition to an Anglo-Soviet agreement

Snow now took a stance of opposing not only an unsolicited guarantee for Finland but also any association with Moscow at all. Commenting on Molotov's suggestion that Finnish suspicions of the Soviet Union would be allayed if British protection came as part of the package, he assessed that the fears of the Finns would not be dispelled and the position which Britain held in Finland would be damaged. 'It would be folly', he declared 'to assume that the effects of one thousand years of first-hand experience or even the memories of the independence war of twenty years ago could be enforced by wishing.' Voicing an opinion which would be repeated by others later, Ivone Kirkpatrick of the Central Department made a marginal comment on Snow's despatch saying that 'we cannot afford to be guided by [Finnish views]'.[45]

The fact that the Chiefs of Staff and Halifax had started to look favourably at an alliance with Soviet Russia led to Chamberlain accepting the possibility of a deal with Moscow. On 24 May he spoke to the House of Commons saying that if, as he expected, all obstacles could be removed, a system of co-operation between Britain, France and the Soviet Union would soon be installed.[46] However, seeing as he proposed that Russian aid could only be enlisted under Article XVI of the League of Nations' Charter, he was clearly intent on erecting a barrier of his own. In a letter to his sister, the Prime Minister explained that this caveat had been included in anticipation that it would give the Soviet connection 'a temporary character'.[47] Molotov, however, read just such an intention into the plan and, after consulting the Supreme Soviet, informed Seeds (and William Strang who had now joined him) that although it seemed as if the Western powers had accepted the principle of mutual assistance, they had made no mention of the three states on the northwestern border of the Soviet Union: Estonia, Latvia and Finland. These states could prove susceptible to German attack and, as Molotov said, none of them, including

Finland, would prove able 'to defend their neutrality in the event of an attack by aggressors'. For this reason, his government had to insist that Britain and France join them in guaranteeing the security of 'all the European countries bordering upon the USSR, without exception'.[48]

Collier and the Moscow talks

The fact that the talks had not been conducted *in foro publico* did not prevent rumours of their substance permeating the capitals of Europe. Gripenberg called on Collier on 22 May to enquire whether the Soviet Government had reformulated its demands since his last visit to the Foreign Office. Avoiding a direct answer, Collier replied that, as far as he knew, HMG was determined not to join a Soviet guarantee of Finland and the Baltic States. He thought that a promise to help the USSR if it was attacked through any of these countries could be given, but not a guarantee to the countries themselves. Gripenberg accepted this but added that his government needed strong assurances that HMG was not contemplating any pact which would be unwanted by Finland.[49] The views of the Finnish Government were made explicit when Erkko spoke to the Eduskunta, the Finnish parliament, on 21 May, saying that any 'so-called assistance' would be regarded by his government as aggression.[50] However, Molotov did not see things this way. In a speech to the Supreme Soviet on 31 May, he condemned the Anglo-French proposals as doing nothing to address the question of guarantees for the states on the USSR's northwestern border which might not be able to look after themselves 'in the event of aggression'.[51]

Attempts to find a mutually acceptable formula

A means of satisfying both Finland and the Soviet Union was beginning to prove impossible. Ivan Maisky, the Soviet Ambassador in London, told Halifax on 12 June that the problem of the three Baltic States (according to his definition these were Finland, Estonia and Latvia) 'was the fundamental problem without which negotiations could not be brought to a successful conclusion'. In reply, Halifax told Maisky that he appreciated the Soviet requirement for security in this respect but repeated the now familiar objection that 'we could not impose assurances on states which did not require them'.[52] For all Chamberlain's transparent optimism in May, it now seemed as if British policy was to refuse the important concession of guarantees to Moscow. The Prime Minister himself told a meeting of the Cabinet's Foreign Policy Committee on 9 June that the British Government should not put Estonia and Finland in the same position in regard to guarantees as Greece or Romania.[53] This gave the two named states a higher priority in the eyes of the British Government than Finland.

In actual fact, the real importance of Finland and Estonia lay in their proximity to German trade routes in the Baltic Sea. Memoranda on German dependence on Swedish iron ore had been prepared by the Industrial Intelligence Centre since January 1937 and in February 1939 it recommended that 'strike action' be taken to prevent this 'most important commodity of all [from] reaching our enemy'.[54] Collier, as noted in a previous chapter, had also pointed to the importance of Swedish iron ore for the German economy. This reasoning did not, however, figure in the Prime Minister's assessment. Whereas Collier and some of his colleagues felt that the Soviet Union would be the most significant ally in depriving Germany of this vital raw material – witness their arguments over the Åland Islands question – Chamberlain was far from being convinced that it should be given the chance.

The Prime Minister may have failed to consider the possibility of the disruption of Germany's Baltic trade but those who were better informed on Baltic affairs did not overlook the possibility. Snow feared that the strategic importance of Finnish territory for both Germany and the Soviet Union – trade routes in the case of the former, a jumping-off point for invasion so far as the latter were concerned – had given rise to the belief in Moscow that Finland, in common with the Baltic States, could not survive a major war and would come under the domination of either the German or Soviet Government. This being the case, 'he could understand the Soviets' anxiety to obtain a position in which they would have as free hands as possible' in regard to the countries in question. Unfortunately, he lamented, if the Finns were faced with a choice, they would choose Germany. Finland's previous subjugation by the Russian Empire meant that no Finnish government could choose otherwise. He finished with a warning that if the British Government decided to accommodate Soviet wishes regarding Finland, then Britain's future position in Finland would not be rosy. German influence would grow, and any hope of retaining Finnish sympathy in wartime would disappear. There was not much anyone in the Northern Department could say to this. Barclay minuted that the Department was fully aware of the feelings of the Finns, but nobody at this stage was prepared to take it further than that.[55]

The impressions of C.G. Mannerheim and other soldiers

The Northern Department may have been aware of the feelings of the Finns but they clearly hoped that Finland would not stand in the way of an agreement between Britain and the USSR. For its part, the Finnish Government was responsible for making and implementing decisions relevant to the acceptance of a guarantee, but appreciation of the British position was not lacking in important circles in Finland. General Sir Walter Kirke of the British Army arrived in Finland on 17 June to renew acquaintances made on his previous visit in the 1920s and was met at the airport by Field Marshal Mannerheim. This gesture was more fully appreciated the following week when Mannerheim declined to greet the German General Halder on arrival. At a dinner given in General Kirke's honour on 18 June, Snow struck up conversation with Mannerheim, telling him that while Finland's unfavourable impression of British negotiations in Moscow was understandable, he hoped that the Field Marshal realised that the intention of HMG was to create a deterrent to further German aggression in Europe, and that all guarantees issued would remain purely hypothetical. Mannerheim replied that he did indeed understand the British position. He then outlined his own thoughts on the matter. Of the three alternatives on offer – (1) an agreement between the USSR and Britain; (2) between the USSR and Germany; and (3) no agreement at all – the best would be that between Soviet Russia and Britain. From Finland's perspective, the worst option would be an arrangement between Moscow and Berlin. If Russia entered into no agreement with anybody, then Stalin would be left with a free hand after the combatants in the certain Western-Germanic war had exhausted themselves. He added, however, that he was speaking from a purely 'theoretical and international' point of view, and that as a Finn he could not possibly welcome a guarantee from the Soviet Union, who would certainly insist on a say in Finland's defence policy once a guarantee had been granted. The Central Department's Frank Roberts, a future Ambassador in Moscow, expressed satisfaction that Mannerheim 'clearly realised the wider issues at stake'.[56]

Influential as the Field Marshal was, he did not hold a current post in the Finnish military. Worry was expressed by both Colonel Vale, the military attaché in Riga, and Snow that a guarantee to Finland which involved the USSR in any way could lead the Finnish military to seek a German alliance. The Acting Commander of the 2nd Finnish Division had said as much to Vale when he visited Tampere with General Kirke. Snow commented that he had heard similar rumours, admittedly from a source 'which is not altogether reliable' that conversations had taken place during General Halder's visit in regard to Finland being given Luftwaffe protection in the event of war with Russia.[57]

'Indirect aggression'

The insistence by Moscow that Finland and the Baltic States constituted a vital interest to its security and should therefore be protected by guarantee, and the resolution of the Finns that such a guarantee would constitute a near warlike act meant that no ideal solution was available to British negotiators. Moscow could only be brought into the anti-Hitler fold at the price of upsetting the Finns and probably sending them in the opposite direction. If, on the other hand, the Finns were to be placated and any advances to the Soviet Union discontinued, then the deterrent which the Western Allies wished to place before Hitler would be seriously undermined. At the end of June, in an apparent attempt to have it as many ways as possible, Halifax instructed Seeds to approach Molotov, agreeing to guarantee all states bordering Finland and the Soviet Union, including Finland and the Baltic States, but asking that they should only be included in a secret protocol, as any intimation that they had been included against their wishes could play into German hands and prove 'very prejudicial to the solidarity of the peace front'.[58] This seemed to offer the Soviet Government just about everything it had been asking for, but after considering the new Allied offer, Molotov raised a new demand. So-called 'indirect' aggression became the new stumbling block. The Kremlin's definition of this term reflected a concern that a pro-German *coup d'état* in any of the bordering countries, achieved without German intervention, could lead to a deterioration of the Soviet security position without activating the pact with the Allies. The fear of the British and French governments was that the Soviet Government could feel tempted to view any changes in government in these countries as a hostile act.[59] When Maisky explained the Soviet position to a prominent official in the City of London, he said that his government needed this clause because of German and Italian actions in Spain, Czechoslovakia and Albania.[60] He could have thrown in the Estonian and Latvian adherence to a non-aggression pact with Germany as further examples.

So far Snow had not been informed officially of the major concessions Britain had made to the USSR regarding guarantees, for fear of the Finnish Government finding out. On 8 July he cabled London requesting 'further particulars' as to the 'rights' which were to be granted to Soviet Russia, and repeated his argument that nothing should be done which could justify the Finnish reproaches that they were being traded away. 'To start by placing Finland under what might appear to be Russian protection', he contended, 'might be difficult to reconcile with the suggested explanation that the Anglo-Soviet agreement is designed to assist the Finns to maintain [their] independence.'[61]

This was undoubtedly an accurate assessment of the feelings of the Finnish Government, who presumably had more than an inkling of the substance of the latest proposals in Moscow. The fact that Maisky felt able to mention the substance of the discussions to a non-government figure in Britain showed that confidentiality with regard to the Moscow talks was now being honoured more in the breach than the observance. Gripenberg called at the Foreign Office on 7 July, without the knowledge of his government, but with the conviction that Britain had accepted Molotov's terms regarding a guarantee for Finland. He was told by Collier that the British Government was merely recognising that the Soviet Government had a vital interest in the territorial integrity of the Baltic States (within which it included Finland) in the same way that the preservation of the Low Countries was essential to the strategic defence of the Allies. Collier explained that neither Holland nor Belgium required a guarantee but that had not stopped HMG from asserting that they composed a vital interest, and the Baltic States and Finland were just as important to the USSR. The recognition of this fact did not mean that an unsolicited guarantee had been forced on Finland or anyone else. When Gripenberg replied that his government had no fears of a British guarantee but would decline one from a government which aimed at 'infiltration and penetration' (as this was more or less how the Soviet Union later extended its rule over Latvia and Estonia, his fears were justified) he was told that Europe faced a real and immediate peril, which emanated from Berlin and not Moscow. If Poland was reduced by Germany to the level of Czechoslovakia, then the Baltic States would become German protectorates. This eventuality, Collier admitted, might be preferred in Helsinki to Russian domination but he believed that the policy HMG was following was much more likely to preserve Finnish and Baltic independence. Furthermore, if it was Germany rather than the Allies who reached agreement with the Soviet Union, then the position of Finland and the Baltic States would become hopeless. The British negotiators were aware of the Finnish fears and did not want to drive the Finns into the arms of Germany but 'had to take into account the immediate perils which confronted us'.[62] Collier's argument was in line with both Halifax's directive to Seeds and Mannerheim's unofficial assessment of the situation. What he now seemed to believe was that a choice based on moral considerations based on a small state's right to choose its own allies was a luxury Britain could not afford.

His tone was echoed by his immediate superior, Sir Lancelot Oliphant, a Permanent Under-Secretary with responsibility for the Northern Department, who justified the proposal for the inclusion within a secret annexe in a communication to Snow. Admitting that the effort to reconcile Soviet demands with Finnish susceptibilities represented 'a choice of evils', he went on to argue that 'unless we are prepared to forego completely the prospects for any Russian agreement – a course which would have the gravest military and political consequences – we must annoy the Finns and the Baltic States'.[63] Oliphant had previously held grave doubts regarding the benefits of a Soviet association. Two days before the announcement of the Polish guarantee, he minuted that Admiral Sir Hugh Sinclair had informed him that the Soviet armed forces could do nothing of real value.[64] The purges of the Red Army during the 1930s had created an impression that the military strength of the USSR was inconsiderable. As late as 31 May, Cadogan made a diary entry expressing amusement at Oliphant's tendency to convince his colleagues that 'his Bol[shevik] friends are as black as he paints them'.[65] His new outlook did not mean, however, that he thought Britain should provide the USSR with an excuse to interfere in the internal affairs of its neighbours.[66] An idea of Snow's, which he sent to the Northern Department on 3 July, but which Oliphant did not address, was whether the Finns would feel more amenable to a guarantee if a satisfactory deal could be reached over the islands of Lauanssarri and Seiskari in the eastern Baltic which had been the subject of the Stein mission a few months earlier (see Chapter 2). Lascelles doubted that an agreement over these islands was likely and questioned the advisability of offering mediation in the matter, even if an Anglo-Franco-Soviet pact could be secured. Collier, on the other hand, thought that the Finns could, and should, ask for mediation after a pact between London and Moscow had been signed and in this case it should be granted.[67] Collier seemed to believe that an acceptable compromise between Finnish and Soviet interests was possible, but he was rightly committed to a policy which elevated British interests above the moral consideration of upholding a political consensus in the Baltic.

Gripenberg, who even by the middle of July had still not been informed officially of the latest developments in Moscow, felt worried enough by the rumours to approach a higher level at the Foreign Office, and on 14 July he called on Under-Secretary of State for Foreign Affairs, R.A. Butler. Butler has been represented as an opponent of any association with the Soviet Union and a public servant who worked to undermine any moves towards rapprochement with the USSR.[68] However, his reaction to the presentation of a note by Gripenberg on behalf of his government, in which his replies carried no semblance of an anti-Soviet stance suggests that, in this instance at least, he may have been familiar with Northern Department arguments, as his reply to Gripenberg was very similar to the views being expressed by Collier. Gripenberg's note laid out the Finnish Government's policy in five points, which read as follows:

1   The Finnish Government are decided to adhere to a policy of strict neutrality and to defend their neutrality with all means at their disposal.
2   The Finnish Government cannot admit the right of any power to come to their assistance for the purpose of resisting an alleged direct or 'indirect' aggression on Finland in any other cases other than when they themselves have asked for such assistance.
3   The Finnish Government will consider as an aggressor any power, who, without their consent, attempts to render them armed assistance.
4   The Finnish Government hope that His Majesty's Government will not enter into an international agreement to introduce provisions which in some way or other might adversely affect their policy of strict neutrality.
5   The Finnish Government consider that the notion of 'indirect aggression' might encourage other powers to inadmissible interference in the internal affairs of Finland.

The note demonstrated quite clearly that the Finnish Government was unhappy with the British Government's policy towards Moscow and was thoroughly opposed to any agreement between the great powers which would compromise its neutrality. In addition to this written communication, Gripenberg asked orally why a simple tripartite pact between Britain, France and the USSR could not suffice. Butler told him that this would not have had any application to the immediate problem of aggression on Poland. Once the projected agreement had begun to address this local application, it had become necessary to enlarge the discussions to make reference to the Baltic States which were as important to the Soviet Union as the Low Countries were to Britain. The problem of Polish unwillingness to enter into alliance with Soviet Russia was glossed over by Butler in his attempt to repeat the justifications outlined above by others to the Finnish Minister.[69] Since he later recorded his distaste for the Polish guarantee, which by pledging military support to Germany's eastern neighbour 'gave Russia just the excuse not to defend herself against Germany',[70] the advocacy of a conclusion of a pact for Finland against its wishes seems inconsistent. Butler opposed an alliance with the USSR, played an important role in the creation of Chamberlain's League of Nations clause, and tended to follow up any opportunities for Anglo-German understanding. He was usually more amenable to seeking agreement with Berlin than Moscow. These views appear inconsistent with the arguments he presented to Gripenberg. They were certainly unusual for Butler. No documentary evidence is available to explain his attitude at this interview. However, as he was articulating views which were held at the Northern Department, most importantly by Collier, it is difficult to believe that in this instance he was not under the temporary influence of their arguments.

The above comments, conveyed by Foreign Office members to the Finnish Minister in London and the British Minister in Helsinki, demonstrate a belief in the Northern Department of the need for full Soviet participation in an anti-Hitler coalition. Such a coalition could deter Hitler from going to war in the first place, and if he did initiate hostilities, the USSR could play a big part in defeating him. They were fully aware of the unpleasant consequences which could possibly ensue from agreeing to Moscow's demands and did not try to condone them, but their main concern was the immediate threat to Europe posed by the German Reich.

The possibility of German-Soviet rapprochement

The Germans also posed a threat to the chances of a successful conclusion of the Moscow talks, although it was not widely realised at the time. Cadogan had observed early in the negotiations that if agreement were not reached, then the door would be open for the Soviet Government to 'make some kind of non-intervention agreement with the German government'. He did not think this possibility likely, however. R.A.C. Parker has noted how Cadogan minuted as early as February 1939 the need to monitor the 'development of any tendency towards a *rapprochement* between Germany and the Soviet', yet was unable to bring himself to trust his own observation.[71] Cadogan was not alone in believing that the chances of a Soviet-German friendship were remote. This belief was also held at Cabinet level, where the conviction that the supposed ideological gulf between Germany and the USSR militated against any agreement with each other held sway. In any case, 'the cool, controlled, inflexible mind and the cold-blooded defensive pragmatism of the *Realpolitiker*'[72] meant that Stalin, for one, did not see ideological differences as a barrier to advantageous political settlements. More importantly, Germany was in a position to make offers to the USSR which the Allies could not match. Hitler had made a decision to cultivate better relations with Moscow in May, and at the end of July Karl Schnurre, the head of the Eastern Section of the German Foreign Ministry, summed up the attractions of the German case in a memorandum circulated to Russian diplomats which was phrased:

> What could England offer Russia? At best, participation in a European war and the hostility of Germany, but not a single desirable end for Russia. What could we offer on the other hand? Neutrality and staying out of a possible European conflict and, if Moscow wished, a German-Russian understanding on mutual interest, which, just as in former times, would work out to the advantage of both countries.[73]

In other words, the concessions which the Soviet Government was trying to extract from the British and French, which would probably only be granted for the length of the emergency, could be granted by Germany at a much cheaper price. This would then leave Hitler free of the worry of Soviet animosity to his eastern plans and the fear of war on two fronts. It would also mean that the Soviet Union would get the 'free hand' in the Baltic which had so worried Erkko, Gripenberg and Snow. Naturally, the concept of 'indirect' aggression would lose its meaning if agreement between the Russians and Germans were reached.

The continuing difficulties in satisfying both Helsinki and Moscow

The notion of 'indirect aggression' was still causing frustration and concern among British officials. Chamberlain told the House of Commons on 31 July that Britain was looking to find a satisfactory definition of 'indirect aggression'. Speaking for Halifax in the House of Commons on the same day, Butler seemed to rule out the imposition of an indirect aggression clause in any future agreement with Moscow, saying that Britain was now unwilling 'to encroach on the independence of the Baltic States', but admitted that 'the violation of the neutrality of [Finland or the Baltic States] would be a matter of vital interest to the three governments concerned'. Three days later, Halifax spoke to the House of Lords on the same subject, regretting that no formula on indirect aggression had been agreed upon.[74] These three statements show that the most senior of British foreign policy-makers retained a concern for the aspirations of Finland and its small neighbours, despite a recognition that there was no way around granting the Russian requests if an agreement was to be reached. The noises coming from Moscow made it clear that an acceptance of both the imposition of a guarantee and the concept of indirect aggression were pre-requisites to any progress. In August, Molotov protested to Seeds and to the French Ambassador M. Naggiar about Butler's remarks, and his negative attitude led to Seeds reporting the negotiations as having suffered 'a severe setback'. Indeed, the political negotiations ended at this point, with the question of 'indirect' aggression still unsettled. By this time, however, the British and French governments had complied with a Soviet request for the despatch of military missions to Moscow, and plans for their departure were in progress.[75] Even though the political negotiations had stalled, the military talks were still going ahead.

Collier had just as much sympathy for Finnish interests as his superiors, but held a much more realistic attitude on what sacrifices were necessary for the creation of a credible defence front. Replying to Sir Norman Vernon of Spillers Ltd who had received an urgent communication from a M. Søren Berner, the Finland-based agent for the Spillers company, highlighting Soviet untrustworthiness, urging Britain to 'keep Finland as its friend' and requesting the support of *The Times* for these policies, Collier spelled out the overriding importance of an Anglo-Soviet alliance. It was unfortunate, he argued, that Berner shared 'the prejudices and misconceptions which seem to be current in Finland at the present moment' and suggested that Sir Norman reply by referring M. Berner to speeches made by the Prime Minister and R.A. Butler, notably those highlighted above. His explanation went further and encapsulated his own attitude to the talks. In replying to Sir Norman in this way, Collier was acting as the spokesman for the Foreign Office and articulating its policy but his tone indicates clearly the differences in emphasis which separated his own views from those of his superiors. For this reason, his remarks are worth quoting at length:

You can therefore assure Mr Berner that so far from having sold his country to the Bolsheviks, Great Britain has done nothing to imperil its sovereignty and neutrality. We have in fact risked the preservation of the peace of Europe by insisting on our point of view. After all, Finland has just as great an interest as any other country in the preservation of peace; and a war in Eastern Europe, whatever the result, would probably jeopardise the independence of the smaller states. It does not seem to be sufficiently recognised in Finland that the danger of war in Europe has been and is an immediate one, which can only be met by immediate measures. Hence our general policy of the last few months, of which our negotiations with the Soviet Union are a logical outcome. If a war were to arise over Danzig in the near future, Finland and the Baltic States might be in the position of having to choose between Soviet and German domination. We fully appreciate that in such circumstances they might prefer German domination; but our policy is designed to preserve their independence and neutrality, which we naturally assume they would prefer to either of the above eventualities.

There has been a considerable amount of talk in Finland and other countries that we propose to 'guarantee' Finland or allow the Soviet Union to guarantee her. There is not in fact any question of a guarantee, either Soviet or British, but we cannot reasonably object that the Soviet Government assert that the independence and integrity of the Baltic States and of Finland is of vital interest to them, in exactly the same way that the independence and integrity of the Low Countries are of vital interest to us. We have not therefore compromised the neutrality of the Netherlands, nor have we given her a guarantee. It is a statement of fact. The position of Finland is similar, and her neutrality will not be compromised if the British, French and Soviet governments declare they will fight Germany if Germany violates Finland's neutrality. The neutrality, in that event, will already have been compromised by Germany. One of our main objects in our negotiations with the Soviet Government, as shown in the parliamentary statements quoted above, has been to devise a suitable formula which would recognise the vital interest of the Soviet Union in the independence and integrity of these states without permitting the signatories of the agreement to arrogate to themselves any right of interference in the internal affairs of those states.[76]

These remarks contained frustration at the manner in which progress in the Anglo-Franco-Soviet talks was being impeded by the very people whom Collier thought would benefit most from their successful conclusion. The notion that Finland and the Baltic States constituted an area of importance to the Soviet Union every bit as great as that of Belgium and the Netherlands to Britain had been voiced before, most prominently by Butler. Yet whereas Butler's comments to Gripenberg suggested an alternative manner of looking at the problem, Collier's assessment asserted that a recognition of the importance of the region was the only starting point if war was to be averted, and bitterly attacked the denial of what he saw as an uncontested fact. His earlier belief that, while Soviet support was desirable, Britain could not afford to drive the Finns into the Germans' arms,[77] had been modified to an opinion that a Soviet connection, with its prospects for denying movement to the Germans in the Baltic, was an utter necessity. His sympathy with the dreadful position which seemed to be facing the Finns could not be doubted but his assessment was based on a realistic and pragmatic consideration of the situation. Henry Kissinger, in an address to a group of Nobel laureates in 1988, explained to the gathering that the policy-maker who has to deal with reality soon learns to strive for the best that can be achieved, not the best that can be imagined, all the while attempting to avoid the greatest immorality, meaning world war.[78] Collier's attitude suggests a belief that the result of failing to realise the best that could be achieved would lead to the very worst that could be imagined.

The end of the Moscow negotiations

The worst, however, was the likeliest outcome by the time that the British military representative, Admiral Sir Reginald Plunket Ernle-Erle-Drax, arrived in Moscow to take up military talks in the hope of establishing the breakthrough which had eluded the political negotiators. Having no plenipotentiary powers, the Admiral was always unlikely to achieve this aim, through no fault of his own. The fact that anything and everything discussed had to be referred back to London militated against the possibility of swift progress. He was in no position to match the speed with which Ribbentrop moved in obtaining a Russian stance favourable to his government's position. Secret negotiations between German and Russian representatives took place throughout August. They culminated in the pact of non-aggression signed between Molotov and Ribbentrop on 23 August. A secret annexe to the pact assigned Latvia, Estonia and Finland to the Soviet sphere of influence, thus delivering to the Soviet Government that which the Allies had failed to. This result represented not just the worst fears of Collier, but also those of Mannerheim and indeed Erkko. They were not to realise the full extent of Nazi-Soviet collusion, however, until the Soviet Union began making demands on its Baltic neighbours in October.

The Government and Halifax had been pursuing a policy whose ends were compatible with Northern Department thinking. The means that they used were not. The lethargy which seemed to characterise their efforts, symbolised most dramatically by Drax's lack of full negotiating powers, contrasted with the priority which Collier assigned to an agreement. Collier was in full realisation of the dire consequences of failure in Moscow. He demonstrated a conviction that a pact with the Soviet Union was essential to preserve Britain's position in Europe. Collier has been accused by historian Richard Lamb of failing to pass on information which he received suggesting that a Nazi-Soviet pact was a possibility.[79] This criticism seems unfair when Collier's views outlined in this chapter are taken into account. The urgency which he displayed in his communications to Gripenberg and particularly Sir Norman Vernon show how seriously Collier viewed the conclusion of a pact and how strongly he saw Finnish opposition as threatening the peace of Europe. An agreement with Moscow was something he placed great value on. As Louise Shaw has noted, while he 'did not state specifically his support for the acceptance of Soviet proposals', he did encourage the British Government to make an agreement with Moscow.[80] Significantly, his superiors, Sir Lancelot Oliphant and R.A. Butler, spoke in a very similar fashion, despite holding reservations about a Moscow connection. While the British negotiators had conceded most of the Russian demands regarding Finland and the Baltic States, it appeared as if their actions did not carry a great deal of enthusiasm. The final sticking point of 'indirect' aggression, with its implication of interference in the affairs of sovereign states, was particularly distasteful to British policy-makers. Collier's conviction that Finland and its small neighbours would not be spared from catastrophe if war broke out implicitly questioned the benefits of such a moral stance to anyone. His desperation for a pact should not, however, cloud the fact that neither he nor any other British policy-maker was in a position to offer such favourable terms to Stalin as was Hitler. Collier could perhaps be criticised for not impressing his views strongly enough on the Finnish Government but he was initially hopeful that some compromise between the Finns and the Russians could be arrived at, and he could not be accused of misleading Gripenberg with false promises. Snow, although sympathetic to the Finnish position, and unmovingly hostile to the idea of granting any Soviet right to determine 'indirect aggression' in his messages to the Foreign Office, told Erkko at an early stage that an Anglo-Soviet understanding would be in the best interests of Helsinki as well as London. The failure of the talks meant that these best interests could not be met. Policy in future, including the question of meeting Finnish rearmament requests, had to be decided with the new Nazi-Soviet friendship firmly in mind. The implications which it held for Finland were ominous and were to prove a distraction to more people than Collier and Snow.

The Northern Department, and Snow, understood Finland's reluctance to allow itself to fall into a Moscow-led system of guarantees. However, they also believed that British interests would be threatened, and that

German expansion would be an inevitable consequence, if an agreement could not be reached with the Soviet Union. The Northern Department's influence was limited during the negotiations but it remained the section of the Foreign Office with responsibility for Finnish affairs, and was left with the task of explaining British policy to Finnish representatives. The sympathy which it had for Finland is evident, but it is also clear that, with Hitler threatening, it emphasised the British national interest above any consideration of the integrity of a small state.

The Northern Department was more eager than the government or the Foreign Secretary for agreement with the USSR.[81] It understood the arguments which were presented by Molotov regarding Soviet security, as well as it understood the fears which existed in Finland of Russian encroachment. In order to prevent the expansion of German influence in the Baltic, and to reach an agreement with the USSR which would be aimed at Germany, the Northern Department was reluctantly willing to compromise the expressed wishes of the Finnish Government. It did not want any obstacles standing in the way of the prize of an alliance with the Soviet Union. It did its best to convince the Finns that such an alliance would be in Finland's best interests, but its priority at this stage was British security against Hitler. Finland represented a problem, not a priority.

5

THE AFTERMATH OF THE NAZI-SOVIET PACT

The Northern Department and the deterioration of Finno-Soviet relations

The Nazi-Soviet pact meant that the Soviet Union could no longer be considered a possible ally against Germany. Unknown to the Northern Department, or anyone else outside the Soviet and German Governments, it also meant that Finland had been assigned a place within Moscow's sphere of influence. This chapter shows the reaction by the Northern Department to the growing tension between Finland and the USSR which was one consequence of the pact, and also demonstrates the divergent opinions between Collier and the Northern Department in London and Thomas Snow in Helsinki. While the latter saw Soviet aggression as something to be resisted, the former viewed it as something which was almost to be welcomed.

Prior to the Nazi-Soviet pact, Collier and others at the Northern Department had argued in favour of Britain making a contribution to some of Finland's defence requirements. This was despite the opposition of the War Office, the Air Ministry and the Admiralty. The Northern Department's reasoning had been based on the political consideration that Finland should be encouraged to keep its distance from Germany and this could only happen if Britain and not Germany acted as Finland's quartermaster. The agreement between Moscow and Berlin, however, eliminated any possibility of Finnish co-operation with the Third Reich. It also precluded any chance of British collaboration with the Soviet Union to guarantee the former frontiers of Finland and the Baltic States. The hope in the Northern Department that Britain could help to foster better Finno-Soviet relations through its policy on the Åland Islands and rearmament suffered a bitter blow. Instead, thanks to a secret annexe to the document signed by Ribbentrop and Molotov on August 24, Finland had been delivered into the Soviet sphere of influence.

Despite the fact that the reasons advocated by the Northern Department for assisting in the Finnish rearmament programme had now been rendered sterile, interest in the topic within the department did not disappear. The focus, however, changed. Rather than pursuing its political line, the Northern Department began to advocate military aid to Finland for the more traditional purpose of defending its territory. This change in emphasis did not lead to a break in the consistency of the Northern Department's outlook. For the previous few months, its policy in relation to Finland had been aimed at containing or reducing German influence in that part of the world. Since 3 September, the previously likely, if hypothetical, supposition that war would break out with Nazi Germany had turned into a proven fact. The need to contain German influence was, therefore, more urgent than ever, and the means of acting on this proposition needed to change. Whereas in peacetime, Collier had thought it desirable to bring Finland and the Soviet Union closer together for the purpose of strengthening the British position, once war had been declared, he expressed stronger backing for Finland. This ran the obvious danger of creating friction with the Soviet Union, but the hope was that once Moscow engaged in hostilities in the Baltic region, events would soon run out of control and conflict between Germany and the USSR would ensue. Collier's recommendations, detailed in this chapter, can be interpreted as seeking to exploit tension between Finland and the USSR as a means of combating German influence in the Baltic. What had not changed, however, was the attitude of the service ministries which continued to oppose the proposals of the Northern Department.

The beginnings of Soviet aggression

On 17 September, Red Army troops moved into the section of Poland assigned to them by the annexe to the pact and took control of the area. The Soviet Government then went about bringing the other areas which the pact had allocated to it under its control. Between 28 September and 10 October Moscow concluded mutual assistance pacts with Estonia, Latvia and Lithuania. Hoping, and probably expecting, the Finnish Government to acquiesce in the same manner as its Baltic neighbours, Molotov issued an 'invitation' to Finland to enter into talks on 5 October. Equally ominous for the Finns was a speech made by Hitler the next day in which he omitted Finland from a list of states with which Germany enjoyed friendly relations. The Finnish delegation which paid three visits to Moscow between 12 October and 9 November were to receive no support of any kind from Germany.

The significance of Finland

Not surprisingly, it was expected in London and Helsinki that the Soviet Government would make demands on the Finns as it had on the Baltic republics. On the day of Moscow's announcement of its mutual assistance pact with Estonia, Snow warned the Northern Department of Russia's 'territorial ambitions in regard to Finland'. The Soviet Government, he assessed, was in a good position now that Germany would not oppose its moves in the Baltic. Estonia's new status had worsened Finland's position, a fact which D.W. Lascelles, the First Secretary at the Northern Department, also noted.[1] It was clear that Finland's range of choices was limited. It could surrender to Soviet demands in the manner of its Baltic neighbours. It could attempt to negotiate acceptable terms with the Russians. If these options seemed unattractive, it could resist. There was no doubt now that any armaments which the Finns procured could only be intended for future use against the Soviet Union. This was a scenario which the Northern Department had hoped could be avoided but the European situation which it had hoped for was an impossibility in the aftermath of the Nazi-Soviet pact.

The Finnish Government and the Northern Department had been disappointed in the response of the service ministries to Finnish enquiries in the first nine months of 1939. The War Office had attached stringent conditions to the sale of ammunition to Finland and the Air Ministry had been unco-operative over the attempts to arrange a visit to Britain by the Chief of the Finnish Air Staff. The general sense of frustration which the Northern Department felt towards the service ministries continued following Britain's declaration of war on Germany. Such feelings were inevitable when the service ministries attempted to deprive Finland not only of material which it wanted but material which it had ordered and actually paid for. As well as these material grounds, the Northern Department was frustrated by the lack of awareness on the part of the service ministries of the political benefits which could be derived from supplying Finland.

In a previous chapter it was related how Finnish requests for the latest model of tank had been refused by the War Office, despite protestations by the Northern Department of the benefits which their export to Finland could bring. The decision was probably wise on military grounds, but a matter of three years had made a big difference to the War Office's attitude to Finland. In 1936, the Finnish Government had placed an order for six British tanks after intensive pressure to buy from the War Office. In 1939 this order still had not been delivered. A message from the War Office on 6 October informed Lord Halifax that while the Army Council fully appreciated the desirability of maintaining good relations with Finland and giving it the encouragement it needed to defend its independence, it was firmly of the opinion that the six tanks now urgently requested by the Finns ought to be retained by Britain. The reasoning was that, in the near future, the tanks were likely to be offered to Turkey 'or some other ally or prospective ally'. The tanks, although obsolete models, were still rated as having an important training role by the War Office. This being the case, neither the tanks nor any other war material could be offered to Finland. The War Office's message stirred up hostile comment in the Northern Department. C. Barclay minuted his dissatisfaction as follows:

We bully the Finns into ordering the tanks and then refuse to supply them. The Finnish Minister has shown ... how much [they] have set their heart on this material. The War Office no doubt consider that six tanks in hand are worth more than Finnish good-will. I might have agreed before today, but now I think that we must consider Finland as part of the Scandinavian bloc.

Collier added his own contribution to Barclay's assessment to the effect that the War Office case seemed to be poor. He predicted that the value of Turkey as an ally would decrease if, as seemed likely, Stalin expressed alarm at the prospect of an active British-Turkish treaty.[2]

Collier's attempts to discourage the Finns

Despite his sympathies for the position which Finland now found itself in, and his attempts to persuade the military authorities to supply armaments to Finland, Collier did not allow these feelings to be made obvious to the Finns themselves. This was demonstrated when Gripenberg called at the Foreign Office to request that 36 Bofors anti-aircraft guns which Britain had purchased from Sweden but had been refused export licences by the Swedish Government, be diverted to Finland. Collier promised to raise the matter with Halifax but pointed out to Gripenberg that Britain still hoped to secure the guns and, if it could not, would probably ask the Swedish Government to send them to a potential British ally such as Turkey. Finland, he remarked, was not even a potential ally. Collier also argued that such a small quantity of guns would hardly make any difference to Finland.[3] The differing positions which he expressed to his own colleagues and the representative of a foreign government do suggest that Collier saw the logic in the military arguments but are not proof that he subscribed to them. His own views on the best policy in the Baltic for British interests was set to become more prominent as events developed.

Rearming Finland

At a Chiefs of Staff meeting on 13 October, a report by Captain N.C. Moore, the naval adviser in Helsinki, regarding Finnish orders for tanks and boats was considered by the Allied Demands Committee. It decided that the holding up of the supply of war material to Finland might induce the Swedish Government to release the Bofors guns. Collier was pleased that the question of Finnish war material had gained the attention of the Allied Demands Committee, but was horrified at the idea of linking it to the matter of the Bofors guns which he feared would lead to 'unnecessary complication and delay'. It was quite clear, he minuted, that the Swedish Government had no intention of allowing the guns to come to Britain, and as the guns were probably already in Finland, holding up supplies to the Finns would do no good. 'I hope, therefore, that this particular suggestion will not be allowed to complicate the question of supplying arms to Finland,' he concluded.[4]

Collier was correct in thinking that the guns would find their way to Finland shortly, if they were not already there. The withholding of legitimate Finnish orders, therefore, would be a pointless exercise. Nonetheless, there was no sign of the tanks leaving Britain. After hearing rumours from Gripenberg that Finland was on the point of buying weapons from Germany, Collier drafted a letter for Halifax to send to Lord Chatfield, the Minister for the Co-ordination of Defence. The letter stated that it seemed 'difficult to believe that the War Office would be making such a very great sacrifice in allowing only half a dozen tanks ... to a country which has urgent need of them and which it is much in our interest to encourage and strengthen at this time'. He added that Chatfield should make the Secretary of State for War, Leslie Hore-Belisha, aware of the political reasons 'why it would be better for us to let the Finns have these tanks now than to hold on to them with a view to a possible future offer to the Turks'. Cadogan found himself in agreement with Collier, writing a similar letter to Sir Arthur Street at the Air Ministry, stressing to him the desirability of putting the Finns in a position to stand up to the Russians.[5] This political desirability related to the belief held by Collier that the denial of assistance to Finland would be 'playing the German game'.[6]

The attractions of a Soviet-Finnish war

Collier had stressed this view as a response to an assessment by Snow that the 'best course' and 'most useful service Finland could render was to temporise with the Russians' and to avoid resorting to force unless there was 'some prospect of success'. Snow felt that the Finns were unlikely to choose the peaceful option and concluded that Finland 'if left to its own devices, is heading for catastrophe'. As the relative strength of Finland compared to the Soviet Union was not very impressive, this seemed a reasonable assumption. Back in the Northern Department it was generally agreed that this was the case, but the interests of Finland were not his primary consideration. Lascelles, allowing that British advice was unlikely to hold much sway over the Finns, doubted that 'Finland's best course (i.e. from her own point of view)', and 'the most useful service which she could render (i.e. to us)' were the same thing. 'A war with the USSR would be a dreadful prospect for Finland and could lead to Soviet occupation.'

However, from the British perspective, there would be some interesting possibilities. Collier considered that military action by the USSR would absorb Soviet oil, food and war material which might otherwise be sent to the Germans; that Soviet aggression might stir up anti-Soviet feeling in the

United States; and that armed intervention by the Russians could lead to their coming into conflict with Germany. Collier elaborated on this point. He had sought and gained the agreement of the Swedish Minister that, 'in the interests of [Britain] ... it was desirable that the Finns should fight'. As for the resistance which Finland could be expected to put up, Collier was reasonably confident that the Finnish army could field a large number of soldiers thanks to conscription.[7]

Lascelles and Collier both set store on the long-term assessment that any military disturbance in the Baltic region would make the onset of hostilities between Germany and the USSR more likely. If this happened, then British interests would be served, in their opinion. A disaster for Finland could well turn out to be an advantage for Britain. In the immediate future, however, there did not appear to be much hope that the two dictator states were about to fall out over Finland, despite inaccurate reports coming out of Moscow that the Germans were disturbed at Soviet Baltic policy.

On 10 October, Halifax was visited by Prytz, the Swedish Minister in London, and Eric Boheman of the Swedish Foreign Ministry, who wanted to know what plans Britain had for helping Finland. Halifax told them that while it was in the interests of the British Government to do what it could to assist Finland to resist Soviet pressure, there was not a lot of practical good that they could do. 'In the interests of Anglo-Soviet relations', he explained, 'diplomatic action would clearly do more harm than good, and in any case ... the Soviet threat was very possibly "bluff" and the worst might not occur'.[8] In one sense, nothing much had changed since the summer; the Foreign Office still did not want to damage prospects with the Soviet Union on Finland's account. Nothing also seemed to have changed regarding Finland's orders for military equipment. Halifax confessed to Gripenberg that the Finnish Government had a genuine grievance over the missing equipment, particularly the six tanks and wrote to Chatfield urging him to use his powers to get the weapons released.[9] It was hardly surprising that Halifax neglected to tell Gripenberg of the near relish with which Collier and Lascelles viewed a Finno-Soviet conflict. However, by not espousing this position himself in his conversation with Prytz and Boheman, it can reasonably be supposed that Halifax did not share the perspective of his subordinates.

Snow and the British attitude

Meanwhile, in Finland, Snow had been explaining to Finnish Foreign Minister Erkko that the British Government could not voice its disgust at the Soviet proposals, as Erkko hoped, as it did not know what these proposals were. However, when he contacted the Northern Department he put on his Finnish hat, and warned that the British Government 'are already exposed to criticism for the absence of moral support at Moscow and that if eventually aggression should take place, the reactions of idealist anti-aggression front will be still more critically examined'. It had taken less than a week for Snow to alter his position that the best course for the Finns would be to 'temporise' with the Russians. He was now advising the Foreign Office that it should be giving the Finns moral support during their time in Moscow. Collier minuted his own worries in response to Snow's communication but they were of a different hue to the Minister's. He argued that the Finns were trying to induce President Roosevelt to intercede with:

> [a] general "peace move" regardless of our interests. In these circumstances we are under no obligation to do more for the Finns than is needed in our own interests; but what may be needed in those interests is, of course, a different (and a difficult) question.

He then advanced an idea that the Scandinavian states, Norway, Sweden and Denmark, should actively lend support to Finland, while being guaranteed by the Allies against German intervention, which was a possibility if the Scandinavians allowed themselves to get involved in a conflict.[10] Collier had not changed his opinion that Germany was Britain's only enemy and his idea regarding Finland, that a Finno-Soviet war would benefit Britain, was not inconsistent with this view. Three days later, after the Finns had made their request to Roosevelt and found him unresponsive, Collier felt that Britain was now absolved 'from considering anything but our own interests in deciding what we should do for the Finns'.[11] What was clearly not in British interests, so far as Collier was concerned, was a settlement whereby Finland peacefully surrendered to Soviet demands. If it were to do so, German worries regarding violent disruptions in the Baltic area would be allayed. He furthered his assessment of the relative threats of the Soviet Union and Germany when responding to a claim that the Soviet Union posed more of a threat to Europe than Germany. Collier dismissed this view, saying it was 'not tenable by anyone who knows the comparative efficiency of the Russian and German forces'.[12]

Collier was, at this stage, expecting, even hoping, that war would break out between the USSR and Finland. In this appraisal he differed from his chief, Lord Halifax. The Secretary of State did not believe that the Soviet Government wanted to go so far as war to achieve its objectives, and assured Gripenberg of his hope, adding that he would do his best to make sure that the material, including the six tanks, which was still outstanding, got to Finland.[13] Halifax then contacted Lord Chatfield with the communication referred to earlier in which he stressed the political reasons for meeting the Finnish requests. These political reasons amounted to the need to prevent Finland shopping in Germany and thus strengthening ties with the Reich, although the Nazi-Soviet agreement undermined his argument somewhat. Collier's perspective saw reason for confidence in Halifax's warnings, and argued that if Finland should be armed, then it should be for military, not political, reasons. He argued that Britain's best hope lay in a conflict erupting in the Baltic region, and if Finland could put up a fight against Soviet advances, then the chances of Germany getting sucked in would be greater. Even if the two dictatorships avoided war, it could at least be hoped that a Baltic war could help to reduce co-operation between Moscow and Berlin. Commenting on a communication from Tallinn, which gave space to the unfounded and unlikely speculations of one Andrea Pitka, a member of an influential Estonian family and a campaigner for support for Finland, that Germany had undertaken to give secret help to Finland, Collier advanced his own views on how British policy in the region should develop. He argued that encouragement should be given to:

> The belief (whether true or false) that the [Pitka] organisation really has the secret backing of Germany. It seems to me that the rift which this would tend to cause in Soviet-German relations would be well worth the small concomitant gain to German prestige, which is at present very low. The encouragement must, of course, be very discreet and entirely local.[14]

No record exists of British subversion along these lines, but Collier's proposal illuminated the kind of thinking in which he was indulging during those days.

The rumours that Finland was ready to sign some sort of agreement with Germany were perpetuated when Erkko told Snow that Germans and pro-German Finns were bringing strong pressure to bear on him to appeal to the Reich for aid. Naturally he didn't want to do this as it would compromise Finland's neutrality. He then stated, as if in contradiction to his earlier point, that Germany was intending to invade Finland to 'force a peace', pointing to the recent evacuation of German citizens in Finland as proof. This notion was scorned by Collier and a colleague from the Central Department who would achieve prominence in the 1950s, Ivone Kirkpatrick. He understood that the Finns, 'like most of us' would want to put their own interests first, hence Erkko's direct plea for major British diplomatic intervention, but felt annoyed that they seemed to be as 'tiresome' as they had been during the Moscow negotiations.[15]

Snow's proposals for an anti-Soviet alliance

Kirkpatrick was, however, mistaken if he thought that the Finnish Government was the only one which held a paramount concern for its security.

Snow contacted the Northern Department on 21 October with a remarkable proposal. He believed that if the Soviet Union were to commit aggression against Finland, then Britain would have to take some action, and would have to choose between breaking diplomatic relations with the USSR or declaring war on it. Snow favoured the latter, stating that Stalin posed a greater threat than Hitler, thus echoing the comments of Finnish politicians. If Finland was invaded, Snow charged that the Red Army might not stop at the western Finnish border but would proceed into Sweden to occupy the iron ore fields, and from there sweep all before them until the Norwegian Atlantic coast was reached. This scenario posed a significant strategic challenge to British interests, and it was with this in mind that Snow recommended a war against the Soviet Union. In order to prosecute such a war successfully, it would be necessary to conclude an arrangement with Japan, who would be in a position 'to deal Russia's criminal policy a sickening blow'. Snow believed that the Japanese would be amenable to such a suggestion as they had sympathy for the Poles, were temporarily suspicious of Germany and had their eye on certain Russian territories. The last Anglo-Japanese alliance, which had ended in the 1920s had, he reasoned, been beneficial to both nations and Japan had prevented Russia from expanding into Manchuria in 1905. A new alliance would force Hitler and Stalin into a closer dependence on each other, would intensify frictions and would 'powerfully assist the process by which German and Russian peoples will be one day wary of their leaders'. Assessing this proposal, Fitzroy Maclean, a Northern Department official known for his expertise on Russian affairs, thought that the idea had some possibilities as Japan was the only power in a position to take action against the USSR. Lascelles thought that the measures Snow was suggesting were far too extreme and that there would be no need to break off diplomatic relations with Moscow, never mind declare war, even if it did commit an act of aggression against Finland. He minuted his presumption that the Cabinet would not want to make a complete break with Russia and turn it into a German ally. Collier wondered exactly what incentive Japan, who had just concluded a truce with Moscow, would have to attack the Soviet Union, unless Britain provided a significant *quid pro quo,* such as a free hand in China, which would be just as immoral as acquiescence in a Soviet attack on Finland. R. Howe, an official with experience in the Far East, agreed with Collier, saying that such an alliance would mean the withdrawal of British support for China and might drive Chiang Kai-Shek into the arms of the Russians. In any case, he argued, Japanese troops would be so bogged down in China that they couldn't possibly go on the offensive against the Russians. Sir Lancelot Oliphant, the Under-Secretary with responsibility for the Northern Department, was aghast at Snow's suggestion and decided that no reply should be forwarded to him on the matter.[16]

Nonetheless, part of Snow's thesis was, apparently, worth considering. Halifax reported Snow's communication (minus the Japanese proposal) regarding Norway and Sweden to the War Cabinet, where it was agreed that the Chiefs of Staff Committee should be asked to prepare an appreciation of the relative advantages and disadvantages 'which would accrue to us' if Britain was involved in war with the Soviet Union over Finland or Scandinavia.[17]

Snow was unaware that his idea to revive the Anglo-Japanese alliance was being virtually ignored, and it wasn't long before he was to contact the Northern Department with an elaboration of his plan. He proposed that if Japan were to invade the USSR, then Britain should agree to recognise Japanese conquests in the east, plus the puppet governments in Manchukuo and Nanking. Lascelles thought this 'very wild stuff'. Maclean, while acknowledging that while 'indirect' and 'discreet' encouragement for Japan to attack the Soviet Union might be in British interests, thought it would be a bad idea 'to proclaim our readiness to condone one act of aggression in the hope of avenging another'.[18] As no act of aggression had yet been committed by the USSR against Finland, talk of vengeance was a little premature, but the Northern Department officials had recognised that to follow Snow's plan could lead to political disaster, without any commensurate strategic benefit.

The future for Anglo-Soviet relations

The Nazi-Soviet pact and the Soviet occupation of eastern Poland had not removed British hopes of a productive trade agreement with Moscow, and efforts had been continuing to make advances in this area. Strangely enough, the pressure which the Soviet Government was believed to be exerting on Finland had more of an effect in British governmental circles than the atrocities in which they were indulging in Poland. In Patrick Salmon's evocative description, 'in a sense ... Finland had already acquired a status in British eyes higher than that of Poland, where the Soviet occupation of Poland had occasioned only a formal protest'.[19] This seemed to be borne out when Maisky was told by Halifax that the proposal for the initiation of wider Anglo-Soviet trade negotiations would be withdrawn if the USSR was to adopt too intransigent an attitude towards Finland. When Halifax reported this stance to the War Cabinet, the ensuing discussion noted that from a purely strategic angle, an increase in Soviet naval strength in the Baltic through the acquisition of additional ports was to Britain's advantage, as Germany would have to take greater precautions in the Baltic, thus weakening its resources west of the Kiel Canal. On the other hand, however, the political danger that the occupied areas might be bolshevised had to be considered.[20]

Four days later, on 1 November, the Cabinet received the report it had requested from the Chiefs of Staff Committee on the implications of a declaration of war on the USSR. This report concluded that 'Great Britain and France are in no position to undertake additional burdens and that we cannot, therefore, from a military point of view, recommend that we declare war on Russia'. They added that, while a Soviet attack on Norway would have serious implications for Britain's strategic position, the invasion of Finland would present no military threat to the Allies.[21] The political doubts as to the expediency of adding another major enemy to those currently lined up against Britain had already been outlined by the Northern Department. Now, it seemed, there was no military benefit to be gained from following Snow's advice either. The Chiefs of Staff's report could be easily reconciled with Northern Department thinking. While Collier was hoping for war between the USSR and Finland, he was not recommending that Britain form an immediate alliance with the underdog. The military assistance that he was suggesting should go to Finland was intended to give the Finns enough strength to put up a decent fight against any invaders on their own account, and create enough of a disturbance to disrupt German-Soviet relations.

The release of equipment to Finland

The six tanks, whose non-delivery had proved such a bone of contention in the preceding months, were finally given clearance for release on 1 November by Leslie Hore-Belisha, the Secretary of State for War, who had been influenced by the political reasons urged upon him by Halifax.[22] These reasons, of course, had been to demonstrate that Britain was a reliable partner who would prove more trustworthy than Germany. Collier was also anxious to supply the Finnish military with war material, but for different reasons, as has been shown. This was not such a cynical outlook as it may appear. He genuinely believed that the tanks in particular should be delivered because three years earlier the Finns had been bullied into ordering them in the first place. Yet his arguments were not framed in a moralistic, simplistic, manner. He believed that any tension in the Baltic had to act as a distraction to the Germans. As things stood at the moment, Russia possessed most of the important eastern Baltic ports, and as the Germans had not dared to attack Russia via the Baltic in the Great War, the chances of them wanting to do so now were low. The strategic interest of Finland for the Germans had become 'correspondingly small'. This being the case, Collier didn't believe that the Germans would dare to 'double-cross the Russians'.[23]

The Finnish-Soviet negotiations

It was widely known in governments all over the world that Finnish representatives were engaged in talks in Moscow, although the substance of these conversations was still secret. This circumstance changed on the last day of October when Molotov, for reasons known only to himself and his associates, made a speech at a session of the Supreme Soviet, revealing the details of the Soviet demands on Finland. These demands included the leasing of the Finnish port of Hankö to the USSR for a period of 30 years; the ceding of a number of islands in the Gulf of Finland; and the moving of the Soviet-Finnish frontier on the Karelian Isthmus further north from Leningrad. In return, the Soviet Government offered to cede a district in Soviet Karelia twice as large as the combined territories to be given up by Finland. In addition, the Soviet Government was prepared to allow Finland to fortify the Åland Islands, provided it did not attempt to do this itself, but worked in conjunction with Sweden.[24] Gripenberg told Halifax, who was by now sufficiently interested in Finnish matters to see the Finnish representative on a frequent basis, that he was convinced that his government could not accept the Soviet demands, particularly for the naval base at Hankö.[25] This was an accurate assessment of the Finnish Government's position. While J.K. Paasikivi and Väinö Tanner, the two Finnish negotiators in Moscow, were inclined to reach a settlement with the Russians, their superiors in Helsinki, including Prime Minister A.K. Cajander and Foreign Minister Eljas Erkko, were against granting too much in the way of concessions and resolved to remain firm. Paasikivi and Tanner were instructed to merely restate their government's position, even when the Soviet line appeared to be softening. On 3 November, Molotov made an ominous comment to the two Finnish delegates that 'we civilians don't seem to be making progress; now it is the soldier's turn to speak'. This was the first threat of violence that the People's Commissar had uttered throughout the negotiations.[26]

The disclosure of the terms on offer to the Finns occasioned a discussion in the British War Cabinet. Not surprisingly, Winston Churchill, the First Lord of the Admiralty, argued that the Soviet demands appeared very reasonable, especially since they involved territory which the Russians had lost as a result of the Great War. It would be in British interests, he argued, that the USSR should increase its strength in the Baltic, 'thereby limiting the risk of German domination in that area'. On these grounds, he warned against any 'stiffening' of the Finns. Halifax gave him support, up to a point. He believed that it was essential to maintain a tolerant policy towards Moscow, and did not think that the Finns should be encouraged in their opposition, but 'he was not prepared to press them to make concessions which they themselves regarded as vital to their national independence'.[27]

This discussion in Cabinet led to Collier composing a minute in response. He contended that German domination of the Baltic would not be appreciably affected if Finland accepted the Soviet demands as Germany controlled the exit from the Baltic into the North Sea. The presence of Soviet naval bases in the Baltic had not caused the Kriegsmarine to transfer a single ship from the North Sea to the Baltic. He went on to advance the argument that the Germans were conniving in Soviet pressure on Finland in order to frighten the other Scandinavian countries and make them 'more amenable to German pressure directed against ourselves ... and from that point of view an increase of Soviet strength in the Baltic would be a political disadvantage to us'. Churchill was, in Collier's opinion, mistaken in believing that the USSR could be induced to take a hostile line against Germany. Until the issue of the war was decided, Moscow was likely to remain benevolently neutral towards the Reich. If that was so, it was in British interests to see the USSR involved in difficulties of its own, thereby rendering help to Germany more difficult. 'With all respect to the First Lord's opinion', Collier still felt that the policy of his department, to encourage 'within limits' Finnish resistance to Soviet demands was still valid. These arguments were convincing enough for Halifax to use them as the basis for a private letter to Churchill, outlining this alternative.[28] Collier and Churchill were divided only by tactics. They both aimed at the disruption of Soviet-German relations. Where they parted was in their vision of how the Moscow government should be treated, Churchill believing in a conciliatory and obliging line, while Collier, interpreting the bonds between Berlin and Moscow as being strong and close, saw a Nazi-Soviet split arising only out of violence. They were both agreed on the point that any distraction to the Germans in the Baltic could only be of benefit to Britain.

However, if the Finns were expected to put up sufficient resistance to divert Soviet raw materials away from a German destination, they would need to be well armed. Now that the question of the six tanks had been settled, the most pressing requirement for the Finnish armed forces was for aeroplane parts, and Wing Commander Johnson, air attaché in Helsinki, delivered an urgent message for the Finnish orders to be met, a request which met with immediate satisfaction. On the bright side, Johnson reported that pro-German elements in the Finnish armed forces had been discredited and the standing of the Anglophiles, General Ohqvist and General Lundqvist, had risen.[29] The reason for this was probably due to the actions of the German Government since the conclusion of the Nazi-Soviet pact. Johnson explained that an agent of the German Government, who had come to Helsinki in early October for the purpose of selling Messerschmitt aircraft, had suddenly received orders not to sell any and had returned home. Johnson thought that this must be due to German reluctance to offend the USSR.[30]

The different interpretations of the Soviets by Snow and the Northern Department

Even at this stage, however, it was not seriously expected that the Soviet Government would resort to war in order to achieve the fulfilment of its demands. In Finland Erkko believed that the breakdown of negotiations and the return of the delegates to Helsinki would occasion nothing more that 'a week of angry utterances in Moscow'.[31] In London, Lascelles and his colleague Maclean both agreed that articles published in *Pravda* suggested that the Soviet intention was to intimate the threat of violence, thus keeping the Finnish army in a state of mobilisation and imposing a severe strain on the Finnish economy.[32] Only Snow entertained suspicions of more sinister intentions on Moscow's part. Summing up the recently terminated Finno-Soviet discussions, Snow asserted that the fears which the Finnish Government had expressed during the Anglo-Soviet Moscow negotiations were obviously well founded and had not been based on some form of irrational hysteria. He also pointed out that the demands which the Soviet Government had made on Finland constituted the same 'indirect aggression' which the Kremlin itself had so ostentatiously claimed to be against during the summer.[33]

Snow was clearly more perceptive about the implications of a Finno-Soviet diplomatic impasse than were the other observers. His concern was vindicated on 26 November when Soviet radio announced an incident on the border with Finland near the village of Mainila. Shells were alleged to have been fired from the Finnish side, killing and injuring a number of Red Army troops. Northern Department officials now had to agree with Snow's assessment that a Soviet attack on Finland was imminent. They additionally agreed that the incident had, in all probability, been manufactured by the Soviet side to justify hostile actions.[34] Naturally, the Soviet Government denied such allegations. Maisky, in London, told Halifax that the Finns had opened fire from their side of the border and that the Finnish Government seemed determined to provoke the USSR into action. Halifax warned the Ambassador that if the dispute were to develop into open hostilities, it would make it very difficult for London to improve relations with Moscow, and that trade arrangements would be the first to suffer.[35] These threats could only have carried little, if any, weight. Events had moved too quickly, and it was an illusion to believe that anything could persuade the Soviet Government to modify its course of action at this stage. War in the Baltic seemed inevitable and there was nothing that Britain could do to prevent it. Halifax, in a letter drafted by Collier, summed up the British position in a letter to Snow, rejecting the Minister's repeated calls for the renewal of the Anglo-Japanese treaty and its application against the USSR, and pointing to the limits of British influence. Britain had become involved in a 'life-and-death' struggle, as a result of the commitment to Poland, and if the British Empire were to succumb 'through taking on more than we could achieve, there would be no hope left for *any* small power in Europe'. Halifax assured Snow that if Britain was blessed with adequate resources, then there would be no hesitation in taking on Russia in the last resort, but, as things stood, no great assistance could possibly be forthcoming.

Snow had not advocated an unholy alliance with Japan simply for moral reasons. He was also aware of the dangers of bringing Germany and Russia into closer contact. However, he believed that this would not necessarily be a bad thing, as they were 'two poisonous but mutually destructive elements' and that there might 'be much to be said for their being thrown into the closest possible contact with each other under the disconcerting pressure of a Japanese attack on Russia'. There was a certain degree of *Realpolitik* in his assessment, but, in a letter drafted by Collier, Halifax told Snow that such a pragmatic reasoning would have a disastrous effect, both in the United Kingdom and overseas. In order to bring the Japanese on board, Britain would have to agree to Japan being given a free hand in China. If that were to be done, then Chiang Kai-Shek would throw himself over to the Russians completely. Even if material advantage could be accrued from an alliance with Japan on these terms, which was by no means certain, acquiescence to 'Japan's rape of China' would be no less immoral than to acquiesce to 'Russia's rape of Finland'.[36]

It was probably just as well that some moral, rather than merely pragmatic, justification could be found for not helping Finland. Snow's unacceptable suggestion had allowed Collier and Halifax to retain some form of moral perspective. Even when national considerations dictate policy, it is convenient to summon up a moral imperative to justify action.

The Soviet invasion of Finland

On 30 November, Soviet troops of the Leningrad district crossed the border with Finland as the advance guard of a military invasion. Bombs were dropped on Helsinki and its airport by aeroplanes of the Red Air Force. On 1 December, a new 'Finnish Government' was announced to be in place at the town of Terijoki, which had been overrun by Soviet forces within hours of the invasion. It was announced that the Head of the Government was to be Otto Kuusinen, a Finnish communist who had spent the previous 20 years exiled in Moscow, and had somehow managed to avoid becoming a victim of Stalin's purges in the 1930s. A day later, the Soviet Government recognised Terijoki as being the legal government of Finland.

Collier had hoped for a Soviet move of this nature since the announcement of the Molotov–Ribbentrop pact. Such a disturbance in the Baltic, he believed, would serve to disrupt and even antagonise relations between

Germany and the USSR, and this could only be to Britain's benefit. At the very least, it was hoped that Russia's ability to supply Germany with oil and other raw materials would be disrupted. This reasoning lay behind his pressure for military equipment to be delivered to Finland. As well as securing a political benefit of improving relations with Finland, the delivery of equipment would help to stiffen Finnish resistance in negotiations with Moscow. Six obsolete tanks, only fit for training purposes with the British Army, were never going to be able to hold the full might of the Red Army at bay, but it was hoped that the symbolic value representing a measure of British support for Finland and an upgrading of the Finns' military equipment, would reinforce the Finnish will to resist. Unfortunately, the matter did not unfold in the way Collier would have liked. Neither the preliminary incident at Mainila, nor the invasion and bombings of 30 November, marked the occasion of any German protest to their newfound partners in Moscow. Likewise, in Helsinki, no comfort was given to the Finnish Government by the German representative.

The hopes entertained by Halifax, for a *rapprochement* with Moscow, led by productive trade agreements, was an early casualty of the Soviet military aggression. The already slim chances of weaning Moscow away from Berlin through diplomatic means had ended, and relations with Moscow in the future had the background of an aggressive military campaign to contend with. Ironically, the political objectives, which had seemed so important before the Nazi-Soviet pact, of keeping Finland clear of German influence, had been achieved. Britain and France were now Finland's most trusted European friends. Sadly, the more immediate need of a conflict in the Baltic detrimental to Germany's strategic position did not come to pass. Relations between Helsinki and Moscow, which Northern Department officials had attempted to normalise from early 1938 until Hitler's invasion of Poland, had broken down completely, and the worst possible scenario, a Finno-Soviet conflict, with Germany adopting a passive stance towards the USSR, had come about.

6

THE LEAGUE OF NATIONS
DEBATE IN GENEVA

There was very little that Britain could do in response to the Soviet invasion of Finland. Indeed, Neville Chamberlain privately thought that the
invasion was not such a serious matter at all.[1] Collier, on the other hand,
was aware of the urgency of Finnish needs and the opportunities for the
British which the Soviet action had opened. For some time he had been
arguing that the Baltic could be the region which could lead to disagreement between Germany and Russia, and any military disturbances in the
area were, he thought, likely to occasion such an eventuality. He had been
urging the service departments for some time to meet requests from the
Finnish armed forces, but even he realised that there was a limit to what
could be supplied to a rather distant country at a time when the survival of
the British Empire was at stake. The options which were open ranged
from an outright acceptance of the Soviet action along with recognition of
the Kuusinen 'government' to the more drastic option of military intervention against the Red Army. In between these poles lay less extreme
forms of protest, such as the continued supply of military equipment to the
Finnish armed forces and the raising of the issue at the League of Nations.
These latter options were followed by the British Government in the days
following the invasion (albeit reluctantly in the case of bringing the issue
before the League).

Changes in attitude at the Northern Department

As the senior British resident in Finland, it was natural that Thomas Snow
would be quick in reporting his assessment of the Soviet invasion. His
reaction to the invasion was to restate his earlier call for action against the
Soviet Union in co-operation with Japan, with the possible help of the
United States and Italy. Snow believed that the reported Italian indignation at the Soviet action had increased the possibilities for such a combination. A Japanese connection had already been ruled out by the Foreign
Office (see Chapter 5), and it was widely known that the USA had no
intention of getting mixed up in a European conflict. For these reasons,

Collier characterised Snow's proposals as 'obviously impracticable'. Nonetheless, Collier hoped that events would 'make it possible to organise a purely European *bloc* against Germany and Russia'.[2] In hoping for this, Collier had reversed his earlier policy of attempting to maintain an understanding with Moscow and also his idea that Germany and the USSR could be brought into conflict over developments in the Baltic region. His outlook had been influenced by a visit he received at the time of the invasion from M. Prytz, the Swedish Minister in London. Prytz had contended that the situation of two nominally independent wars being fought in Europe at the same time could not exist for long. He hinted that Italy and the Balkan nations were ready to act against 'both the robbers'. If that was the case, Prytz believed that it would be 'worth [Britain's] while to have Russia as [its] enemy as well as Germany'.[3] As Sweden had no intention of engaging in hostilities with anyone, it was a little presumptuous for Prytz to make suggestions for the sort of battlefields he wanted British troops to visit. It was also a rather casual assumption that a declaration of war on Russia would place no great burden on British resources. His visit had, however, swayed Collier sufficiently for him to think in terms of a 'European bloc'.

Developments in the new Finno-Soviet conflict had changed the way in which Soviet actions could be interpreted and, therefore, the manner in which a British response could be assessed. By the time the Kuusinen 'government' had been established at Terijoki on 1 December, Soviet intentions could not be doubted. Any hopes that Moscow might be aiming at limited goals gave way to a realisation that they now wanted the entire country. The so-called Finnish Democratic Republic was proclaimed on 1 December. Fitzroy Maclean was quick to note that it would become a 'people's republic' along the lines of Outer Mongolia when the time suited the Kremlin. Daniel Lascelles predicted that this 'puppet government' ruled out any chance of a 'peaceful compromise'.[4]

This much seemed certain the following day. Molotov informed the US Ambassador in Moscow that the reconstituted government in Helsinki, where banker Risto Ryti had acceded to the Presidency, appointing the leading Social Democrat, Väinö Tanner as Foreign Minister, was a bad one. Sir William Seeds, the British Ambassador in Moscow, reported Molotov as citing Tanner as the 'evil genius of Soviet-Finnish negotiations', a comment on Tanner's role as one of the Finnish negotiators in Moscow a month earlier. He also claimed that if matters had been left to J.K. Paasikivi, the other Finnish negotiator, peace would have been concluded.[5] Molotov certainly had a point about Paasikivi, the moderate right-wing politician who had made no secret of his belief that Russian security demands should be met, although he disregarded the fact that neither Paasikivi nor Tanner had been accorded plenipotentiary powers. His attack on Tanner, however, suggested that he was a man in need of an enemy to pin the blame on. Lascelles noted this and condemned Molotov's 'gross hypocrisy'. Tanner had befriended Stalin before the revolution, Lascelles remembered, and could hardly be taken to be an archetypal anti-Soviet 'evil genius'.[6]

On 2 December, Stalin and Otto Kuusinen, the leader of the 'Finnish Democratic Republic', signed a Treaty of Mutual Assistance and Friendship in Moscow. Kuusinen, it appeared, had not even made the effort to visit his newly acquired state. By the terms of the treaty, the new Finnish 'government' was awarded the Finnish-speaking territories of Soviet Karelia, and in return granted all the demands made by the Soviet Government on Finland over the previous two months. The signature was seen as a farce in the Northern Department, where the gift of Karelia was seen as a sign that the whole region would come under Moscow's control. It believed the Terijoki 'government' had only been established to meet the contingency of a Finnish referral of the matter to the Council of the League of Nations. The Soviet delegate at Geneva would be able to claim that his country was not at war with Finland and had signed a peace treaty with the Finnish Government to prove this.[7] This fear was borne out by Molotov's statement on 3 December that:

> The USSR is not at war with Finland and does not threaten the Finnish nation with war. Consequently, reference to Article XI, paragraph 1 is unjustified. The Soviet Union maintains peaceful relations with the Democratic Republic of Finland whose Government signed with the USSR on 2 December a Pact of Assistance and Friendship. This pact settled the questions which the Soviet Government had fruitlessly discussed with delegates of the former Finnish Government now divested of its power. By its declaration of 1 December, the Government of the Democratic Republic of Finland requested the Soviet Government to lend assistance to tha republic by armed forces with a view to the joint liquidation at the earliest possible moment of the very dangerous seat of war created in Finland by its former rulers.[8]

The call for the assembly of the League of Nations

In fact, one of the first actions of the new Ryti Government in Helsinki was to cable the Finnish delegation in Geneva, instructing them to 'summon the General Assembly on account of the Soviet aggression', a request they duly complied with. No other state had been consulted by the Finns before taking this action. The General Assembly had not met since before Hitler's invasion of Poland. Any condemnation of Germany's action would have been pointless since it was not a member. The Soviet Union was a member, however, and on 3 December Joseph Avenol, the

Secretary-General of the League of Nations, requested members of the League Council to meet in Geneva on 9 December, and informed them that he had proposed that the General Assembly be convoked on 11 December. In making a request to Avenol, the Finns were in fact conversing with someone who had wanted to find an excuse for expelling the USSR from the League for a long time. Avenol, 'a devoted Roman Catholic in the political sense rather than the religious sense'[9]quickly seized the opportunity he had been given, believing that it would increase the prestige of the League.[10] The British Government accepted the invitation.[11] Halifax, however, was not impressed with the arrangements. He believed any League meetings, whether of the Council or General Assembly, on the matter of Soviet aggression, would be pointless, as they could not produce any useful result. The fact that he ordered his deputy, R.A. Butler, to attend the Geneva sessions, to resist the imposition of economic sanctions on Moscow, suggests that he did not particularly seek a 'useful result'.[12] He clearly did not, at this stage, wish to raise tensions between the British and Soviet governments, who, despite the Molotov–Ribbentrop pact of August, were not actually on antagonistic terms with each other.

Apart from sanctions, the other possible punishment which could be inflicted on the USSR by the League was expulsion. This again was something which the British did not want. A.W.G. Randall of the Northern Department composed a minute on 4 December highlighting the problems which a referral to the League could cause. If Britain voted for the expulsion of the Soviet Union from the League of Nations, then the Poles would be encouraged to raise their claims against Moscow 'and the Assembly may at once be in full cry against a hare which we have tried to keep safely caged!'.[13] This was a reference to the rather restrained condemnation of the Soviet invasion of Poland in September which had been made by the British. Using the wording of the Anglo-Polish treaty concluded in August, which referred to aid being given by the British Government in the event of an attack by a European power, Britain had been able to avoid taking strong action against the USSR by pointing to its Asiatic status. According to Randall, the only possible advantage that a referral to Geneva could secure was that proceedings there would make German recognition of Terijoki impossible. Both he and Collier agreed that while the Soviet Government should be condemned by the League, any greater punishments should not be imposed. Cadogan added that Britain would not be able to oppose the decisions of the League Council or Assembly but regretted that matters were to be taken there, predicting correctly that the impotence of the League would be highlighted and it would be brought into greater disrepute.[14] Presumably, he felt that the League was already an object of some ridicule, otherwise he would not have felt the need to interpolate the adjective 'greater' into his statement. On the other hand, it is interesting to note a figure of the British policy-making establishment exhibiting such sensibilities for the international standing of the League of Nations. It would seem that he wished to maintain an illusion of the League as an important body in world affairs. It was, however, an illusion which could only be kept up if the League was not requested to involve itself in any problems. It had, after all, been silent over the German conquests of Austria and Czechoslovakia.

The League sessions had the potential for embarrassment in other ways. There was the possibility that the Sino-Japanese conflict, which had claimed thousands of lives since 1937, and where Japan had assumed an aggressive persona, could be revived at the Council; that Britain would get taken to task over Palestine; and more worryingly, that the Soviet Union could raise the matter of the Munich Agreement with its subsequent desertion of Czechoslovakia and accuse the Western powers of leaving Albania and Ethiopia to the mercy of the aggressor states.[15] Equally serious was the possibility of driving the USSR closer to Germany. Expelling the Soviet Union would, after all, put it on an equal standing with Germany as *persona non grata* in League circles. These considerations all played a part in forming opinions at the Foreign Office, and explained why a moderate resolution, similar to the one adopted over the Chinese question in 1937, was favoured. Being able to carry such a line in Geneva, however, was never going to be a simple matter.

In reality, there was no chance whatsoever of any of these other issues being raised. Swiss fears of antagonising its German and Italian neighbours, and Joseph Avenol's distaste for bringing up these matters, meant that the only item on the agenda would be the Soviet aggression against Finland.[16]

The French position

It was clear from the moment that Finland referred the matter to the League of Nations that Paris had definite opinions on it. In supporting a statement by M. Mistler in the Chamber of Deputies who said that the League would condemn the Soviet aggression, Prime Minister Edouard Daladier commented on what he hoped would happen at Geneva. He trusted that 'even among the enemy states there were men who ... protested against the crime of which a noble country was the victim'. Germany, the state that he ought to have counted as his principal enemy, was not even represented at the League of Nations. He concluded his statement with another confusing reference:

> For the first time since September 1 there seemed to be a certain awakening of the universal conscience which has appeared to be somewhat deadened in the face of the brutal use of force. That was perhaps the greatest service Finland had rendered to humanity.[17]

Perhaps Daladier was being ironic, but not only did he seem to have forgotten the violence which had been inflicted on Poland since 1 September, he also seemed to be confusing the priorities of the Allied cause between a conflict which had broken out on the very periphery of Europe and one which was likely to engage them in a fight for their own existence.

As Finland's role had so far been passive, the only rendering which had been done was by the Soviet Union, although to state this would not have embellished the point he was trying to make so well. The conflict was not of Finland's choosing and it would gladly have foregone the chance to render such a service to humanity. Daladier was, in fact, giving the first indications that he saw the crisis in Finland as more important than the one facing France across its western frontier. Or rather, he was displaying an early manifestation of the French desire to create a northern front which would relieve French fears of a replay of 1914–1918. The League Council met twice on the morning that Daladier had spoken and, at the request of the Finnish delegate, had remitted the appeal to the General Assembly, which was due to meet on 11 December. In view of the stance which the French seemed to be adopting, Cadogan contacted Butler in Geneva, telling him that the French wanted Britain to take a 'bold line', which Cadogan interpreted as meaning imposing sanctions on the USSR and expelling it from League membership. Cadogan made it clear to Butler that he should try to avoid the imposition of sanctions, but, if the matter were raised, he would regretfully have to vote for expulsion, which represented a lesser evil.[18]

It would have been difficult and impolitic for the British to have broken ranks with their ally in the war against Germany over an issue which was of no strategic value to them. The French were certainly exhibiting great enthusiasm for demonstrating an anti-Soviet position. The stance of prominent politicians like Daladier was echoed in sections of the French press, where thunderous calls for a tough line at Geneva were commonplace. The attitudes of this section of French opinion was beginning to make inroads at the Foreign Office. Daniel Lascelles, who had displayed moderate tendencies in matters concerning the USSR before the war, now believed that Britain had to insist on a firm line being taken at the League meeting. It would, he argued,

> [be] a great mistake to assume that a reasonably firm line at Geneva with possibly a break in diplomatic relations would necessarily entail war with the Soviet Union. A feeble line at Geneva is likely to bring that about, by convincing the Russians that they can get away with anything.[19]

Lascelles might have been advocating a resolute attitude towards the Soviet Union over its aggression against Finland, but he was not suggesting that

Britain should take up arms against the red menace. There was no suggestion in his argument that the Allies ought to transfer their belligerence from Germany to the USSR. Indeed, his argument implied that the pursuit of 'a reasonably firm line' at this stage would prevent a possible Anglo-Soviet conflict in the future.

There were differences in what action the British and French Governments would have preferred to take. Despite Lascelles' minute calling for a tough line, Halifax favoured a policy of condemning the Soviet action but stopping short of implementing sanctions or expelling the Soviet Union from the organisation. The French, on the other hand, hoped to invoke both these possibilities.[20] As well as the imposition of sanctions and expulsion, the French also wanted to mobilise the League behind a programme of military aid to Finland. Reporting from Geneva, Butler explained that the French stance had considerable support. The South Americans in particular wanted to punish the Russians as much as possible, without risking their own security of course. They were sufficiently far away from the conflict to feel secure from Russian reprisals, and their attitude seemed to conform to the image of the anti-communist banana republics which has become such a stereotype today. Their attitude and 'the not unconnected feeling in the United States make it difficult and even undesirable for us to hesitate on the expulsion issue'. In the light of this intelligence, Butler was given government approval to support the expulsion of the USSR if it were to prove necessary.[21]

The British might have been reluctantly coming round to the idea of expelling the USSR from the world organisation, but the Swedes, who were a lot closer to the action, were not. As much as they deplored the invasion, and sympathised with the plight of the Finns, they were concerned about their own safety. The Secretary-General of the Swedish Foreign Ministry had told E. Monson, the British Minister in Stockholm, that expulsion could well lead to a state of war being declared between Britain and the Soviet Union. If this were to happen, he predicted that Germany and the USSR would find themselves on the same side and divide Scandinavia. Collier, admittedly from the relative safety of the United Kingdom, dismissed these Swedish fears, arguing that such displays of nervousness would increase rather than diminish the chances of the Soviet Union declaring war on its own account.[22] The Swedish Foreign Ministry had no basis for predicting such an outcome if the Russians were expelled from the League. The USSR would not be the first government to leave the League of Nations and such resignations had not led to war in the past. It was also true that the League of Nations, by this stage, had an aura of powerlessness, and that expulsion would hardly affect the position of the Russians in reality.

The League of Nations Resolution and the expulsion of the Soviet Union

The League Resolution on the matter, when it came up before the General Assembly, was relatively mild. This probably reflected Swedish influence in its framing. It restricted itself to naming the aggressor as the USSR, but left help for Finland to the consciences of individual governments. There was to be no compulsion to aid the party which the League itself had identified as being the victim of a great crime. However, contrary to Swedish hopes, the Soviet Union was expelled from the organisation. In a vote taken on the USSR's future status at Geneva, it was decided by a majority that it should be expelled in accordance with Article 16, paragraph 4, of the League Charter. Finland, as a party affected by the decisions made, abstained from voting, along with Greece, China and Yugoslavia.[23]

Butler recognised the futility of what had been achieved, commenting that 'it was a pity [the Council and Assembly] was called at all'. All that had been gained was an acknowledgement that the Soviet Union was committing an aggressive action in Finland, a fact which was evident in any case. The action taken at Geneva would be unlikely to lead to a change in Soviet policy and it would certainly have no bearing on Britain's war with Germany. The French, however, were pleased with the outcome. Over the next three months, representatives of the French Government demonstrated an increasing enthusiasm for intervention in the Finno-Soviet conflict. The referral to Geneva had given them the opportunity to develop their thinking in this way. Joseph Avenol was also satisfied with the turn of events, although he had no right to be. He displayed a remarkable optimism along with a matching lack of prescience when he declared that the League had been given a new lease of life.[24] Its next important action was to disband itself in 1945.

The recourse to the League of Nations had been completely pointless. The Finnish Government had not wished to see the USSR expelled from the organisation and neither had the British Government. This, however, was the outcome, and it is difficult to see the proceedings as anything other than a means by which supporters of the League could attempt to demonstrate their importance. As a way of stopping the war, the convening of the Council and Assembly was useless and this was surely evident to all realists at the time. The League had proved useless in resolving conflicts throughout its brief history. Its major success story was in reaching a settlement over the Åland Islands in the early 1920s (see Chapter 1) but this had been a relatively simple matter involving two nations who had no intention of entering into armed conflict with each other. The Greco-Bulgarian War of 1922 might have been settled with League input, but the Greeks withdrew their armies only when threatened by the superior military forces of Great Britain and France. Japan and Italy had showed their contempt for the League by withdrawing from membership in the face of resolutions hostile to their aggressive policies. The Gran Chaco War between Paraguay and Bolivia ended by the exhaustion of the combatants rather than through any well-meaning League resolutions. Nothing which could be decided at Geneva was ever going to have any real meaning when it came to resolving an armed conflict, and the Finnish debate and resolutions only confirm this assessment. The League could not rescue Finland and its only hope lay in intervention by major powers acting out of their own sense of interest. The question was whether Britain would play this role.

The decision of the League to sanction assistance to Finland by its members, along with the expulsion of the USSR, gave some legitimacy to British attempts to aid Finland, but these attempts would doubtless have been made in any event. The action taken at Geneva went further than many at the Foreign Office would initially have liked, but it did not affect the attitude of the British authorities to the invasion. Collier had been campaigning for an increase in material support to the Finns before the League Council and Assembly met. He continued in the same vein after the League's work was done. It was appropriate that Britain did acquiesce in the decision to bring the matter up at Geneva, however. It was a British official, Laurence Collier, who had been the driving force in having the Åland question brought before the League, in order to honour international obligations and to assuage the suspicions of the Soviet Union regarding the Finnish move. In both this instance and the one regarding the Soviet aggression, British officials generally felt that a referral to the League could not have many practical benefits, but went along with the decisions in order that their allies, both real and potential, did not feel let down. Collier had nothing to do with the December 1939 meeting, but it was ironic that the British officials, while still concerned about the sensibilities of the Soviet Government, felt that this time it was the Finns who needed the reassurance.

7

THE WINTER WAR: THE FIRST MONTH

While the League of Nations had been meeting to determine what punishment was most appropriate to inflict upon the Soviet Union for its aggressive act, Finland was having to contend with less academic problems. It was engaged in a state of war, no less real for its being undeclared, and its armed forces were fighting for the nation's survival. The British authorities had to decide what was the most meaningful assistance which they could afford to send to Finland. The expulsion of the Soviet Union from the League of Nations had done nothing to improve Finland's military position, nor to persuade the Red Army's commanders to call off their offensive and head back to base. In considering the situation, British officials had to deliberate on what aid they could supply, and how they could avoid permanently antagonising the Soviet Government. They also had to ponder the implications of the Finno-Soviet Winter War for the Allied conflict with Germany. The possibility that Finland's predicament might provide an opportunity that could be turned to Allied advantage could not be overlooked. At the same time, it was not generally believed that the Finns had much of a chance against the Soviet forces. This chapter considers the British response to Finnish requests for assistance, from the Soviet invasion until the close of 1939, and the part that the Northern Department played in formulating policy.

The assessment of Britain's ability to aid Finland

When military opinion was canvassed, the initial feeling of the Chiefs of Staff was that Soviet expansion in the Baltic would not have an adverse effect on the Allies' position. Their fear was, however, that the move against Finland could be a prelude to action elsewhere. They warned that if Russian aggression occurred in the Balkan region, then 'we might be forced to declare war on her whether we liked it or not'.[1] As Russian aggression was not apparent in the Balkans or elsewhere outside the Baltic area, this statement by the Chiefs of Staff can be taken as saying that the Soviet Union posed no strategic threat to British interests at that time.

Nonetheless, Gripenberg still hoped that Britain would extend the maximum possible assistance to his country in its hour of need. He called on Halifax on 1 December, asking that British Contraband Control should allow goods to go to Finland as there was no longer any possibility that they would be re-exported to Germany. In addition, he hoped that Sweden would be allowed to import British supplies to replace the ones which it had sent itself to Finland. Halifax was sympathetic to Gripenberg's position and managed to secure the agreement of the Ministry of Economic Warfare for such transactions to take place.[2] The Ministry of Economic Warfare was happy enough to comply with the request. In its view, assistance to Finland would help it in its own negotiations over war trade with the Scandinavian nations.[3]

The adaptation of the contraband laws was a fairly easy concession to make, but not all of Gripenberg's requests proved so easy to deal with. On 4 December, Gripenberg called on the Foreign Secretary once again, this time asking for the urgent delivery of 30 fighter planes of any model.[4] Halifax thought that the supply of fighter aircraft to Finland would have an important political impact, both in Finland and in the neutral countries, and he had the backing of Prime Minister Chamberlain. They faced opposition from the Air Ministry, where the Chief of the Air Staff and the Secretary of State for Air both thought it impossible for Britain's available air resources to meet such a request.[5] However, Halifax had his way. The next day the Air Ministry decided 'on political grounds' to let Finland have up to 20 Gladiator fighters.[6] The Gladiator was not the most advanced plane in the Royal Air Force but it did have the advantage of being able to take off and land on water, a facility which, coupled with its Bristol engine which was used extensively in the Finnish Air Force, made it an ideal plane for Finland. It was not likely to make much of an impact against the Red Air Force in the quantities in which it was planned to be delivered, however.

Nonetheless, the Finns were extremely grateful for the offer. The offer had received some publicity which was aided by Erkko's public thanks for the planes on 8 December. The decision to publicise the supply of the planes was made to forestall criticisms from within the UK and from neutral countries that Britain was doing nothing to help the Finns in their predicament. Unfortunately, this type of publicity caused anxiety within the Swedish Government, who were afraid that it would make its own position, in regard to transit and assembly of materials, more delicate. The more covert approach which the Swedes seemed to favour was taken up by the Finns as well. On 12 December, Collier was told by Gripenberg to ensure that Britain did not give supplies publicly, as this 'made difficulties for purchases elsewhere'.[7]

The Northern Department's attitude to Italian aid to Finland and the effect of the conflict in Germany

Certainly the Finns were attempting to acquire weapons from other sources. Italy, unlike its Pact of Steel partner Germany, had expressed outrage at the Soviet invasion at an early stage. The attitude of Mussolini's Government led Finnish officials to believe that here was a government that would extend all possible assistance. It seemed for a while as if they were right. The Italian authorities dispatched 50 warplanes for use by the Finnish Air Force.[8] Sadly for the Finns they had to be transported overland across Germany. The German authorities refused permission for the planes to go any further, and stopped their transit on 11 December. The next day they allowed a few of the planes to go through. These actions by the Germans led to conflicting interpretations among British officials. Monson, in Sweden, seemed convinced that the German action had been taken in order to appease the Russians. Collier, relying more on the news that some planes had been allowed through, thought that this more benevolent attitude indicated that the Goering faction was gaining the upper hand over the Ribbentrop faction. He still felt that the allegedly pro-Finnish sensibilities of Goering could prove decisive and be turned to Britain's advantage.[9] This notion that Goering's sympathies for the Finns were so advanced that he was prepared to usurp the authority of his own government was a feature of Collier's thinking at this time. He had given credence to a report which stated that Goering had prevented Hitler from extending diplomatic recognition to the Terijoki 'government'[10] and saw in the Luftwaffe leader a possible replacement for Hitler. He seemed convinced that two factions, a moderate wing led by Goering and an extremist group led by von Ribbentrop were engaged in a struggle for power within the Nazi state. This belief led him to welcome the idea, put forward by Samuel Hoare, for a leaflet drop over Germany. The leaflet would be completely concerned with the Finno-Soviet conflict. Dr Tancred Borenius of London University believed it was a good idea, emphasising the need to impress on the Germans that their government was acquiescing in the destruction of a small nation which had won its independence thanks to German arms only 20 years previously. As Borenius pointed out, senior German officials, such as Admiral Raeder, had given direct assistance to Mannerheim in 1918. The indignation which such men might feel at their work being undone could, Borenius hoped, lead to a change of policy towards Finland on Germany's part.[11] His optimism was rather misplaced. The fact that Goering had told Swedish friends of his, on 30 October, that Finland would not be attacked, suggests that other opinions, more sympathetic to the Soviet Union, held sway in Berlin.[12]

Uncharacteristically, Collier was entertaining thoughts that German and British goals could be compatible. This naturally assumed the overthrow of the Hitler/Ribbentrop group. Compiling a minute after receiving intelligence from a Swedish industrialist via Monson that Germany would not intervene in the conflict unless Russia crossed the Swedish border, Collier leapt to the conclusion that the Germans were adopting a passive attitude to Swedish assistance to Finland and were even thinking in terms of helping the Finns themselves.[13] There had been nothing in Monson's despatch to encourage such ideas. Monson had merely quoted the industrialist as saying that Sweden would give every assistance to Finland, short of declaring war, and that if the Red Army crossed the Swedish border, Germany would occupy the south of Sweden. As this would have given the Germans complete command of the iron ore routes, it is difficult to comprehend the grounds for Collier's optimism.

Collier's hopes for a Soviet-German conflict

However, for all his concern about the security of the Finns and his seemingly newfound confidence in German policy-makers, Collier had not really lost sight of Britain's real interests. His enthusiasm for supplies from Axis sources arriving in Finland can only be interpreted as showing an interest in Finland's survival. When given information from the US Embassy in Rome that Italy had sent 80 fighters and 50 bombers plus crews to Finland, he commented that he wished he could believe this intelligence but 'definite statements' from both Finland and Sweden exposed the news from Rome as a massive exaggeration.[14] If anything, Collier's statements confirmed his desire to see Germany (and possibly Italy) embroiled in conflict with the USSR over Finland. His attitude to the suggestion by Finnish Foreign Minister, Eljas Erkko, that Polish warships be despatched to the nickel-rich Petsamo region of North Finland to attack Soviet supply lines, shows that he had no desire to go to war with the Russians. In arguing against allowing the Poles anywhere near Finland, Collier and Lascelles pointed out that as the Polish ships had been incorporated into the Royal Navy, any act of war committed by them would constitute an act of war by Great Britain.[15] Clearly, such aggression was not on his agenda. His views were in step with those held at the Admiralty. In a memorandum commenting on the request for Polish warships to be despatched, J.A. Philips, on behalf of the Lords Commissioners of the Admiralty, explained that if the Polish ships were sent to Petsamo, they would have to be maintained by the British Government and this would lead to the Soviet Government justifiably asserting that the British were actively assisting the Finns in their war against the USSR.[16]

Collier still believed that direct German-Soviet collaboration was unlikely, although his earlier belief that the two 'gangsters' would come into conflict with each other was wavering.[17] He also believed that the erroneous perception, extolled by Snow, of collaboration between

Europe's leading aggressor states was deterring the Swedish Government from extending greater help to their neighbours. It was now imperative to make the Swedes believe that Germany and the USSR were not that close, and that Sweden could afford to assist Finland without fearing an attack from the south. The image which Snow wished the Northern Department to 'inculcate', of a Nazi-Soviet alliance, would work against any moves to reassure the Swedes that they were under no threat from the Germans.[18] The Swedes were only likely to get involved if they could be convinced that they did not face extermination from a totalitarian Russo-German monolith.

The problems of supplying Finland

At best, Snow's schemes for an anti-Soviet alliance, first broached before the Russian invasion, could be described as fanciful. He was right to highlight the potentially calamitous situation which the Finns faced, and was also correct in assessing that Finland's plight could only be relieved by large-scale assistance from abroad. The plan he constantly put forward was, however, politically impossible and logistically improbable. The Finnish forces were in dire need of immediate munition supplies and did not need time-consuming negotiations towards a possible formation of an anti-Soviet front, involving two nations – Italy and Japan (see pp. 91–93) – whose own interests were likely to conflict with Britain's at some point. Finland's needs were far more immediate. The British service departments fortunately chose this moment to show their generosity. They had been so reticent at supplying the Finnish forces a matter of months earlier but now allowed themselves a little more flexibility. The Army decided to make available 100 Vickers machine guns, 100 anti-tank rifles (but no anti-tank cannon), 5,000 anti-tank mines, 10,000 hand grenades plus sundry other equipment.[19] Three days later, on 19 December, they announced the further provision of ammunition, with more anti-tank mines and grenades, plus a consignment of 25 howitzers. The War Office also let it be known that four of the six tanks, whose status had been so disputed a matter of weeks earlier, were being shipped with the other material.[20] As the release of the tanks had been agreed in principle already, this hardly constituted a major concession, but the supply of howitzers assumed greater importance when it was learned that Germany had held up an order for 54 howitzers which the Finnish Government had placed with German factories. Snow interpreted this action as further evidence of German connivance in the Soviet invasion.[21]

The Air Ministry also began to appear more receptive to Finnish requests. Before either Britain or Finland had been involved in war, they had even seemed cool about extending an invitation to the Chief of the Finnish Air Staff to visit the UK. The Gladiator planes which they had supplied were less modern than the Hurricanes and Spitfires used by the

RAF, but the Ministry didn't even seem to be raising the objection that they could be used for training purposes in the UK. Even so, the number of Gladiators which could be sent had, they claimed, reached an optimum number. As an alternative to the Gladiator, the Air Ministry officials suggested that the Gauntlet might fit Finnish needs. The problem here was that all available Gauntlets had been promised to the forces of the Union of South Africa, but the Air Ministry was able to talk them out of their claim.[22] In addition to these defensive aircraft, the Finns also hoped to obtain planes which would enable them to take the fight to their enemy. The Finnish Prime Minister, Cajander, requested the immediate delivery of 12 Blenheim bombers on 21 December. He hoped that they could be used to bomb the Murmansk railway, Russia's primary northern supply route, and to undertake air raids on Leningrad and Moscow. The latter suggestion was a little too extreme to find any favour in the Foreign Office, but the notion of attacking the Murmansk railway found a good reception. Fitzroy MacLean, recently installed at the Russian Desk of the Northern Department, thought it would be a good idea to facilitate the Finns' pursuit of this course of action for a number of reasons. First, it would be relatively easy to accomplish. It was a single track railway, badly constructed, and passed over a number of bridges. Destroying it would mean that land communications between the Red Army operating in the Lake Ladoga area, and the rest of the Soviet Union would be severed. Second, economic life in the Soviet Karelian Republic would be severely dislocated. The resulting disruption would lead to Soviet forces consuming greater quantities of petrol and other materials, which would prevent their delivery to the Germans. Finally, the longer the Russians could be kept busy in the north, the less chance there was of them making advances in the Balkans and Middle East 'where our own interests are directly threatened'. If Britain were to come into conflict with the USSR at some point in the future, this railway would have to be destroyed in any case. By helping the Finns destroy it now, 'we should save ourselves the trouble of doing it in less favourable conditions later on'.[23] MacLean's minute was fairly hawkish. He was not openly advocating war with the Soviet Union, as his views over Snow's proposed alliance with Japan show, but was posting a warning that British interests in other parts of the world were threatened by Moscow more than Berlin and that Britain should prepare to take action against Russia as well as Germany.[24] He found that his immediate superiors, Collier and Cadogan, were in agreement with his suggestions for arming Finland, and his minute formed the draft for Cadogan's message to Sir Kingsley Wood, at the Air Ministry. This called for the urgent despatch to Finland of the 12 Blenheim bombers requested by the Finnish Government. The point was made that Britain's cause could be furthered as effectively by the Finns using these planes against the USSR as by Britain using them against Germany. The Air Ministry acceded to the request.[25]

The supply of war material to Finland, although modest, was reaching levels which had caused disagreement between the Northern Department and the service ministries before the war, and even earlier that month. Equipment and ammunition which the military staff had declared should stay in Britain were now making their way to a war front, to a war in which Britain was not involved. Some orders remained outstanding, however. Gripenberg drew Halifax's attention to the order which the Finnish defence forces had placed with ICI for cartridge cups before the European hostilities commenced. As shown in Chapter 3, the British Government, in the knowledge that its own country was likely to be involved in war soon, invoked a *force majeure* clause in the contract to frustrate delivery to Finland, and the Finns had graciously accepted this situation. They now hoped that the decision could be reversed. Halifax's reply was enough to leave Gripenberg feeling hopeful, but he kept quiet when the Finnish Minister requested the despatch of Royal Navy destroyers to Petsamo to shell Russian troop ships.[26] As has previously been shown, any action of this kind had been ruled out at the Foreign Office. The War Office agreed to allow ICI to release the cartridge cups to Finland two days before Christmas[27] and, in a further boost to Finland, the Cabinet agreed in principle to the Air Ministry's decision to supply the Finnish Air Force with Blenheim bombers on the same day.[28]

Britain's interests in the Finno-Soviet war

Britain's material assistance to Finland was improving, but after the release of the above equipment and ammunition, the Chiefs of Staff Committee reluctantly concluded that, at this time, they could not advise any further assistance to Finland, giving the familiar reasoning that Britain needed its own reserves and had to meet requests from nations like Turkey, who were clearly more valued than the Finns.[29] There were no plans as yet to send troops to intervene in the conflict. The Finno-Soviet war had presented Britain with a problem. There was certainly no desire to see Finland overrun by the Red Army and incorporated as the newest republic in the USSR. However, Britain's main concern had to be with the war it was involved in itself with Germany. It has been demonstrated earlier that certain officials believed that any disturbance in the Baltic would be in Britain's interests as it could have a detrimental effect on Germany's position. At best, Germany would see its own interests threatened and become embroiled in military conflict with the Soviet Union. At least, supplies of war and other raw materials which the USSR would otherwise be supplying to Germany, would become tied up in its own fight for supremacy in Finland. Somewhere in between these two poles lay the hope that in being kept busy in Finland, the Soviet Union would be unable to 'cause trouble elsewhere', an opinion articulated earlier by MacLean and also held by Lord Halifax.[30] These conditions could only apply while the Finno-Soviet conflict continued. Any assistance given to Finland in a war which was not directly connected with Britain's own, would, therefore, have the effect of improving Britain's situation.

The assessments of what this assistance should consist of, not surprisingly, varied. Snow had never given up on his scheme to create an 'anti-Russian concert'. Perhaps the Northern Department should have quashed his suggestions in the first instance as Snow showed no signs of his enthusiasm for this idea abating. He had first suggested enrolling a coalition of disparate nations to stand up to Soviet aggression before the Red Army had even invaded, so naturally his appeals became more urgent once a genuine conflict had broken out and Finnish sovereignty was more than theoretically threatened. On 9 December, he had reiterated his proposal, arguing that an anti-Soviet alliance would have the effect of leaving Moscow and Berlin isolated. He predicted a 'shattering moral shock' in Berlin if Britain took the relatively minor course of breaking diplomatic relations with Moscow. He remained unconvinced by the Foreign Office argument that British intervention would mean that the Allies would 'succumb through having taken on more than we can achieve', and he argued that once Britain got involved, assistance would come rolling in from all over the world. To illustrate his point, he referred, rather confusingly, to the moral stance Britain had taken over Belgium in 1914.[31] This missive was not well received in the Northern Department. Daniel Lascelles complained that Snow's advice on this matter was becoming 'distinctly tedious', and pointed out that neutral countries were highly unlikely to declare war on the USSR. He then picked up on the point about severing diplomatic relations. Far from causing a 'shattering moral shock' in Germany, such an action would have the opposite effect, with Germany and Russia drawing closer together. As for the comparison with Belgium in 1914, Lascelles was distinctly unimpressed. Britain's vital interests had been directly threatened then, 'a small point which Mr Snow seems to have overlooked'. The high state of Lascelles' emotions over this matter made it unwise for him to reply in person to Snow. Instead, Fitzroy MacLean drafted a more moderate version of Lascelles' minute, explaining to Snow that while Britain did not condone the Soviet invasion, an anti-Soviet combination was not practical politics, and that a war with the USSR would be disastrous for the Allied cause.[32]

Snow wrote back on 14 December, arguing that Finland could not be saved by the development of differences between Germany and the Soviet Union. He felt sufficiently threatened by the Red Army himself to have evacuated the British Legation to Grankulla, and urged that the British Government should at the minimum take the step of severing diplomatic relations with Moscow. 'Diplomatic action' would, he argued, isolate Russia and Germany from the rest of the world, although he did not, as

MacLean noted, specify exactly what he meant by this term. Snow pointed to what he called 'the moral effect of Russian isolation in the last world war', which 'had shattering results on the Germans'. He believed that a similar result could be obtained in 1939. Orme Sargent articulated the Northern Department's confusion at this interpretation of the events of 1918. Germany had benefited, not suffered, from Russian 'isolation'.[33] Collier pointed to the inconsistencies in Snow's argument that the Soviet-German combination could be broken by the isolation of these two powers, when Snow had been arguing that they were in 'indissoluble collaboration'.[34] Sargent replied to Snow with a rather terse note. There was no possibility of enlisting any other nations in an anti-Soviet combination. Events at Geneva had proved that, where little enthusiasm had been shown for taking anything but the minimum action. He appreciated Snow's anxiety to help Finland and isolate Russia, and he himself was under no illusions about the difficulty of actually separating the Germans and Russians. However, all that the British Government could do was supply war materials and try to encourage the Swedish Government to extend greater help to its neighbours. Snow's advice had been considered but it had been deemed impossible to act on it. Sargent finished with an apology for sounding so discouraging, but assured Snow that the Northern Department's stance was dictated by considerations over which it had 'little or no control'.[35]

Snow was hardly discouraged by the unenthusiastic response which the diplomats in London had given him. On 17 December, he contacted the Foreign Office. Once again, he urged the conclusion of a pact with Japan and Italy, which could be turned against Soviet aggression.[36] Halifax replied to Snow, informing him once again that there was no possibility of such action. Japan, in particular, would demand too high a price, one that Britain could not afford to pay.[37]

Snow was not alone in assigning a symbiotic relationship to Moscow and Berlin. The impression gained by the American Minister in Finland, Schoenfeld, was that the British media and the BBC in particular were portraying the Germans as being responsible for the Soviet aggression against Finland. He attacked this attempt to 'distort events and distract attention away from the red criminals', which would have the effect of dissipating sympathy for the United Kingdom in America. Schoenfeld seemingly suspected that the British were, in some way, covering up for the Russians, but in fact, the Foreign Office News Department had instructed the BBC to broadcast a report stating that the Soviet attack could only have taken place with German connivance because there had been a danger that outrage at the Russian action would lead to the USSR becoming public enemy No. 1.[38] This was a valid point. The plans which evolved from this point on for Allied intervention in the Finno-Soviet conflict showed just how easy it was for policy-makers to overlook their prime cause for concern, namely, their war with Germany. Certainly the mood in the country was growing more belligerent. The Labour Party was sufficiently outraged by the Soviet invasion to prepare a paper, which was published in February 1940, attacking the aggression and linking it to German instigation. The paper railed against the perfidy of the USSR, against the mutual friendship between Berlin and Moscow, and also against the fellow travellers, or 'Stalin's men' in the UK who were prepared to tear up their old slogans and manifestos, follow their master's instructions, and denounce the French and British 'warmongers'.[39] The Labour Party clearly had its eyes on its pre-war communist enemies as well as the Red Army, although such concerns might not have been evident to the readership of the pamphlet at the time.

Early plans for intervention

M. De Castellane at the French Embassy in London explained to Collier his government's proposals for a démarche at Stockholm and Oslo. He hoped that the démarche would force the Scandinavian governments to co-ordinate their measures for helping Finland with those of the Allies. This would, hopefully, involve them in the war on the Allied side, if the Soviet Government appealed to the Germans to help them.[40] The great attraction of Scandinavian involvement on the Allied side was that the Swedish iron ore, which was thought to be so vital to the German war effort, would be denied to the enemy, and the war brought to a swift conclusion. The importance of the Swedish mines had been realised before war broke out, and once installed in the War Cabinet, Churchill lost no time in drawing up plans to isolate this precious mineral from the Germans. It was nothing new, therefore, for such importance to be placed on the ore now. The urgency for taking control of the mines appeared greater though. It was feared that the Russians might not content themselves with Finland and march on to conquer the Scandinavian peninsula. The Chiefs of Staff had previously noted that while Finland itself was of no strategic value to the UK, any attack on Sweden and particularly Norway, could leave Britain dangerously exposed.[41] On 31 December, the Chiefs of Staff were once again asked for their opinions, this time on whether British interests would be served if the Allies went to war with the USSR. Their reply is discussed in the next chapter (p. 126). In the Northern Department, it was believed that, in theory, some benefits might accrue. On the same day, Maclean gave his views on the matter. He believed that it was not in British interests to deliberately provoke a breach, but at the same time 'we are not going out of our way to avoid one. Indeed, our policy is to do what we can to damage Soviet interests without going to war (in which, no doubt, it exactly corresponds to the policy of the Soviet Government towards Great Britain).' He thought it unlikely that any action taken by Britain would drive the USSR and Germany closer together, as their interests diverged in a number of spheres. It did not seem to occur to him that this same argument had been made right up to the signing of the Nazi-Soviet pact in August. He concluded by saying that a declaration of war or even the breaking of relations should be avoided, and thought that the use of 'non-intervention' as practised in Spain, would be more effective.[42] During the Spanish Civil War, allegedly non-combatant nations had managed to hide behind their neutrality and supply both sides during the conflict. The support which Italy gave to Franco's forces was particularly significant and effective.

Of course, there were potentially great disadvantages as well. The Northern Department's dismissal of Snow's plans had been partly based on the argument that any move which could be seen as being directed against the Soviet Union could drive Stalin even further into Hitler's embrace. This was a reasonable assumption which was also held by such notables as the Italian Foreign Minister, Count Ciano. The Count, Mussolini's son-in-law, advised Sir Percy Lorraine, British Ambassador in Rome, on 29 December, that the Russo-German alliance was far from solid, but could well be consolidated if the Allies pushed the Russians too far. He believed that a declaration of war on the USSR would be a grave mistake.[43] Collier's minute on Ciano's advice was rather strange. He thought that Ciano disliked the idea of a Soviet-German alliance as it could force Italy into a position of hostility towards Germany. This would, he remarked, make it positively desirable for Britain to be at war with the Russians.[44] It is surprising that the normally thoughtful and pragmatic Collier could believe that an alliance with Italy, whose most efficient wartime activity was raising the white flag, could compensate for the problems which hostilities with the USSR could cause. On the same day, he gave further evidence of his new perspective during a conversation with M. Charbonnier of the French Embassy. He learned during the course of his meeting that the French Ambassador in Moscow had declared that the Finno-Soviet war would not lead to a breach between Hitler and Stalin as they both needed each other. This being the case, the Ambassador believed that Allied prestige was at stake and a Soviet victory would be a serious blow to the Allied cause in the eyes of the world. Adding to this assessment, Charbonnier commented that the half-measures applied by France during the Spanish Civil War should not be repeated. Instead, the Allies 'must "go all out" to help Finland, regardless of Russian reactions and regardless, also, of the timidity of the Swedish and Norwegian Governments'. They must be willing to take risks. Collier agreed, composing a minute on the conversation, which brought the retort from Cadogan that the 'risks' seemed to mean 'denuding the Western (and Home) front of material'.[45] On the same day, Collier informed Gripenberg that hopes of creating a rift between Germany and the Soviet Union had disappeared.

Formerly, Hitler could not afford to break with Stalin, now it was the other way around, and the Allies had to find the best way of fighting the 'Russo-German combination' without getting into a war with the USSR.[46] From appearing as the archetypal advocate of a conciliatory policy towards the Soviet Union, he was now speculating on the benefits of going to war with it. Essentially, though, his ideas had not changed. He had never regarded any country but Germany as Britain's major enemy, and his advocacy of a possibly aggressive policy aimed at the USSR was put forward in the hope that it could strike a blow at German interests. Unlike Snow, he was not suggesting that a total breach with Moscow would strike a devastating moral blow at Germany, nor was he naïve enough to think that the example which Britain would set in so coming to Finland's assistance would mobilise world opinion, especially that of the United States. The Soviet Union had not replaced Germany as Britain's principal enemy, in his eyes.

Nonetheless, it seemed at this point as if Collier had given up on the hope of enlisting the USSR to Britain's cause through kind actions. Before the war, in the debates over the Åland Islands, he had advocated a conciliatory policy towards Moscow, urging that the Soviet Government should not be left feeling isolated in Europe. His hope then was that London and Moscow could come closer through common interests, exhibiting respect for each other's security concerns. Such an approach was out of the question by the end of 1939. His adaptation to the changing circumstances still retained an overriding concern for British interests, rather than any kind of explicit anti-Soviet philosophy.

Whatever reasoning lay behind Northern Department's views on the Finno-Soviet conflict, they did nothing to make a termination of the war likely. 1939 ended with the Red Army still very much encamped in Finland, despite its crushing defeat at Suomussalmi. The war was not going as Stalin and his advisers had anticipated. The quick, roll-over victory, aided and abetted by the 'working-class uprising' which Kuusinen had assured them would take place, was being replaced by a battlefield where more and better resources would have to be deployed. So far, the Finns had done well to keep the Russians at bay, but 1940 could be expected to be another story. It was noted in the Northern Department at the end of the year that while material aid to Finland would help the cause, it was useless without the commodity that the Finns were most desperate for – manpower. It was no good sending over equipment and then 'washing our hands'.[47] This was the problem which British policy-makers had to wrestle with in the first three months of 1940.

8

THE WINTER WAR: THE
SECOND AND THIRD MONTHS

Britain supplied lavish amounts of sympathy and modest amounts of arms to Finland in the month following the Soviet invasion of 30 November. The Allies' own war with Germany was proving so far to be a very quiet affair, the naval action off the River Plate notwithstanding, and the Finno-Soviet conflict stood as Europe's most violent current affair. It had always been hoped in the Northern Department that the course of the war in Finland could be turned to Britain's advantage, either through a Russian encroachment in the Baltic leading to a clash with Germany, because it would prevent the USSR from extending military assistance to Germany, or because it could distract Russian attention from other potential trouble spots. The Finns had managed to confound informed opinion by keeping the Red Army at bay and winning some important defensive victories but limited military resources meant that they could not hope to fare well indefinitely.

By the beginning of 1940, interest in Finnish affairs had grown at the highest levels of government, and policy towards that region was now being discussed at Cabinet level and in Cabinet Committees. British policy towards Finland therefore in this phase 'was in the first place Cabinet policy'.[1] The decisions and suggestions which the Cabinet made cannot be avoided in any discussion of British policy during the Finno-Soviet war but the focus of the chapter is mainly on the Northern Department, and how its own views, opinions and recommendations were affected by the heightened interest in the conflict in the top political circles.

Nobody at the Northern Department now believed that Finnish and Soviet aspirations could be reconciled with the light facilitating touch of the British. The motives of Collier and the Northern Department had always been guided by the desire to improve Britain's position in relation to Germany, even before war had broken out. That basic goal had not changed, but the means for achieving it had simplified enormously. Whereas diplomacy and a delicate balancing act had been the weapons used during the Åland dispute and the dissensions over Finnish rearmament, it was now accepted in the Northern Department that military force against the Soviet Union was inevitable, although its desirability was embraced more enthusiastically by Maclean than his superior Collier. However, the latter's views were to grow more harmonious with those of his assistant as time went by. Collier's change of mind is demonstrated in the rest of this chapter.

Unlike Chamberlain and his close political colleagues, Collier and his staff had a familiarity with Finnish politics and experience of dealing with Finnish representatives, most usually in the relationship which had developed with Georg Gripenberg, the Finnish Minister in London. It should be noted also that Collier had built a reputation before the war as an opponent of appeasement. In February 1940 he still insisted that a stand be taken against appeasing aggressor powers, even though the identity of the rogue state had changed from Germany to the USSR. As Britain was at war with Germany, the doctrine of appeasement had clearly not fulfilled its goals, even if the time had not yet arrived for it to become the discredited concept so familiar in numerous polemics, beginning with 'Cato' and popularised by the first volume of Churchill's war memoirs. Being proved 'right' about Hitler had not done Collier's credibility any harm. Nonetheless, as this chapter shows, in calling for British forces to fight in Finland, he was fighting a losing battle. His views were not in harmony with those of the Cabinet or the Chiefs of Staff who saw assistance to Finland in the context of the war against Germany. Nonetheless, they did represent an alternative and articulated option, one which has been left out of previous histories. It also shows that he was consistent in his anti-appeasement. Winston Churchill was the most famous critic of the government's appeasement policy before the war but he was not so vocal in arguing that his pre-war line should be followed in relation to the Soviet Union. Collier, on the other hand, made no discrimination between the wrongdoings of Hitler and Stalin.

Previously, Collier and Maclean had regarded the Finnish theatre as one where British interests in their war with Germany could be furthered. They now relegated the concerns of *Realpolitik* behind a concern for Finland as the victim of aggression, as this chapter relates. Their concern for Finland and their desire to harness British power to the struggle to expel the Red Army from Finnish territory were not motivated by any anti-Bolshevik notions. Maclean was no friend to the communist regime in Moscow but he did not allow his political views to determine his line on the Finnish war. Instead he wanted Britain to intervene in the Finno-Russian conflict because he believed a wrong had been committed and that Britain had the power to rectify the Russian transgression. By this stage, Collier was also motivated by moral and humanitarian considerations. He had made it clear before the war that he held Nazism to be a more pernicious system and a greater threat to the British Empire than communism (see pp. 32–33). His opposition to the Soviet Union in 1940 was determined by its act of aggression, not by the political complexion of its rulers.

In this, Collier and Maclean differed greatly from both the British military staff and their superiors in the diplomatic and political world. While such luminaries as Lord Halifax, Neville Chamberlain, and Winston Churchill were in sympathy with the Finnish predicament, they perceived the conflict essentially in terms of how it could be used to bolster and improve Britain's own fortunes in the war against Germany. So while these politicians were anxious to pursue policies which would benefit Britain, Collier, while still retaining his desire to see Germany defeated, began to advocate military assistance to Finland as an end in itself. This was not the first time that Collier had found himself at variance with his superiors. The policies which he had advocated before the war regarding such matters as the Åland Islands and Finnish rearmament had not always been in accord with other political or diplomatic opinion. The irony was that, whereas before the war, Collier had called for the British authorities to extend aid to Finland to isolate Germany, reassure the Soviet Union and bolster Britain's own position, now that both Britain and Finland were involved in conflicts of their own, his attitude actually became more idealistic, although his considerations of the national interest did not disappear.

Swedish iron ore

In December 1939, the first month of fighting, the Soviet forces had all been supplied by the local Leningrad garrison, but reinforcements and the appointment of the formidable Marshal Timoshenko as commander were a sure sign that the Kremlin did not intend to be complacent. As 1940 progressed, it became clear that a Soviet victory was inevitable, especially after the massive offensive which was launched by the Red Army on February 11 and which succeeded in breaking down the main Finnish defences.

The first month of the new year showed what a dreadful military position the Finns were in. It was clear that they could not survive for long without Allied military intervention of some kind. At the same time, British plans for disrupting the supply of iron ore which Germany received in large quantities from the Swedish port of Luleå, gathered momentum. These plans had been mooted for some time. As early as 1938, the prospect of using a fortified Åland Islands for this purpose had been raised in a Chiefs of Staff Report, which the Foreign Office had requested when the question of Åland remilitarisation had first arisen.[2] It was, however, in the early days of the war against Germany that the suggestion was discussed at Cabinet level. The matter was raised by Winston Churchill, newly restored to Cabinet rank as First Lord of the Admiralty. In his opinion, Germany would be unable to continue its war effort for long if it were deprived of its iron ore supply. During the winter months, when the Baltic Sea was frozen, consignments of the metal would have to come via the Norwegian port of Narvik, and it was Churchill's view that the surrounding waters should be mined. He had been responsible for undertaking a similar policy in 1918.

Churchill intended that any action taken against the Swedish ore fields would be undertaken as part of the war effort against Germany and not directed against the USSR. The Finno-Soviet conflict could, he believed, supply the pretext for an intervention in Scandinavia. Any potential intervention depended, therefore, on the war continuing. The War Cabinet recognised this fact when, on 4 January 1940, it decided that it was better for the Scandinavian nations to be kept in a state of anxiety than for the Soviet Union to be defeated. The War Cabinet reasoned that the Scandinavian governments were more likely to lean towards the Allied side if they feared for their own safety, even if that feat was occasioned by a Soviet menace rather than a German one. At the same time, it was realised that Britain should endeavour to prevent the Finns from suffering defeat.[3]

Northern Department ideas for taking action against Moscow

This reasoning reflected some of the arguments which had been put forward by Collier before the Soviet invasion. Finland should be given enough support to avoid defeat but not enough to secure an outright victory. This view was further articulated by Orme Sargent on 21 January, who maintained that if the USSR were forced to accept German aid to defeat Finland, the resulting *quid pro quo* would be one of increased German influence in Russia. This would be 'a serious blow to Great Britain and France'.[4] The continuation of the war was detrimental to the interests of the Reich as Moscow would be unable to supply any economic assistance and was prevented from throwing its weight around in the Balkans, an adventure which could throw up serious problems for the Allies. One reason for Allied intervention in Scandinavia, as portrayed above, was also open so long as war in the Baltic continued. This being the case, the Germans could be expected to lean on the Finns to accept a 'Munich' style settlement. It was clearly in the Allied interest to prevent this from happening. The Finns would need to be encouraged to directly appeal to the Allies for military assistance and intervention, otherwise there was little chance that their resistance could be prolonged.[5] Thus, the reasoning was, that the longer the war continued, the greater the inconvenience for both Germany and the Soviet Union and, *ipso facto,* the greater the benefit to the Allies.

Paradoxically, however, British suspicions continued that the Red Army and the Wehrmacht were effectively fighting on the same side.

Snow, whose service to the Finnish cause was truly indefatigable, pleaded for the use of bombers on 10 January. He justified this request by arguing that the sites targeted by the Finnish Air Force would benefit Britain as Finnish military objectives 'are British military objectives also'. On the same day, Captain N.C. Moore, the British naval adviser in Finland, stated that secret sources suggested that the Russians were preparing to build submarines for the German fleet at Leningrad. In addition, they were planning to allow the Germans port facilities at Murmansk. It naturally followed that any bombers which Finland received from Britain could be used to frustrate these plans. Barclay scribbled his agreement to a bombing raid on the alleged German submarine bases in a marginal comment, and contended that the case for taking action in Petsamo had been strengthened.[6] This latter point was a reference to the earlier suggestions that Polish warships be despatched to the Petsamo region to attack the Soviet supply line (see Chapter 7). This scheme had been vetoed by the Admiralty after doubts had been expressed in the Foreign Office in December.

However, the issue resurfaced in early January when the French Ambassador asked Halifax to reconsider sending Polish ships to the Arctic. The Ambassador did not believe that the Soviet Union was likely to declare war as a result of Polish ships operating against their forces in the Arctic region. After all, the action, in his opinion at least, would be no different to sending arms and munitions which the Allies were already doing. Halifax, with the support of the increasingly belligerent Maclean, referred the matter back to the Admiralty.[7] It is interesting to note that even schemes which had been dismissed a matter of weeks earlier were now gaining more currency at the Foreign Office, especially within its Northern Department. Maclean was certainly becoming more strident in his views, which seemed to echo the French calls for increasingly aggressive action. Collier had up to this point managed to temper his criticisms of the USSR but Maclean did not see the point in such restraint. The outlook of the two officials was to actually converge later, as will be demonstrated in the rest of this chapter.

The proposal with respect to the Polish warships was discussed by the War Cabinet on 19 January. Halifax reported the interest of the French in the matter. Dudley Pound, Chief of the Naval Staff, agreed that it was possible, through this action, to inflict considerable damage on Russian shipping.[8] In a further War Cabinet meeting five days later, Winston Churchill expressed his opinion that the Polish naval units could legitimately sink Soviet vessels 'without involving us in the charge of committing hostile acts against the Soviet', as Poland was at war with the USSR. Churchill had a point, although he overlooked the fact that the Polish vessels had been incorporated into the Royal Navy, and that a Polish attack on Soviet interests would be indistinguishable from a British one. The meeting was informed by the Chiefs of Staff that they would look at the possibility of Allied action on the Scandinavian peninsula, and that this would include naval action against Petsamo and Murmansk.[9]

Co-ordination of help for Finland

The Chiefs of Staff delivered a report on allied assistance to Finland on 28 January. The arguments in favour of such action, which were so familiar in the Foreign Office and Cabinet, were advanced, that Soviet supplies to Germany would be retarded, and that while the Red Army were tied up in the Baltic they would be unable to threaten the Balkans. However, the Chiefs of Staff warned that intervention through Petsamo was entirely unfeasible. Its physical location was an unattractive prospect for any possible expedition, which ruled out any Polish naval action. The terrain and exceptionally low temperatures in the area were not amenable to the convoy of large troop concentrations. Any direct military assistance to Finland would have to come via Scandinavia, that is, by transit through Norway and Sweden.[10]

Direct military assistance was not being planned at this stage anyway. In fact, arrangements for relieving the pressure on Finland were not made in a very efficient or effective manner. The Military Co-ordination Committee of the Cabinet had decided on 8 January that the organisation of assistance to Finland should be undertaken by an independent office, distinct from government, which would be headed by Sir George McDonough. This office would handle the recruitment of volunteers for the Finnish forces.[11] The independent status of the office would prevent the British Government from becoming embroiled in any controversies with Moscow. The despatch of the volunteers, or even any publicity associated with them would necessarily be withheld until Swedish and Norwegian approval for their transit had been given. Barclay noted that human resources were what the Finns stood in most urgent need of, and that an 'unofficial' despatch of a relatively small force of 'carefully chosen men' would be valuable and would ensure that any material sent would not be wasted.[12] As the proposals for the recruitment of volunteers stood, they would be so carefully chosen that they would not meet the minimum criteria for service in the British forces. In other words, no regular British troops would be considered and nobody eligible for call up to the forces would be considered either. Such a group would hardly have been likely to have played a decisive part in action in Finland.

It was, however, reasoned that the presence of British volunteers on the Finnish front would have an important moral and political effect in Finland, and that their despatch would show Britain to be complying with the League of Nations Resolution which called for all states to offer appropriate assistance to nations who found themselves to be victims of aggression. However, it was also recognised that the likely poor quality of the volunteers, and their almost certain inability to withstand the Finnish climactic conditions could bring discredit on Britain. The numbers of volunteers was never going to reach particularly high levels, certainly not the 20,000 which it was estimated that the Finns were in need of. That amount could not be raised unless Britain accepted the risk of general hostilities with the USSR and organised a full-scale military expedition, consisting of regular troops.

There are two interesting points to extract from this particular meeting of the Military Co-ordination Committee. The first is that this committee stressed the *political,* rather than military, reasons for helping the Finns, something which the Northern Department had done before hostilities commenced, albeit for different reasons. While Collier and his colleagues had advocated arming Finland to keep them away from the German influence, and to increase the chances of Soviet-German disruption, this Cabinet Committee were more concerned with how British assistance would be interpreted in neutral countries, particularly the United States. They hoped that Britain would be seen to be fulfilling its obligations under the League of Nations Resolution and would receive a more benevolent opinion from uncommitted nations as a result.

The second interesting point is the conclusion of the Military Co-ordination Committee that the risk of entering into hostilities with the USSR might be worth taking and 'might prove our best point of attack on the whole structure of the enemy's defences'.[13] This was a clear admission that elements within the Cabinet were accepting the French interpretation of the significance of Finland to the war with Germany, and were therefore assuming a close Soviet-German collaboration. The French had contended for some time that the German and Soviet causes were nearly indistinguishable. Intriguingly, a similar view was reported to the Auswärtiges Amt, the German foreign service, by the German Minister in Dublin, who reported fears in the Irish Foreign Ministry that the evident Russian weakness in their Finnish war would stimulate Allied inclination to carry on their war against Germany.[14] The French certainly conveyed the impression that Germany and the Soviet Union should be regarded as a single and common enemy, and sources at the Quai d'Orsay were suggesting that a Finnish defeat would represent a major blow to the Allied cause. This argument was accepted as valid by Barclay in the Northern Department, an indication of how little credence his department was beginning to place in any future co-operation with Moscow.[15]

However, it would be wrong to assume that this interpretation represented the views of the War Cabinet as a whole. In mid-February, it was discovered that Leslie Hore-Belisha, who until recently had served as Home Secretary, had written an article for publication in *The News of the World,* entitled 'Shall we fight for Finland?' Hore-Belisha clearly felt that

Britain should, pointing to the friendship which seemed to exist between Berlin and Moscow and advocating Allied landings in Norway and Sweden. This was similar to the ideas laid out by the Supreme War Council, but there were problems with Hore-Belisha's article. In the first place, his status as an ex-Cabinet member could confer a measure of authority on the work as far as the public was concerned and this would not be desirable in Cabinet. Second, both the Cabinet and Foreign Office feared that Hore-Belisha's argument that Allied assistance to Finland could allow the Finns to take the offensive and capture Leningrad risked confusing the issues for which Britain was actually at war, not to mention the enemy which Britain faced. Even more specifically, in response to an appeal by Maclean for the immediate despatch of RAF pilots to Finland, the Secretary of State for Air, Sir Kingsley Wood pointed out that Britain was at war with Germany, not the Soviet Union, and that it would be dangerous to send men and material to Finland when they might be needed at any time in the struggle against the Germans.[16] Wood could also have added that it was no straightforward matter to send assistance to Finland, as permission for transit had to be secured from the Norwegian and Swedish Governments.

Maclean's endorsement for direct action was not dampened by Wood's mild reprimand. In fact, he received confirmation of his own views from Sir Orme Sargent, a senior Foreign Office official, within a week. Sargent believed that the time it would take to train Finnish pilots to fly British planes could prove fatal to Finland's cause and thus recommended that RAF pilots be despatched to the front as 'volunteers'. He didn't think that Britain would run any great risk in pursuing this path as, in his view, it was not in Moscow's interest to go to war with the United Kingdom at that time and Soviet reaction could, therefore, be ignored.[17] Similarly, Maclean refused to be discouraged by the physical and political obstacles which lay in Scandinavia. Nor was he unduly concerned by the problems presented by British law. The scheme for the recruitment of volunteers ran the risk of contravening the Foreign Enlistment Act, 1870. This statute, which had been introduced at the time of the Franco-Prussian War, stated that any British subject 'accepting military or naval service with any state at war with any foreign state at peace with Her Majesty, without the licence of Her Majesty', would be liable for punishment under the terms of the Act. This created a dilemma for the British Government. Any offence to the USSR could be minimised by reference to the unofficial status of the volunteers. However, to allow the recruitment of such volunteers would amount to the granting of a licence by the government, and would thus constitute a *de facto* act of hostility towards Moscow. This did not, however, deter Maclean. After concluding that the Foreign Enlistment Act could be disregarded, he drafted a statement for the Prime Minister saying that the British Government would not stand in the way of any individuals who were ineligible for service with the British forces, but wished to offer their services to the Finnish Government.[18]

The turn of the tide against Finland

The Finnish need for troops was certainly pressing. Brigadier Ling, who was observing the action at the Finnish battlefront, believed that Germany would invade both Finland and Sweden if the Red Army moved too close to the Swedish border or the Åland Islands. This eventuality would be prevented, he contended, if the Finns were able to hold the Russian forces back. For this task, they needed weapons but the more urgently required resources were human.[19] If the Finns were able to keep the Soviet forces at bay without major allied assistance, it would also have meant that Allied forces would be denied their pretext to occupy Sweden themselves. The Brigadier clearly did not have such schemes in mind. He commented that Mannerheim did not want direct Allied intervention for fear of provoking Germany. Allied intervention, and German reaction, were exactly what Collier, and indeed Churchill, had long hoped for. The Finnish historian, Jukka Nevakivi, has identified the middle of January 1940 as the turning-point of the Winter War in terms of British policy. Certainly, from this point, the War Cabinet accepted the need for British involvement.[20] The Northern Department, as has been shown in the previous chapter, also advocated assistance to Finland. Its more belligerent line had pre-dated the Cabinet's position by some weeks. However aggressive a posture was adopted, British assistance to Finland was never taken out of the context of the war with Germany at this stage. Collier's attitude, however, was soon to change.

Dubious allies?

At this time, Collier deployed an uncharacteristically illogical line of argument. On 13 January, after hearing that the Italian Government had plans to send airmen with experience of the Spanish war to Finland, Collier urged Sir Percy Loraine, the British Ambassador in Rome, to approach Count Ciano, the Italian Foreign Minister, urging him to send fighter aircraft to Finland immediately.[21] Encouraging other powers to intervene in the conflict would reduce the justification for Britain's own intercession. If Finland received adequate help from Italy, enough to fulfil its immediate needs, then the excuse to occupy Scandinavia would be removed. On the other hand, it could be argued that he was working to create the kind of international coalition which could be turned against both Soviet and Nazi aggression. If this was the case, then Collier's intentions seem to carry a touch of irony. After all, he had been scathing of Snow's appeal for the creation of an international front involving Italy and Japan only a matter of weeks earlier. Not surprisingly, in view of his recent statements, Maclean was also in favour of enlisting the sort of allies for Finland, who might earlier have been categorised as slightly dubious. By the beginning of February his enthusiasm for attracting support for the Finnish cause led him to describe an alleged offer for service at the front by General Franco's Spanish Air Force as 'tempting'. It would, he decided, fit in nicely with any British plans or efforts 'for taking over the good will of the anti-komintern (sic) pact'.[22] There is no evidence of any particular efforts on Maclean's part to realise such an ambition, but it was a strange comment for him to make. After all, Britain was at war with Germany not the USSR, and was certainly not at war with an ideology, either communist or fascist.

The Anti-Comintern Pact had been indelibly associated with Hitler and the Nazi state during the 1930s and to invoke its legacy was a dangerous path, seeing as Britain was now at war with Germany. It would, however, be unfair to interpret Maclean's comments as a desire to take up the mantle which Hitler had worn so successfully as leader of the Anti-Comintern Pact before the war. While Maclean's comments clearly welcomed international collaboration against the USSR, he did not entertain any ideas of Germany changing sides to join in. The Russians had certainly become a *bête noire* to him, and his opinions were definitely running ahead of Collier's, but such remarks reflect the frustration which he was undoubtedly feeling at the time. Britain was taking no initiative in the war against Germany, which was in its 'phoney' stage. The Finno-Soviet conflict stood in total contrast to the 'phoney' or 'twilight' war in Western Europe. As Maclean was to give up his desk job for a life of action at the first opportunity, his comments at this time reflect a desire for Britain (and he himself) to be heartily involved, rather than a wish for Britain to become Nazi Germany's ideological successor. It could also be said that the anti-Soviet feeling now emanating from the Northern Department reflected the growing disenchantment with the Soviet Union felt in the country at large, which can be gauged by the newspaper coverage of the time and, more interestingly, the Labour Party pamphlet discussed earlier.[23]

In any case, Maclean was not reading the signals correctly. While Rome did indeed sympathise with Finland's predicament, it was never likely to conduct a policy contrary to the one held by Germany. A minor Italian nobleman had given Loraine excuses of cold weather for the withholding of Italian volunteers, but Collier had rightly concluded that this meant that Mussolini's attachment to Germany was greater than his distaste for the USSR, and that, if pushed, he would do what Hitler asked.[24] The Spanish offer, if it truly existed, could not have overcome the transit problems which were facing the Western Allies' own efforts to send meaningful assistance to Finland, through its potential donation of aircraft.

The Petsamo plan

There were only two directions from which aid could reach Finland. The Baltic Sea was effectively closed because of the presence of the Kriegsmarine, so supplies had to go either overland, via Norway and Sweden, or through the port of Petsamo in the Arctic. As the Russians held that port, and used it to facilitate the supply of weapons and manpower to the Finnish front, it would be necessary to take it from the Red Army first. Such an action would, of course, make war with the Soviet Union likely, a fact which policy-makers could not fail to be aware of. Nevertheless, French opinion seemed to be in favour of running the risk of increasing the number of enemies which the Allies faced. The French General Gamelin signalled his optimism that military action in the Petsamo area could help the Allied cause at the end of January, and the British Chiefs of Staff went to Paris to discuss the matter with Gamelin and his staff. Before leaving, the Chiefs asked the Foreign Office to draw up an aide-mémoire on the possible political repercussions of such action.[25]

Collier immediately complied with this request. On 29 January, he composed a memorandum detailing his impressions of the likely impact of British military intervention elsewhere. Limiting his answer to the Scandinavian peninsula, Collier contended that the Allies would need to be ready to move into the Swedish ore fields fast, before the Germans could get there. In his opinion, there would be no objection to such British action from the Norwegian or Swedish governments, providing it appeared that Germany was about to attack the Finnish rear, in collaboration with the USSR. In such a case, they must recognise that Scandinavian territory would have to be used by the Allies.[26] Collier's assessment of the situation ignored the Petsamo option. Military action at Petsamo could only have been aimed at the Soviet Union, the ore fields were too far removed from this port. The combination of aid to Finland and the cutting off of the ore transports could only be achieved through an overland expedition through Norway and Sweden. It would seem, therefore, that Collier did not view assistance to Finland as an end in itself, at this stage at least. Alexis Léger, Secretary-General of the French Foreign Ministry, had argued with a degree of deception that the Petsamo plan was intended to provoke Germany into invading Sweden, who would then turn to the Allies for help, but this reasoning was far from convincing.[27]

The British military staff were not happy with the idea. They preferred the more direct route to Finland, across Norway and Sweden. The advantage of this plan, apart from the major imperative of seizing the iron ore fields in Sweden and blocking Norwegian waters to Germany, was that it offered little danger of British forces coming into contact with the Red Army. The French scheme for the seizure of Petsamo was, therefore, dropped on 5 February, and the British plan adopted.[28] In order to use this route, however, the approval and permission of the two neutral Scandin-avian governments were necessary.

A detailed look at the negotiations, arguments and disagreements that British policy-makers had with their counterparts in Norway and Sweden is beyond the remit of the present study, but the standpoints and policies of the Scandinavians cannot be ignored when considering how the Foreign Office deliberated over assistance for Finland.[29] The Norwegians and Swedes were never happy about the prospect of the transit of Allied forces across their territory, probably fearing rightly that it would be a prelude to the opening of a new front in the Allied war with Germany, a front which would be likely to see more action than the standstill which was currently evident on the Franco-German border. Peace between Moscow and Helsinki was clearly in their own interests, and from February onwards, Sweden began to pressurise the Finns to secure the earliest possible cease-fire.[30] The standpoint of the Scandinavian Governments was to have reper-cussions for the Allied attempts to implement their intervention plans from this time until the conclusion of the Finno-Soviet conflict on 13 March.

Collier was, in fact, beginning to have some doubts about his belief that a 'symbiotic' relationship existed between the USSR and the Third Reich. This much can be discerned from his reaction to an incident in early Feb-ruary. On 3 February Winston Churchill told his War Cabinet colleagues that two German ships loaded with equipment for the USSR were about to embark for Murmansk. Opinion in the Foreign Office, as represented by Lord Halifax and Orme Sargent, contended that the Royal Navy should intercept and seize the ships, based on the League of Nations Resolution, which stated that all League members should take appropriate steps to render aid to the victim of aggression. Sargent proposed that once the seizure had been accomplished, then the weapons should be diverted to the Finns 'to show that we are not acting entirely in our own selfish inter-ests'.[31] Collier's response was to point out that there was no 'reliable' evid-ence of German assistance to the Soviet Union, on these ships or otherwise.[32] The head of the Northern Department gave a further demon-stration of his feelings on 5 February, commenting on a report in a Greek newspaper that there was 'no doubt' that the Red Army's aggression could only have been undertaken with the complete acquiescence of Germany. The report had claimed that the German facilitation of arms to Moscow undermined their claim to be acting as a neutral power in the conflict. Collier dismissed the report, minuting that it read as if it had been dictated to the Greek reporter by a Finn.[33] He clearly doubted the veracity of the Greek newspaper's report, and did not use it in an attempt to justify British involvement in Finland.

Collier's reading of the situation was not tantamount to saying that a breach between Germany and the USSR was imminent or even that such a breach could be engineered. His earlier hopes that the conflict could be used to bring Berlin and Moscow into conflict had not been revived.[34] Nor had his view that world conflict between democracy and totalitarianism was indivisible been resurrected. However, he now seemed to believe that, while freedom and authoritarianism were indeed locked in conflict, they were engaged in *two separate wars*. This line of reasoning suggested that Britain was only involved in one of these. The scheme for British forces to cross Scandinavia *en route* for Finland was therefore, in Collier's opinion, for Britain's benefit and not Finland's. A mild resurrection of the need to avoid antagonising the Russians occurred when the French politician Paul Koster entered into communications with Lady Maureen Stanley, the wife of the newly appointed Secretary of State for War, Sir Oliver Stanley. Koster proposed a scheme to create a 'White Russian' army in Britain who would fight for the Finnish cause under the patronage of Lady Maureen. Koster's choice of Lady Stanley seems to have been decided by her status as the wife of the Cabinet Minister with responsibility for the despatch of British military aid. Collier found the idea appalling. He allowed that individual Russians resident in Britain should not be disbarred from applying to join the groups of volunteers at the Finnish Legation, but he was adamant that the British Government would have nothing to do with a so-called 'white' army. Despite their urgent need for manpower at the front, he was convinced that the Finns would reject such a contingent also.[35] Collier found agreement from the War Office, where it was also felt that M. Koster's suggestion was a poor one on four counts: (1) the Finns would not want this kind of help; (2) the Russian peasants would be scared of the Whites; (3) it would harm relations with the USSR; and (4) it would force an additional commitment onto the shoulders of His Majesty's Government 'which we have no desire to undertake'.[36] It was true that the Finns were unwilling to accept assistance from this quarter. Mannerheim had been approached by exiled White Russian officers in December, but turned them down, in part because he did not want the war to be seen as an ideological struggle, but rather as a small nation struggling against Soviet imperialism.[37]

A prerequisite for intervention

The continuation of the Finno-Soviet conflict was, nonetheless, a prerequisite for the Allied occupation of Scandinavia. The Norwegian and Swedish Governments were hardly enthusiastic about Allied troops on their territory, even with a warzone existing over their eastern borders. If peace were established in the Baltic and the north, then they could hardly be expected to welcome foreign troops who didn't even have the pretext of travelling to aid the victim of aggression. The Scandinavian Governments saw an early peace as being in their best interests, and the Swedish

Government in particular displayed an anxiety for the Finns to reach a deal with the Russians. Fears grew in the Northern Department that the Finnish Government could approach Sweden, or worse Germany, with the request for mediation between themselves and the USSR. The Finnish Prime Minister, Risto Ryti, denied any German involvement. However, Sweden was being used as a base for peace feelers. The Soviet Minister in Stockholm, Alexandra Kollontai began to sound out the idea of a negotiated end to the conflict between Finland and the USSR with Swedish diplomats and politicians. Sweden had made tentative approaches in respect of a cease-fire at the end of 1939, approaches which continued into the new year. In response, Hella Wuolijoki, a well-known Finnish writer with left-wing connections arrived in Stockholm on 10 January, following instructions from Väinö Tanner, the Finnish Foreign Minister. Her mission was to meet with Soviet representatives, notably Alexandra Kollontai, to seek ways of ending the conflict. It was hoped in Helsinki that Wuolijoki's reputation as a socialist would carry some weight with the people she was likely to come into contact with. After numerous meetings with Kollontai, Wuolijoki was introduced to NKVD officials two weeks later.[38] This personal contact may have had some effect because on 29 January the Kremlin turned its back on its protégé Otto Kuusinen and his 'Democratic People's Republic of Finland'. On the other hand, it is entirely possible that it was the course of the war so far that led Moscow to turn its back on the 'government' it had installed. Whatever the reason, at a stroke the message was sent to the Finnish Government that the war aims of the USSR were now limited and that the Kremlin was no longer convinced that replacing the political order in Finland was a viable option. The conditions for a negotiated cease-fire were in place.[39] Perhaps Kuusinen's bogus 'government' could have been destroyed earlier if the Finns had seen fit to denounce Kuusinen as a Trotskyist, as a Swedish diplomat commented,[40] but this turn of events was not good news for Allied planners. The war could easily end before the intervention forces could even be organised.

The Finnish Government was quick to respond to the new situation and immediately offered the Soviet Government the same terms which Moscow had rejected in the October–November negotiations. This left out certain items which the Kremlin remained adamant that it must obtain, in particular the leasing of the port of Hankö. The Kremlin could not accept a proposition which left them without such a key point of their conditions. While accepting that diplomacy was now an option in bringing the conflict to a conclusion, Molotov warned that the Soviet diplomatic stance would be governed by the 'logic of war' meaning that if Finland refused to accept the terms on offer then Soviet demands would become incrementally greater.[41] On 11 February, a massive offensive carried the Red Army through the main Finnish defences, necessitating a retreat and regrouping on the part of the Finns. This military success meant that the 'logic' referred to by Molotov became increasingly obvious.

The decision of the Allied Supreme War Council

Against this background, the Supreme War Council, which consisted of the highest military and political authorities in Britain and France, decided, on 5 February, to implement a series of proposals for assistance to Finland. It concluded that Finland must be 'saved'; that it needed fighting men urgently and quickly. It also recognised that the Allies must send units of their own forces, which could for appearance's sake be disguised as 'volunteers' in the manner of Italian troops during the Spanish Civil War. It also now appreciated that the Narvik route was preferable to Petsamo as it allowed for control of the Swedish iron ore fields; that full preparations should be made immediately for the despatch of Allied troops 'to assist Finns ... and to support Norway and Sweden'; and finally (and crucially) that the Finns be advised to make an appeal for direct assistance at an appropriate moment, at which time the Allies would approach the governments of Norway and Sweden for their consent to passage over their territory.[42] The emphasis placed on the ore fields and the involvement of Norway and Sweden is an indication of where the strategic priorities of the military lay. Finland was important in so much as it allowed for an opportunity to strike a blow against German mineral interests in Sweden.[43] On the face of it, however, Finland appeared to be the beneficiary. Brigadier Ling was assigned the task of travelling to Finland to inform the Finnish Government of the plans. In summer 1939, the negotiations conducted in Moscow between British, French and Soviet representatives had run into problems over the issue of guaranteeing states like Finland against their wishes. It was ironic that the Allies were now adopting the position held by Molotov when they came to deal with the Scandinavian nations.

The prospects of peace, therefore, were not conducive to the Allied plans. Negotiations which appeared to be moving towards a cease-fire were now in place, but worrying rumours began to circulate in Allied circles that peace moves were being mediated by Sweden under German pressure. Mallet, the British Minister in Stockholm was convinced of this. The Swedes, he argued, were terrified of being dragged into a war with Germany and needed to be persuaded to stand up to any Hitlerian threats. This could only be done by demonstrating that Britain was capable of protecting Sweden from aggression and a large body of volunteers would be the best way of doing this. Mallet concluded on a cautious note, however. If a serious military commitment was made and Finland was defeated, then Allied prestige in Scandinavia and elsewhere would suffer disastrously.[44]

Maclean agreed with Mallet's appraisal of the situation and minuted that the only way in which 'we could be certain of affording to the Finns the assistance of which they stand in need is by sending our volunteers to Narvik as a regular expedition'. Maclean saw no reason to wait for a Finnish appeal before approaching the Scandinavian governments for transit rights. In his view, they should be informed of the measures which the Allies proposed to take 'to save Finland' at the earliest opportunity, when they could reassure the Swedes and Norwegians with the methods by which they would be protected from German wrath. If matters were left too late, then the Germans could launch their own pre-emptive raid into Scandinavia. Maclean realised that the Norwegian and Swedish governments could well refuse the Allied request but thought it best to be aware of this possibility in advance in order that plans could be revised accordingly. Maclean also noted that if a refusal were given at an early stage, then the Allies would be able to work on the sensibilities of the Scandinavian Governments concerning their international reputation. They could be apprised of 'how difficult their position would be once their obstructive attitude became generally known'.[45] This notion of placing the blame on Norwegian and particularly Swedish shoulders recurred frequently over the next few weeks. Maclean's attitudes, and desire for action to be taken, seem thoroughly consistent with his adventurous reputation which he later gained through his famous book *Eastern Approaches*. It is interesting to note at this point that in all Maclean's arguments regarding the Finnish conflict in the Foreign Office files, there is little reference to aid for Finland being a mere smokescreen for the seizure of the Swedish ore fields. The strategic reasons for gaining a foothold in Scandinavia and cutting off Germany's iron ore supply were not as major a factor in his arguments from January 1940 onwards. His enthusiasm for assisting the Finns was motivated from the fact that they were in dire need of help and he believed that their fight was also Britain's, and that British interests were being threatened by Moscow.

The proposals of the Supreme War Council (SWC) were, naturally enough, not widely divulged at this stage, certainly not to the Swedes or Norwegians. Key Finnish personnel such as Gripenberg were also kept in the dark. Halifax was able to reassure Gripenberg that Finland had not been forgotten by the Allies and that direct military intervention could not be ruled out, but he was able to limit Gripenberg's expectations by referring to the delicate position of Norway and Sweden. The Finnish Minister was kept in the dark completely as far as the SWC resolutions were concerned.[46] Halifax was similarly guarded in his comments to the Polish Ambassador, M. Zaleski on 8 February. He had to be, as Zaleski seemed too anxious to regard the USSR as the primary enemy, and resurrected the notion of sending Polish troops to Petsamo, as well as suggesting that Russian oil fields in the Caucasus be bombed. Halifax did reveal that any action at Petsamo could be ruled out but then left the Pole with a noncommittal answer that if Allied aid for Finland became too obvious, then the reprisals which the Gemans might then execute on Norway, Sweden and Finland would be disastrous.[47]

The Supreme War Council's plan dictated that Finland be informed of the proposed military intervention first, with a view to encouraging its government to make a direct appeal for assistance. On 12 February the War Cabinet agreed to send Brigadier Ling to deliver in person its intentions to the Finnish Government and also to request the Chiefs of Staff to research the possibility of sending 'volunteers' through Norway and Sweden should the governments of these states refuse to accept official Allied passage.[48] Ling's instructions were to inform Field Marshal Mannerheim that an Allied force was ready to leave for Finland if the approval of Norway and Sweden could be gained. Such permission might be given if the Finnish Government made a public appeal to the Allies. In addition, Ling was to tell Mannerheim that the project should not be prejudiced by the acceptance of mediation by any other power, or by a premature appeal to the world.[49]

While the Scandinavian Governments were not informed of the Allied plans regarding Finland, and while it was firmly intended, despite Maclean's protestations, that they be kept in the dark, it proved impossible to prevent suspicions arising in Oslo and Stockholm. Mallet reported that the Swedish Government were aware of the rumours on 13 February.[50] The next day he informed the Northern Department that the Swedish Government were alarmed at the plans which they suspected the French of making for aid to Finland. M. Wallenberg had expressed his fear of German reaction and invasion if Sweden provided too much support for Finland or allowed Allied troops through. He warned that the Germans would occupy the Åland Islands and invoked the traditional fear of Swedish politicians, quoting Napoleon's description of a pistol pointed at Stockholm.[51] In turn, the Norwegians were concerned that the arrival of 200 aeroplanes at Bergen *en route* to Finland had been announced on the BBC Radio, evidently fearing German wrath if it transpired that British military equipment was finding its way across Norwegian territory.[52] It was clear that the Finns had an inkling of what to expect too. When Walter Citrine and Phillip Noel-Baker, two representatives of the Trades Union Congress who had visited Finland, returned to Britain, they gave an encouraging report of Finnish morale but warned that the Finns were worried that their chances of securing manpower from Norway and Sweden would decrease if Allied help was given so ostentatiously that it embarrassed Norway and Sweden with regards to Germany.[53]

Butler's meetings with Maisky

On 16 February, the Under-Secretary of State at the Foreign Office, R.A. Butler saw the Soviet Ambassador to Britain, Ivan Maisky, at a lunchtime meeting. Maisky advised Butler that it would do Britain no good to increase the aid it was sending to Finland. He warned that if it rose above the level at which it currently stood, then Nazi-Soviet collaboration would, by necessity and common interest, grow. Although Maisky was happy with the Molotov–Ribbentrop pact, he did not wish to make the alliance closer and hoped that Britain would not make it so.[54] This was, no doubt, Maisky's method of advising Britain to keep out of the conflict. It was a warning that if warmer relations between Moscow and Berlin did develop, then any assistance which Britain sent to Finland would be a major cause. Eight days later the two held a subsequent and more important meeting.

At this second meeting, Maisky, claimed the authority of his government, and told Butler that the latter wished to make peace with the Finns on similar terms to those which were offered before hostilities between Finland and the USSR broke out. He then expounded the Soviet demands. These were that the islands in the Gulf of Bothnia currently occupied by Soviet forces should be retained; that Hankö should be leased to the USSR as a naval base; that the whole of the Karelian Isthmus should be ceded to the USSR; and that Finland would be offered no compensation for its lost territories although the Red Army would withdraw from the Petsamo area which it now occupied. Maisky tried to impress on Butler the fact that the Finnish defences had now been effectively penetrated and that if the Finns did not accept these conditions, then the war would have to continue. He then stated that if the Finns were to accept these terms, then it could represent a turning point in Anglo-Soviet relations. This was a clear hint for Butler and his government to use their influence with Finland to bring the war to a swift conclusion. Maisky added that he understood the sympathy for Finland which existed within Britain and accepted the present official British position of providing help to Finland under the cover of a League of Nations Resolution. Nevertheless, he would be interested to hear whether his message made any impression 'upon the mind of His Majesty's Government'. Butler assured Maisky that he would let him know the government's feelings about the proposals as soon as he became aware of them.[55] Other Foreign Office officials were not impressed with Maisky's proposals. Cadogan thought Maisky's attitude was 'both ridiculous and sinister' while Halifax decided that the Finnish Government would not be informed of Maisky's offer at this moment.[56]

The Swedish Government, at least, did appear to be suffering some embarrassment regarding their lack of help for Finland. On 16 February, in Helsinki, Snow heard that Swedish circles were thinking of sending three divisions to the Finnish front, as a possible war with Russia was preferable to the reaction they could face from Germany if the Allies instigated their own intervention. Their fear was that any involvement by the British or French on the Scandinavian peninsula would identify them as a prime target for a German blitzkrieg. The Swedes would, of course, have preferred to keep out of both the Finnish war and the European war. On the other hand, Snow felt that the Swedes might be prepared to help Finland if Britain 'set [an] example' of relevant military action.[57] This may have been because he doubted the intentions of the Swedes to send any form of assistance to their neighbours. Maclean certainly doubted the Swedish willingness to get involved. On the same day as Snow's message, he minuted a response to correspondence from Mallet, who had argued that the Swedish Government were still worried that Germany would attack them if they sent direct help or if the Allies sent assistance to Finland. Maclean protested that there had been no German démarche to this effect so the Swedish excuses were very lame. He concurred in Mallet's assessment that the Swedish Government would put every obstacle in the way of Allied intervention, but argued that they would not dare to flout their own public opinion by refusing passage to British and French troops.[58]

The Swedish Government was presented with a request by Väinö Tanner, Finland's Foreign Minister, for the supply of official armed units on 13 February. They refused the entreaty but assured Tanner that they would still allow Swedish volunteers to travel to Finland.[59] On the other hand, Tanner's predecessor, Eljas Erkko, now Finnish Minister in Stockholm, expressed optimism on 17 February that the Swedes would send significant amounts of material aid and manpower. It was, he argued, in their interests to do so. He felt confident that he would be able to convince the Swedish Government that they had no reason to fear a German attack if they assisted their neighbours.[60] Collier was sceptical of the chances of the Swedes adopting such a position. On 23 February he minuted that the Swedes *were* probably convinced of the unlikelihood of a German attack now but had managed to invent a new excuse for doing nothing, this excuse being that their own efforts to help Finland could never be enough; that ultimately the Allies would have to get involved; and that this would consequently invoke the wrath of Germany. He didn't think that the Swedes actually believed this and made the enigmatic comment that 'their attitude is fundamentally psychological and no more based on reason than is that of a rabbit to a snake'.[61]

It could have surprised nobody, least of all Collier, that Erkko's assessment had been wildly optimistic. Thomas Snow, who had been consistently vocal in his belief that Britain's interests were bound up in the Finnish conflict, was recalled to London during February, in the knowledge that he would not be sent back. His views regarding the Japanese alliance (see Chapter 7) had been largely responsible for this. In his farewell meeting with the Finnish President, Kyosti Kallio, Snow was given confirmation that the Swedish Government had refused the request from Finland. As a final request to Snow, Kallio asked if the British and French Governments

139

could warn the Soviet Union that failure to respect Finland's desire for peace on reasonable terms would have a marked effect on relations between the Allied capitals and Moscow.[62]

The instructions given to Ling were modified on 20 February. The Finns would now be requested to call upon the Norwegian and Swedish Governments to allow passage to Allied troops at the same time as making their appeal for assistance to the Allies themselves. While the appeal to the Allies would be made public, their supplication to the Scandinavian nations would initially be kept secret. A Foreign Office draft indicated that the governments in Scandinavia would then be warned that the appeal would be revealed to the world should they refuse to co-operate in the scheme.[63] However, when Halifax contacted the two governments in Oslo and Stockholm, he omitted to mention any such threat. Collier bemoaned Halifax's exclusion of this warning, arguing that it was 'our one truly powerful lever for overcoming the reluctance of the Swedish and Norwegian Governments'.[64]

The attitudes of the Swedes and Norwegians were, however, irrelevant if the Finns chose not to make an appeal for Allied assistance in the first place. Initial fears that this might happen were eased on 23 February when it was learned that Mannerheim had given the Supreme War Council's plan his approval. Collier hailed this news as 'very satisfactory' and put Mannerheim's approval down to the 'hopeless Swedish attitude' and his realisation that no meaningful help was likely to emanate from Scandinavia. Mannerheim's only hope, therefore, lay with the Allies.[65]

Collier's developing suspicion of the Swedish and Norwegian Governments

Correspondence from the British Minister in Stockholm, Mallet, helped to confirm the unfavourable impression of the Swedish Government which Collier had developed. The Swedish Foreign Minister had informed Mallet that there was nothing which his country could do to prevent Finland from being defeated, and was apprehensive at any possible Allied adventures in Scandinavia. Mallet interpreted this assessment as amounting to a Swedish desire for a 'Finnish Munich'. He informed the Northern Department that the Swedes were frightened of Britain infringing their neutrality and were 'likely to put pressure on Finland to capitulate on terms'.[66] Maclean commented that the Swedes were in 'a deplorable state of mind'. Collier took an even more extreme line: he argued that the Swedes would never take any risks and that it might be desirable to serve them with a *fait accompli* such as landing 'volunteers' at Narvik who would then make their way over to Sweden. He argued that 'to merely *ask*' the Norwegian and Swedish Governments for permission to land would lead nowhere.[67]

Collier took this point further on 27 February when he composed a memo on the projected allied route through Scandinavia. In his view, a *fait accompli* might be necessary where Sweden was concerned. If the Allies sat back and respected a Swedish refusal, then Finland would be defeated and would end up under Soviet domination. Germany would then be free to dominate Scandinavia and get all the iron ore that it needed. If Finland fell due to a lack of action on Britain's part, then the British Government would possibly suffer the same fate as Gladstone's administration after Gordon's death at Kharthoum, when popular outrage shook Whitehall, and Gladstone the GOM (Grand Old Man) of British politics was rebranded as the MOG (Murderer of Gordon). This being the case, Collier thought that the expedition should go ahead even without the consent of Oslo and Stockholm. His argument implied that Britain could not be seen to be doing nothing, even if there were very good practical arguments for withholding assistance to Finland. The journey might take a little longer without the active assistance of the Scandinavian governments but if the Finns could hold out until the spring thaw, then this would not matter as this would leave enough time for the assistance to arrive. He was convinced that, having taken the plans so far, Britain must go through with the action.[68] He received support for his suggestion of a *fait accompli* being presented to the Norwegian and Swedish governments from Gladwyn Jebb, who felt that Allied troops could be landed as 'volunteers' and that the Scandinavian governments would be too ashamed to obstruct their progress or attempt to turn them back.[69]

Collier was given further opportunities to indulge his growing cynicism towards the Swedish Government. On 26 February Mallet, along with Harold MacMillan, met the Swedish Prime Minister, Per Albin Hansson, who told them that he thought the USSR would be prepared to make peace on terms approximate to the frontiers of 1721, which were drawn up at the conclusion of the Great Northern War between Russia and Sweden. These corresponded roughly to the pre-war frontiers of 1939. Collier was unimpressed by this statement, in which Hansson had refused to make any promises regarding assistance for Finland. He believed Hansson was the main problem, adding that Sweden would do nothing effective for Finland so long as this man stayed in office.[70]

It was clearly in Sweden's interests that the war be brought to a speedy and satisfactory conclusion, but their assessment of what this would represent was not in harmony with the views prevailing in Finland. The Finnish Government were none too keen on the fighting continuing either, but hoped to maintain a position of resistance to the Russian invaders in order to compel the Kremlin to offer better terms. Gripenberg approached Halifax on 27 February with a request from his government. He himself had not been inducted into the secret plans and consequently was in ignorance of the nature of this request to the Foreign Secretary. He told Halifax of his government's wishes for the 'scheme' to be accelerated.

Halifax replied that this was unfortunately not possible. He was unable to divulge what was not possible, but it is likely that Gripenberg understood that the question referred to the timescale for getting Allied forces to Finland. Halifax then asked Gripenberg if rumours of German mediation in the conflict, which had come to his attention, were true. Gripenberg did not think so and added that his government could not accept the Soviet terms as they now stood. At this point Halifax informed the Finnish Minister of the talks which Butler had conducted with Maisky. He declined to say what the terms were but remarked that if the Finnish Government wished to know them, they would be informed.[71]

The need for an appeal from Finland

The plans which the Allies had drawn up could not, however, be put into effect until Finland made its appeal. On 29 February, Cadogan heard, via a conversation with the French Ambassador, of some possible movement towards an appeal by the Finnish Government. The Finnish Minister in Paris, Harri Holma, had informed Daladier, the French Prime Minister, that he had received instructions from his own Prime Minister, Risto Ryti, expressing gratification at the Allied plans and asking whether they could be accelerated. The Finnish Government had obviously cabled similar instructions to their representatives in both Allied countries, but Daladier was determined to read more into the enquiry than Halifax had been. Daladier thought that Ryti's phone call should be taken as an appeal for armed assistance and that this should act as the cue for taking diplomatic action with Norway and Sweden. Daladier insisted that if Finland fell, then the blame must fall on the Scandinavian governments and *not* on the Allies, so a démarche would have to be made as soon as possible.[72] A further conversation between Holma and Daladier on the same day initially suggested that Holma's démarche was by way of an appeal, and Daladier was told that Gripenberg would be making a similar approach to the British Government. However, Holma's initial statement that an appeal had been issued was somewhat undermined by his subsequent declaration that the figure of 12,000 Allied troops which he had been given was too small and that his government's decision would be dependent on the number of troops promised and the timetable for their arrival. Cadogan and Corbin both believed that the Finns should be allocated a greater number of forces and that the date of arrival should be brought forward.[73] The clear differences between what the Finns thought was the minimum necessary for their continued survival and that which the British were prepared to offer presented a further obstacle to the fulfilment of the British plan, in addition to the one thrown up by the Norwegian and Swedish Governments.

Gordon Vereker, the replacement for Snow as British Minister in Helsinki, arrived at his post in the final week of February. On 24 February he met the Finnish Foreign Minister, Väinö Tanner for the first time. As an air raid was in progress, the meeting was held in the bomb shelter of the President's residence. Later that day, Vereker and Tanner met once again. At this meeting, the British Minister informed Tanner that a British force, numbering '20,000–22,000' could be despatched on 15 March and could arrive in Finland exactly one month later. He added that the troops could be used on the southern Finnish front, rather than being restricted to the north which had originally been planned. Most importantly, he apprised Tanner of the necessity for a transit right to be secured through Norway and Sweden.[74] On 27 February, Vereker was informed by the Northern Department of rumours circulating in Italy that Finland was about to seek German mediation to end the conflict.[75] On the last day of the month, provided by the leap year, Vereker asked Tanner whether the Finnish Government had made a decision over making an appeal. Tanner replied that the Cabinet Foreign Affairs Committee was considering the Soviet 'peace terms'. If they could be sure that the Allies could supply meaningful help, then they would ask for it. Unfortunately, Tanner did not think that his government could rely on armed assistance reaching them in time. For that reason, the terms proffered by Moscow would receive increasing amounts of attention from Finnish politicians.[76] In retrospect, it is clear that Tanner was throwing extreme doubt on the possibility of his government issuing an appeal. Unfortunately, his message was not interpreted in this way in Allied capitals. Tanner's assessment certainly failed to support the enthusiasm which Daladier had displayed following his talk with the Finnish Minister, but it did not give rise to large-scale sentiments that the projected Finnish adventure should be called off. Nor did it do anything to dispel the notion held by Collier and Maclean that intervention was a desirable objective.

Halifax, meanwhile, had been immersed in a number of conversations with Gripenberg. On 29 February the Finnish Minister arrived at the Foreign Office with the depressing news that Stockholm refused to allow the passage of Allied troops. He expressed his own government's natural reluctance to issue an appeal if the attitude of the Scandinavian governments were going to prevent its being answered. All Halifax could say was that the British Government would do all in its power to persuade Norway and Sweden to co-operate.[77]

The following day the two met on five separate occasions, with Gripenberg presenting Halifax with the conditions which Britain would need to meet in order to prevent Finland from entering into peace talks with Moscow. He had been instructed by his government to attempt to obtain 100 bomber aircraft and 50,000 troops by the end of March. This was much higher than anything which the British Government had contemplated sending. All Halifax could do was to tell him that it was impossible to consider such a high number. In answer to Gripenberg's further enquiry as to whether the Allies would proceed with their plan in the face of Scandinavian refusals, Halifax replied that they hoped to secure the co-operation of the relevant governments but that without the participation of the Scandinavians, and the use of their railways, the transportation of troops would be impossible.[78] In a marginal comment, Collier complained that this sort of outlook was not conducive to winning the war. He argued that if Britain wanted Helsinki to appeal, then it had to convince the Finns that the plan would go ahead in all circumstances. He doubted that the Norwegians or Swedes were likely to put up a show of resistance, although he admitted that there was a certain risk in this assumption. He argued, however, that 'if we never take any risk at all in war, then we shall never get anywhere'. In his opinion, the Finnish Government should be informed that if it made its appeal, then Britain would despatch troops and attempt to land them in Norway. Such a move would be undertaken on the premise that the Norwegians would not open fire upon British soldiers and that even if they did initially refuse to collaborate with the Allied plan, they would eventually have to bow before the weight of their own public opinion. If, however, they did resist a landing by force, then the Allies would withdraw. The Finns would be unable to complain of betrayal at such an outcome, as they themselves assumed that there would be no resistance to transit Allied forces across these territories. Cadogan agreed that there was 'something in this' and even Halifax acknowledged that the argument carried some force.[79]

Collier's remonstration was clearly conditioned by the fear that the opportunity to put the plan into operation could be overtaken by events and that time was running out if it were to have any chance of success. This explains his insistence that the views and wishes of the Scandinavian Governments could be ignored and overridden. He was well aware that the collective will to resist was being eroded in Finland, and he had read the War Office communication which described the current diplomatic activity in Helsinki. This communication had highlighted the divisions which had emerged in Finnish governing circles between those advocating talks with the Russians and those who recommended an appeal to the Allies. The supporters of peace, according to the report, justified their opinions by the attitude of Sweden to transit, a fear of Germany, and the realistic fear that any Allied aid would be inadequate and would arrive too late.[80] Collier's response to the report that 'we know this only too well' indicates his awareness that the Finns would need a very convincing offer before they committed themselves irrevocably to an appeal for Allied assistance, and probable entry into war with Germany. If they were fed the sort of material they had been given so far, regarding the size of the Allied army and Anglo-French intentions with respect to Scandinavia, then the hand of the 'peace' party would be strengthened, and the war would end with Soviet influence firmly extended beyond the Finnish frontier.

There was no escaping the dilemma. It seemed clear that the Finnish Government would only issue an appeal if it was convinced in advance that the attitude of the Scandinavian Governments would not prevent assistance from getting through. Knowing that the Norwegian and Swedish Governments were in no way about to modify their stated position on the matter, the British hoped that they could use a Finnish appeal as a weapon to coerce the Scandinavians into changing their minds. Oslo and Stockholm were in no doubt as to why the British and French Governments had advanced the plan, seeing in it a means whereby they would occupy the vital mineral sites in Sweden and prevent the flow of iron ore to Germany. They also were aware that such action would drag them into the war with Germany, an eventuality which naturally appeared less than attractive to them. This was an accurate reading of the intentions of the British Government. Collier, however, had parted company to some extent with his superiors. He did support the plan for aid to Finland, but unlike the Supreme War Council, he wanted to see Britain extend support to Finland to aid the Finns in their struggle with the Soviet Union as well as seizing strategically important points on the Scandinavian peninsula.

Collier had earlier recognised that the Finno-Soviet conflict was separate to the European war being fought between Germany and the British-French Allies. That view did not change, but by the end of February Collier was contending that Britain should be involved in both the two distinct wars. He believed that the British cause in the war with Germany could be served by the occupation of Norway and Sweden but his arguments and those of Maclean suggested that military assistance to Finland was desirable as an end in itself, not just some selfish war aim. It is noticeable that Germany became conspicuous by its absence from Collier's pronouncements by February 1940. The same could be said of Maclean. The position of the latter can perhaps be explained by his adventurous and restless spirit. As for the more senior Collier, the change in his attitudes coincided with the arrival of Maclean. The Cabinet was, of course, now conditioning policy over Finnish matters, and it is possible that Collier, relieved of responsibility in this respect, felt able to promote ideas in relative isolation. It should also be noted that perhaps Collier felt that the Finnish appeal, necessary for British intervention in Norway and Sweden, would not be made without an attractive and trustworthy offer from Britain. This could also explain his desire for substantial aid and assistance to be promised to Finland during the first few weeks of 1940. Alternatively, there was a definite consistency between his pre-war reputation as an opponent of appeasement and his determination to stand up to the Red Army in 1940. Knowing that the most influential members of the War Cabinet and the Chiefs of Staff favoured a policy which proposed to secure British strategic interests in Sweden without doing much to relieve the plight of the Finns, he was arguably attempting to highlight a discrepancy between such cold calculations of the national interest, and an unwillingness to rectify what he now considered to be a moral outrage. Collier had started the year hoping to see the conflict in Finland turned to Britain's advantage and by recommending aid to Finland on political grounds. Two months later, he was advocating a credible military presence in Finland without outlining any political benefits which could be expected in return. Time, however, was running out on both the Finns and on Collier's hopes.

9

THE END OF THE FINNO-SOVIET WAR AND THE FRUSTRATION OF COLLIER'S HOPES

By the beginning of March 1939, it was clear that Finland could not hold out for long without outside intervention. As Finland's plight grew increasingly desperate, Collier and his colleagues grew correspondingly anxious for Britain to take some meaningful action. In the first place, they had to convince the Finns to issue an appeal for aid, as this was the pre-condition for the despatch of a military force. Once this was made, the problem over the refusal of Norway and Sweden to allow any transit of troops posed a potential hazard. If they maintained their intransigent position, Collier proposed that the blame for the collapse of Finland should be placed at their door, thus avoiding any approbation attaching to Britain.

When March began, Collier and his staff were well aware that the choices facing the Finnish Government were in danger of being severely narrowed. Until recently the Finnish Government had had the options of seeking aid from Sweden, making peace with the Soviet Union, or appealing for military assistance from the Western Allies. It had been clear since Tanner's visit to Stockholm in mid-February that their Swedish neighbour was not going to commit itself to prolonging the war by intervening on Finland's behalf. The sidelining of the Kuusinen 'government' had signalled that the Soviet Government was now willing to entertain a settlement short of outright domination of Finland, and this had provided some incentive for elements of the Finnish Government to seek a negotiated end to the conflict as soon as possible. Those with an inclination to accept the best possible terms included the Prime Minister Risto Ryyti, Foreign Minister Väinö Tanner, and future President Juho Kuusti Paasikivi. Of all the available options, Collier hoped that the Finns would go for an appeal for Allied assistance. This appeal would be unnecessary and irrelevant if a cease-fire was obtained quickly.

Deadlines, ultimatums, and the continuing absence of an appeal

As far as the Finns were concerned, the first fortnight of March 1940 was a period of deadlines and ultimatums. Moscow had given them until

1 March to respond positively to the Soviet peace proposals, the Western Allies had signified 5 March as the date when an appeal for assistance must be made, and variations of these two demands were repeated towards the end of the fortnight. The first deadline, presented to the Finns by Moscow, looked likely to be honoured at the end of February. On 29 February, the Finnish Government decided to accept the peace terms on offer from the USSR 'in principle' and to show willingness to enter into discussions of the details in Moscow. This was hardly a surprising turn of events given the military situation, but news of the Finnish Government's decision caused panic in Paris. Daladier had invested a great deal in the survival of Finland. Previous chapters have demonstrated a marked enthusiasm on the part of the French Prime Minister for taking the war to the Baltic. A Finnish defeat was likely to mean the end of his ministry. Without consulting the British, Daladier contacted the Finnish Government on 29 February with a wild promise for 50,000 men and 100 bombers to be in Finland by the end of March. This was more that the Allies were in a position to supply. However, if Finland were to enter into any negotiations with Moscow, then the offer would be withdrawn.[1] Daladier's unilateral action had a galvanising effect in Helsinki, with Tanner reporting to Vereker that his government was 'heartened' by the reports of the arrival of 50,000 troops in the near future. Tanner explained that the Soviet ultimatum had now expired. Before talking to the Soviet Government, Tanner wished to know if the 50,000 would definitely arrive in March. If so, would they be available for action on all fronts? And could the 100 bombers be sent at once? Vereker was not in a position to give answers, and, in any case, the British War Cabinet did not feel that a reply was necessary. The deadline for a Finnish answer had passed and the war was set to continue. Maclean saw this as a good portent. If the Kremlin agreed to talk after its 'ultimatum' had expired then it would be exhibiting 'an obvious sign of weakness'.[2]

The figures supplied by the French had formed the basis for Gripenberg's request to Halifax, described in the previous chapter. Halifax had at that point told Gripenberg that assistance on this scale was out of the question. He was undoubtedly truthful with the Finnish Minister but did not command the support of all of his staff on this matter. Not surprisingly, Collier and Maclean felt that such a stance was 'unnecessarily discouraging to the Finns'. Collier agreed that the British should not copy the French and make promises which they had neither the intention nor the ability to fulfil but they should, in his opinion, show some flexibility. He then addressed the 'military objections'. The plan which had been drawn up on 5 February by the Supreme War Council allowed for Allied troops to be sent to northern Finland, far away from the Karelian Isthmus where the real battles were being fought. Collier thought that this directive should be overridden, that troops should be available for service on any front and that they should serve under Mannerheim's command. He was aware of the 'excuses' which the military were throwing up. These included the argument that only a small number of troops could be detailed for service in Finland because the supply lines in Sweden needed to be guarded against German attack. He finished with an interesting observation – that the military were not that interested in Finland.[3] This was an accurate assessment of the feelings of the British military and, indeed, politicians. Aid for Finland was only valuable or important in as much as it provided an excuse for the Allies to seize the strategic advantage over Germany in Scandinavia. Aware of, but not solely motivated by such considerations, Collier and Maclean alone held the moral flame aloft for 'superb, nay sublime' Finland.[4]

The problem of the Scandinavian Governments

There was no shortage of problems or obstacles, and the biggest threat to the Allied plan was still the intransigence of the Norwegian and Swedish governments. They had never given any cause for optimism regarding the possibility of allowing Allied troops across their territory and their stance showed no sign of wavering. Gripenberg had expressed the view that if the Allied forces were to land, then they would meet no opposition, regardless of what the Scandinavian Governments were saying in public. This argument found receptive ears in the Northern Department, as was demonstrated by Collier's comments on 1 March. Collier's sanguine assessment of the ultimate complicity of the Scandinavian states in the Allied military action over their territory was clearly not shared in other government departments with a responsibility for external relations. A memorandum composed in the Dominions Office warned of a possible fiasco, with the Norwegians and Swedes destroying the railway lines and thus the Allied capability for crossing the two kingdoms, although Collier felt that this assessment was somewhat alarmist.[5] Whatever the likelihood of the disruption of rail networks in Norway and Sweden, the fact was that, at the moment, the Swedes were putting as much pressure as they could on the Finns to accept terms. If the Finns did not accept readily, then Sweden had raised the threat of withdrawing Swedish volunteers from the conflict.[6] Stockholm's attitude was based on its desire to avoid being drawn into any kind of military conflagration. The notion that Allied assistance to Finland could possibly prevent Finland from being defeated could not have proved an attractive proposition to the Swedes, given that their collaboration in such a project would drag them into the general European hostilities. The reality appeared to be that if British forces were to gain access to Finland, then force would have to be used, or at least threatened.

Attempts to persuade the Scandinavians to allow transit

It was, nevertheless, decided by the British Government to make an attempt at gaining the requisite permission from the Scandinavian Governments. Acknowledging the fears that the two states had of German aggression, military protection against the wrath of Germany was promised. Predictably, this had no effect. The Swedish Foreign Ministry apprised the British that its government would not permit any transit of Allied troops to the Finnish zone. Significantly, it added that the Finns had been 'plainly' told this, and could not hope for any reconsideration or help from that direction.[7] The British Government hoped to bring pressure on the Scandinavian Governments to change their decisions, although it lagged behind the French in this respect. Léger at the Quai d'Orsay, proposed on 4 March that the Allies should now inform the governments of Norway and Sweden that they intended to proceed with their plan. The Scandinavians would be told that if they 'acquiesced passively' then the Allies would refrain from 'mobilising international opinion against them'. If, on the other hand, they created difficulties, then 'we would be obliged to take far more extensive operations as well as taking all possible measures for placing full responsibility at their door'.[8] This fitted in with the policy of making sure that any blame for the fall of Finland would be put onto the Scandinavians, with the Allies absolved of any liability or responsibility. Daladier agreed with his foreign minister. He believed that if the Norwegians and Swedes were to acquiesce, then so much the better but that they should be told that the plan would proceed in any case. This extreme attitude caused some uneasiness in London. Cadogan asked Campbell to make it clear to the French that a Finnish appeal was a necessary precondition for intervention. Without it, the attitudes of the Norwegians and Swedes were quite irrelevant. Once it was received, a benevolent attitude on behalf of the Scandinavians would be desirable. Cadogan realised that the collapse of Finland due to inadequate Allied support would lead to a loss of prestige for Britain and France but he wanted the French to understand that it would be equally disastrous for an Allied force to flounder in Finland because the railway lines had been rendered unusable due to 'passive' resistance on the part of the Swedes or Norwegians.[9] This was not an irrational fear. Mallet had received good information, which complemented the report from the Dominions Office described above, that, while the Swedes would not offer armed resistance to the passage of Allied troops, they would probably remove their rolling stock and disrupt their railway lines.[10] In practical terms, this would present as great an obstacle as military resistance. The vital condition of a Finnish appeal was still not forthcoming, however. Vereker reminded Tanner and Ryti on 4 March that it was vital that it be made by the end of the following day.[11]

However, the signs were that at this stage the Finns were considering accepting Soviet terms more than they were considering requesting Allied help. Eljas Erkko, the former Finnish Foreign Minister and now head of the Finnish Legation in Stockholm, explained why to Mallet on 4 March. He told of his government's disappointment at the realisation of how small the Allied force was likely to be. They had expected a much larger expedition, thanks to the information which they had been receiving from General Ganeval of the French War Department. He had led them to anticipate a force in the region of 200,000 men, rather than the 50,000 which Daladier had quoted. The inflated figures supplied by the French had made their way to Mannerheim at the front and had led to considerable embarrassment for General Ling who was visiting him. Back in London, Fitzroy Maclean recorded his anger towards the French over this matter, attacking their 'mischievous distortion'.[12] The contrast between the figures supplied by the French and those which were feasible in reality had indeed produced a demoralising effect in Finnish policy-making circles. Devious as their misinformation was, however, the motive behind the French action was to encourage an appeal from Helsinki which otherwise was in danger of being shelved. Collier, as has been shown, had come close to an understanding of the French policy two days earlier and was to do so again on 5 March. On that date, he argued that 'however unscrupulous the French had been in making promises to the Finns which they knew they could not fulfil, I confess to feeling considerable sympathy for the French point of view'. He believed that it was of the utmost importance to encourage the Finns to make the appeal. Once they had done this and action was under way, Hitler would be forced to respond and could be defeated in Scandinavia. He also noted that Brigadier Ling had reported that the Red Army in Finland could be completely routed if sufficient bomber aircraft were made available to the Finnish forces. The alternative was capitulation by the Finns to the Soviet demands, and this, in Collier's view, was not an attractive proposition.[13]

The French Government had its own reasons for encouraging the Finns to make an appeal. Daladier had invested his entire authority in a Scandinavian mission, which he and his government hoped would draw German troops away from the Western Front and open up a battlefield hundreds of miles away from French soil. As his major ally was insisting that a Finnish appeal should form a prerequisite for such an adventure, even if it was only a smokescreen for the Allies' true intentions, he was desperate to convince the Finns to make their call for arms.

The British Government did not disagree with the French over the possible advantages to be secured by widening the war to Scandinavia, although they were not about to resort to the same methods to secure the required action by Finland. A report submitted to the War Cabinet by the Chiefs of Staff Committee that a Scandinavian expedition 'gives us the chance – which may not recur – of wrenching the initiative from Germany and of depriving her of a vital raw material'.[14] Not surprisingly, they conceived the mission as part of the war with Germany rather than a means of directly alleviating the suffering of Finland. In this they differed from Collier and Maclean, who while convinced of the benefits that the Chiefs of Staff had identified, and hopeful that a Scandinavian mission would contribute to Germany's defeat, believed that the Finns had a cause worth supporting.

The question of most importance to the Finns was whether any promises made by the Allies could be converted into a war-winning reality. The belief in such a prospect was fading in Helsinki and the realisation that the war was lost and that the best terms possible had to be secured was growing. The examples of Czechoslovakia and Poland did not do much to inspire a sense of confidence that the Western Allies could protect a small state from an aggressive neighbour. The influential triumvirate of Ryti, Tanner and Paasikivi all held that the conflict must be resolved at the earliest possible date, and a peace delegation left for Moscow on 7 March. Vereker described the terms which the Soviet Government had offered as 'proposals for peace which could form an acceptable basis for discussion', and reported that the Finnish Government wanted to consider them. Consequently it would need more time to decide on whether an appeal to the Allies was warranted. Vereker sympathised with the Finns. They had, after all, been fighting a life and death struggle for over three months on very unequal terms. However, he believed that the Finns needed to be given a deadline of 12 March by which time a decision one way or another would have to be made. The Finnish Government was in agreement with Vereker on this matter and informed him that its decision would have to be put on hold until this date.[15]

Late attempts by the Northern Department to secure intervention

Maclean was still advocating the most extreme views, which envisaged engaging the Soviet Union as a *bona fide* enemy. On 6 March he composed a memorandum which considered the possibilities of opening hostilities with the Soviet Union. This, he argued, was a risk worth taking. He considered that British aid to Finland would have the effect of strengthening the Finns and causing further embarrassment to Moscow. This would mean that the Soviet Union would be unable to take any action in the Near or Middle East. It would also be in British interests, he recorded, to bomb the Soviet oil installations at Baku in the Caucasus. This would form part of a more general and co-ordinated strategy aimed at the USSR. He conceded that such a policy could only be undertaken with the co-operation of the Turkish Government and as such it would be necessary to inform Turkey if British troops were to be sent to Finland. Clearly, Maclean did not think that Finland's problems existed in isolation but needed to be viewed as part of a wider strategy directed against the Soviet Union. Maclean's assessment was well received by Orme Sargent who recommended it for submission to the Chiefs of Staff. Fortuitously, Sargent failed to submit the paper in time. When asked if he would like Halifax to submit it to the War Cabinet himself, Maclean declined the offer.[16] Perhaps he now viewed the collapse of Finnish resistance as inevitable.

His views were out of step with military thinking. On 8 March, the Chiefs of Staff issued a report on 'Military implications of hostilities with Russia in 1940'. They commented that the risk of initiating war with the USSR would only be acceptable 'if it led to a result which might cause the early collapse of Germany'. They cited the capture of the Swedish ore fields as an example of this. However, they believed that there was no action 'which we could take against Russia' which would bring about the early defeat of Germany.[17] If such was the case, then there was clearly little point in straining resources in order to despatch troops and equipment to Finland.

All things considered, it now looked likely that Finland would come to terms with the USSR. The fact that Norway and Sweden were totally unwavering in their determination to keep out any foreign troops and thus deny an Allied expedition through their territory, meant that the Allied plan could only be undertaken with the risk of coming into conflict with previously friendly countries. This fact, allied to the likelihood of German intervention in their rear, and the certainty of a major collapse of their armed resistance to the Red Army, was instrumental in convincing the Finns to make the journey to Moscow. Unlike their visits in October, this time Paasikivi and Tanner knew that resisting unpalatable concessions was not an option. Tanner had assured Vereker that his government would only make peace on acceptable terms, but the Finns were not in any position to be so choosy about the conditions offered to them, something which Collier was not slow to pick up on. By 9 March, he was resigned to the reality that the spirit of resistance, so long exemplified by the Finnish Government and its armed forces, had dissipated and that even a 'Nystad' peace, similar to the one which was forced on Sweden at the end of the Great Northern War in 1721, removing all of Finland's Karelian possessions, would be accepted now.[18]

Collier's hopes were clearly fading, but they had not been completely extinguished. He was comforted by the telegram which Halifax sent to Vereker, which requested him to inform the Finnish Government that Britain was ready to supply 50 Blenheim Bomber aircraft within two weeks, and would soon be in a position to send its expeditionary force. Naturally, the despatch of planes and troops was dependent on the receipt of an appeal from the Finnish Government. If the Finns decided against an appeal, then, Halifax informed Gripenberg, Britain would close its offer.[19] Chamberlain gave similar information to Gripenberg, although he insisted that British troops would *not* fight on the southern front, which was the very area where the Finns stood in dire need of reinforcements.[20]

Moscow's demands on the Finns

Such information was hardly likely to be of much encouragement to the Finns and an end to the war was now inevitable. The Finnish negotiators in Moscow were presented with demands far harsher than they had been asked to agree to the previous October, but they were in no position to prolong resistance. On 8 March, when the signing of a peace treaty seemed to be only a matter of time, the Bishop of London suggested to the Foreign Office that British intervention should take another form. Instead of sending planes and tanks and soldiers across Scandinavia, the Bishop suggested that Britain should become a party to the negotiations. Other-wise, he reasoned, the war would come to an end as a result of a Russo-Swedish-German collaboration. As a result of this, Allied influence in Scandinavia and Finland would be finished. Not surprisingly, given his recent views, Collier disagreed. He thought that any association with the harsh terms which Moscow was demanding would be certain to discredit the government involved. Without Swedish help, which was not going to materialise, the Allies could not approach the table and tell the Russians to be more reasonable.[21]

Perhaps it was fortunate that Collier was ignorant of the fact that Neville Chamberlain had decided on 8 March that, as the Finns were about to capitulate, there was no point in sending any further aid. If assis-tance were to be despatched, then it could only be considered if the Scandinavian states decided to co-operate, something which Chamberlain knew was highly unlikely.[22] All the considered arguments which Collier was propounding were completely negated in the face of the opinion of Chamberlain. Equally, any ambitions which Collier entertained regarding British military action in Finland were irrelevant when confronted with the views of the Prime Minister.

The terms of the Treaty of Moscow

In any case, it was already far too late to expect the Finns to give the signal which would put Allied invasion forces on action stations for a landing in Scandinavia. A peace treaty between the USSR and Finland was signed on 12 March, leaving the Allied plans in tatters, and causing Daladier's government to fall. The terms accepted by the Finns were more punitive than those they had been offered the previous autumn. The territory ceded to the USSR was extensive and included the Karelian Isthmus, the city of Viipuri which had been Finland's second largest, the western and northern shores of Lake Ladoga and parts of the Rybachi and Sredni peninsulas in the north. In addition, the port of Hankö, close to Helsinki, was to be leased to the Soviet Union for a period of 30 years. Most ominously, the Finnish Government agreed to develop a railway line to connect Kemijärvi on the Swedish border with Kandalaksha.[23] This would increase the potential for efficient and effective Soviet intervention in Finland in the future. While Finland had retained its sovereignty, the terms were onerous and boded ill for the future, yet it had been deemed preferable to accept them rather than pursue the option offered by the Western Allies. A lack of confidence in any meaningful Allied aid arriving quickly enough to reverse the military tide which was flowing against Finland, was instrumental in the reticence of the Finnish Government to issue a public cry for intervention. At the same time, even if an appeal had been made, the determination of the Scandinavian Governments to prevent the transit of Allied troops across their territory would not have wavered. The crossing of Norway and Sweden by Allied troops, without the consent of the Norwegian and Swedish Governments, would have posed significant problems both militarily and politically for Britain and France in the future. The Chiefs of Staff as good as recognised this problem when they declared that a 'test' landing could be made at Narvik but, if the Norwegians contested it, all such plans should be immediately abandoned as the issue could not possibly be forced.[24]

Disenchantment within the Northern Department

Perhaps in the end the Norwegian and Swedish Governments did the Allies a good turn. The fiasco which later occurred following Allied landings in Norway suggest that the planned adventure through Scandinavia, ostensibly to relieve Finland, would have been equally calamitous. Nonetheless, the Norwegian disaster could not be foreseen at this stage, and as far as Collier was concerned, passing the blame for the collapse of Finland onto the shoulders of the Scandinavian Governments seemed the most appropriate mode of action. On 11 March, with time swiftly running out on the Allied plan, Collier had drafted a note to be given to the Norwegian and Swedish Governments following a Finnish appeal. It stated that once the Finns had made the call and confirmed their need and desire for Allied forces, troops would be despatched. The Allied Governments therefore trusted that Norway and Sweden would act in the spirit of the League of Nations Resolution of the previous December and would refrain from placing any obstacles in the way.[25] As peace was on the point of being concluded, it would appear that Collier's motivation for the message was to counterpoise the British Government's willingness to save

Finland with the reluctance of the Scandinavians to facilitate such a salvation for their neighbour. His aggravation with the Swedes in particular was reinforced on 14 March, two days after the ending of the war, by a statement made in the Swedish parliament by its Foreign Minister, who claimed that Sweden had not applied pressure on Finland to accept the Soviet terms. This announcement was too much for Collier, who minuted a strong attack on the Swedish Government and its general lack of support for Finland over the past couple of months.[26] In a separate address, he minuted that the world would be looking for a scapegoat for the Finnish collapse, and if that role was not quickly assigned to Sweden 'it will soon be fixed on us'.[27] The performance of the Swedish Government, therefore, needed to be identified as a significant cause in the obstruction of the flow of British assistance to Finland, and consequently a major factor in the ultimate defeat of the Finnish forces. The Norwegians were also a target for Collier's ire. On hearing that Koht, the Norwegian Foreign Minister, had accused Tanner of giving contradictory statements to the Allies and the Scandinavians, Collier blasted back that Koht himself was guilty of misrepresentation. While Finland had only made one direct enquiry regarding Allied transit to Norway, it had made several to Sweden, which Koht would have been well aware of. Collier surmised that Koht was suffering from a guilty conscience and that his vehemence could be explained by his realisation that Norway and Sweden would get the blame for the Finnish collapse.[28]

As Collier's superior Alexander Cadogan had already realised, world opinion was unlikely to react in this way. Cadogan criticised the belief held by Collier that 'our great weapon with the Scandinavians is the opprobrium [they] will incur from stopping us *helping Finland*. They will incur no opprobrium for defending their own orefield; in fact they will have the world behind them!'[29] The permanent Under-Secretary was clearly of the opinion that the world at large would not have viewed British intervention and 'help' for Finland as a philanthropic act on behalf of the Finns, but as a cynical device in the war with Germany. Collier can, to some degree, be exculpated from this criticism. He at least was advocating assistance for Finland to help the Finnish war effort as well as looking an excuse to seize important mineral assets in a neutral state. A charge of losing sight of vital British interests would be less easy to defend him on.

It would have been easy enough for anyone to have lost sight of British interests if they had lost sight of Germany as the 'ultimate villains', to use Orme Sargent's description. Seemingly, Collier had temporarily forgotten this, obsessed with the spectacle of a small nation bravely protecting its frontiers from foreign incursion. Perhaps too, he had felt the influence of his new colleague, Fitzroy Maclean, to advocate the pursuit of a more aggressive and interventionist policy. He had certainly rejected his pre-war belief in the desirability of an association with the Soviet Union. Fortunately, however, the end of the Finno-Soviet war gave the Northern Department an opportunity to reassess relations with the USSR. In the immediate aftermath of the Moscow peace, Gordon Vereker contacted the Northern Department informing it that Finland hoped eventually to regain all the territory it had lost, possibly as a result of Allied action elsewhere. He recommended that further Finnish requests for war material be met unconditionally and that Finland be regarded as an ally. Maclean, in the cold light of peace, questioned this assessment. If the USSR were to be regarded as a potential enemy, then Britain should assist in building up Finland's military capability, he reasoned. However, if a rapprochement with Moscow were sought, then there would seem little point in undertaking such a policy.[30] A fortnight later, in a report to the War Cabinet, the Chiefs of Staff Committee took a similar view, stating that it was impossible to tell what effect the treaty terms would have on Soviet-German relations, but that British response to any moves by Finland or the Scandinavian countries should be determined by whether there was reason to believe that Germany was involved.[31]

Finland's war had ended (for now) but Britain's had not. Any ideas of using the Finnish conflict to further Britain's own strategic position had vanished. Needless to say, the opportunity of pursuing an 'ethical' or 'adventurous' intervention on Finland's side had also disappeared. The plan devised by the British military staff to deprive Germany of its iron ore supplies from Sweden had come to nothing. Collier and Maclean's calls for substantial aid to be despatched to the Finns, regardless of the wider European context, had not been given serious consideration by their superiors. Therefore, two justifications for intervention in the 'Winter War' existed and had failed to come to fruition. Given the later experience of Allied military intervention in Norway, perhaps a similar expedition in March 1940 would have ended in fiasco. Even if this was, in retrospect, a likely outcome, the plans of the Chiefs of Staff can be excused due to the emphasis they placed on the national interest. On the other hand, Maclean and to a lesser extent Collier, had lost sight of their country's needs, overcome with moral and adventurous zeal and a desire to take the fight to the 'enemy' in a place where war was not 'phoney'. The military plans which had been drawn up meant, even in the event of Allied intervention, that a major incident between British and Soviet forces could probably be avoided. The plan of Collier and Maclean meant that a war with the USSR was a prospect which might need to be embraced. Such an outcome would have been disastrous for British interests. Collier had come a long way since 1938 and his attempts to reconcile the Finnish and Soviet positions in the Baltic.

10

CONCLUSION

In the spring of 1940, Allied forces were driven from the territories they had planned to occupy through the pretext of assistance to Finland. In June of that year, France collapsed ignominiously in the face of the German invaders and Britain's own survival was under threat. The defeat of France meant that it was now unthinkable that Britain could score a military victory over Germany without an alliance with other parties. In June 1941, the British Government did indeed begin the diplomatic moves which would lead to an alliance with the USSR, one which would ultimately lead to victory, following Hitler's 'Barbarossa' offensive. The existence of a common enemy, and the threat of possible destruction at the hands of the German forces, no doubt concentrated many minds, making alliance possible.

The co-operation with Moscow which emerged after 1941 was, however, very different to that which had first been envisaged by Laurence Collier and others in the Northern Department back in 1938. At that stage, the British officials attempted to keep both the USSR and Finland contented. They pursued a course which, it was hoped, would satisfy Finnish security concerns, while allaying Russian suspicions. By the end of 1941, London and Moscow were allies in a fight to the death with Germany, with Britain accepting a state of war with Finland as an inevitable consequence of the alliance with Stalin. The hopes entertained earlier had failed to be realised. So too had the recommendations put forward by Collier and Maclean in February and March 1940 for the granting of immediate and substantial aid to Finland in its struggle with the Russian invader, and Britain and Finland were now enemies.

This turn of events was by no means inevitable. If the differences between Moscow and Helsinki had been reconciled successfully by British efforts in 1938–1939, then the mutual benefits to Nazi Germany and the Soviet Union of a friendship treaty might not have existed. Poland was always the main stumbling block in the way of an agreement between the Western powers and the USSR, but Moscow's interest in the Baltic States and Finland was also important. If Finland and the USSR had been able to reconcile their differences, then a way might have been open for Britain to enlist the support of the USSR without the threat of Moscow infringing Poland's territorial integrity. On the other hand, if the advice of Collier and Maclean had been followed in 1940, conditions for the Anglo-Soviet alliance would have been severely compromised. It is, of course, only hindsight which allows such alternatives to be weighed up. At the time, Collier and his associates had no notion of how events would turn in the future, and acted according to their assessment of conditions at the particular moment. The important point is that, in many instances, the recommendations of the Northern Department were overlooked or overruled. An alternative to their advice was preferred.

It would, however, be incorrect to say that the Northern Department was without influence. Its advice on the Åland Islands was followed, despite reservations from even within the Foreign Office itself. The problem it faced over these islands had no easy solutions. The Åland Convention of 1922 which confirmed the demilitarised status of the islands had, initially, posed no threat to British interests. Even in 1938, the Baltic Sea did not represent an area of vital strategic significance to Britain. Despite this, Collier and the Northern Department engaged with the issue of remilitarisation and refortification when it arose. The international situation had changed considerably since the early 1920s, and the potential threat of a revitalised Germany had to be taken into account. So too did an emerging Soviet Union, which, in its former Tsarist guise, had exercised control over the Åland archipelago. From this point onwards, Britain's policy towards Finland had to be conducted with the security needs of the Soviet Union in mind, and it was hoped that influencing Finnish policy would lead to a more accommodating outlook from Moscow. Influence, like treason, can be a matter of timing.

Finnish rearmament was a major issue which unsettled the USSR. As far as they were concerned, any build-up of Finnish military power could only be aimed at themselves. This fact was recognised in the Northern Department. The policy of the Northern Department towards Finnish rearmament aimed at keeping the Finnish military at a safe distance from their German counterparts. Equally, they aimed to reassure the Finns sufficiently through assisting in meeting their defence needs, that Moscow need not be feared as a potential aggressor. If Finland's requests were met in the field of defence, they would conceivably have been more amenable to Soviet aspirations in the political field. The policy of the Northern Department at this time was determined by a pragmatic assessment of what they considered to be Britain's needs. It was clear that Collier and his officials saw war with Germany as imminent and they were attempting to build the best possible platform for British success in the coming conflict. This meant isolating Germany from any potential allies in northern Europe. Finland was an obvious place from which an attack on Leningrad could be launched, a fact not lost on the Soviet Government, or indeed Carl Gustaf Mannerheim. It was in British interests to prevent any presumption in Moscow that Finnish territory could be used as a launch pad for an invasion of Russia. Britain needed to be viewed by Finland as a better state to associate with than Germany. Consequently, Collier and his staff endeavoured to persuade Finnish military and political opinion through assisting in its rearmament programme. Unfortunately, the service ministries did not think that Britain's military capacity extended to furnishing the military needs of a nation which was not a British ally and which was out of the area of immediate strategic interest. In the view of the service ministries, any military supplies which could be spared from Britain's own rearmament programme should be targeted at nations allied with Britain, or those in an area of strategic importance for Britain. The political reasons put forward by the Northern Department to assist Finland did not harmonise with the strategic outlook favoured by the service ministries, a predictable outcome perhaps.

The policies of the Northern Department with regard to the Åland issue and Finnish rearmament were conducted with the same goal in mind. This was that Finnish and Russian objectives in the Baltic should not be conflicting. When Ribbentrop made his famous journey to Moscow on 23 August to conclude a pact of non-aggression with his Soviet counterpart, Vyasheslav Molotov, the Northern Department's policy became irrelevant. Finland had not fallen into the German camp but the USSR had and could no longer be expected to join an anti-Hitler coalition. The secret protocol attached to the treaty ominously assigned Finland to the Soviet sphere of influence. Moscow had not hesitated in staking out its claim to its allotted sphere of Poland on 17 September 1939. It was not surprising when the Soviet Government approached the governments of the Baltic States with proposals for entering into a security arrangement. It was equally unsurprising that the Baltic Governments accepted the terms. When Finland was approached to enter into similar relations with the Soviet Union, British opinion was divided over what course the Finns should take. Thomas Snow, the British Minister in Helsinki, initially favoured a course whereby the Finns would be encouraged to 'temporise' with the Russians. On the other hand, Collier and Alexander Cadogan both believed that the Finns should stand up to the Soviet Government. At this stage, Collier thought that denying assistance to Finland would be 'playing the German game', clearly identifying Soviet interests with those of Britain's enemy, Germany. While Collier thought that it was in German interests to see Moscow expand its sphere of influence without having to resort to a show of force, he also felt that if the Kremlin had to send its armed forces into action against Finland the resulting disturbances would increase the possibility of Germany and the USSR coming into conflict. He was backed up in this belief by his immediate subordinate, D.W. Lascelles, the First Secretary at the Northern Department. This was to prove a forlorn hope, as Berlin refused to offer any comfort to Finland and allowed the Soviet Union to pursue its aims without any interference.

It is appropriate to consider what the motivations of the Northern Department were. The recommendations of Collier and his associates went from attempting to reconcile Finnish and Soviet interests in 1938 to advocacy of war with Moscow in 1940. Collier was known as opponent of appeasement in the 1930s and continued as such in 1940. The object of his anti-appeasement had, however, changed from Germany to the USSR. Before February 1940, an assessment of British national interest had underpinned the opinions of Collier and most of his colleagues. After British and French policy was pointed in the direction of intervention following the Supreme War council meeting of February 1940, Collier's application of *raison d'état* was modified. This was not down to any ideological reason. At no point were the arguments of Collier and others within his department swayed by ideology. In many ways this was not surprising: British foreign policy had long been characterised by an emphasis on the pure national interest, summed up by Lord Palmerston in the nineteenth century.[1] As the Finno-Soviet conflict progressed, the Soviet Union was certainly identified as an evil to be confronted by Collier and Maclean but the charges levelled against Moscow were generally not motivated by a disdain for communism. At the beginning of the conflict, it was hoped that Russian aggression could bring the USSR into conflict with the forces of Germany. However, by the time the 'Winter War' reached its conclusion, the arguments emanating from the Northern Department were couched in more idealistic, moralistic, and adventurous terms. This did not mean that the arguments had no pragmatic basis. Maclean certainly felt that the USSR could pose a threat to areas of the British Empire. However, it should be noted that some of the arguments emanating from the Northern Department by the time the conflict reached its conclusion were given an idealistic slant, that is to say that no ulterior justifications were made, and that these arguments advocated aid to Finland to help the Finns defeat the Russians, not just to help the British defeat the Germans.

Initially, it had been an assessment of Britain's own needs and interests that had informed Collier's thinking. He minuted his hope that the Soviet Union would embroil itself with Finland in November 1939. As he pointed out, the best interests of the Finns and the British were not identical at that moment. He had joined in the chorus of disapproval which met the suggestion of Thomas Snow to form an anti-Bolshevik front with Japan and Italy in order to drive the Red Army out of Finland. Such a move would have jeopardised Britain's relations in many parts of the world, most importantly with Australia and the United States, who had their own worries about Japanese expansionism. It would have risked losing sight of Britain's principal concern, the war with Germany. In any case, the price demanded by the Italians and especially the Japanese would have been far too high for Britain to pay. Additionally, there was a moral concern. Any indignation felt about the Soviet invasion of Finland would be undermined by a policy which acquiesced in Japan's 'rape of China'. Collier was happy enough to see such arguments supported by not only his department but also Lord Halifax. The moral anxieties regarding the notion of a Japanese connection were reinforced by the political arguments which were used. When Collier came to stress his own moral case for assisting Finland later on, there was no such political standby to back his argument up with. Indeed, if the contentions of Collier and Maclean had been followed to the letter, the likelihood of the USSR being added to Britain's list of enemies would have grown. A 'moral' or 'humane' application of policy would, therefore, have undermined Britain's vital needs and interests in its war with Germany.

So far as morality went, Britain had done its job at the League of Nations meeting in December 1939. The League had hardly distinguished itself as a vehicle for influencing international disputes during the 1930s, and its discussion of the Finno-Soviet conflict was always unlikely to compel the Russians to withdraw. It was fully realised by the Northern Department that the League meeting would have little impact on the situation but Britain's freedom of movement was now conditioned by its French ally, who made it clear that it wanted to take a tough line at Geneva. By voting for the expulsion of the USSR from the organisation, Britain had taken an action which met approval from neutrals around the world without endangering future Anglo-Russian relations to any real extent. The resolution calling on members to send appropriate assistance to Finland was ambiguous enough to prevent its interpretation as an anti-Soviet act, while allowing it to serve as a pretext for the projected invasion of Norway and Sweden in February and March 1940. In the event of facing criticism for not sending assistance to Finland as per the terms of the resolution, the British could always claim that they were prevented from doing so by the Scandinavians. This is what Collier attempted to do in the aftermath of the Finno-Soviet cease-fire. He hoped that the moral condemnation of the neutral nations of the world could be averted. As Britain was engaged in what he himself had earlier termed 'a life and death struggle' with Germany, such notions of blame avoidance seem at best quaint. Finland, for all the emotion it had evoked during its hour of darkness, was of no value to Britain, and scoring points against neutral Scandinavian Governments who had protected their own vital interests by keeping their distance from the conflict was of no benefit.

The Soviet Union, and indeed the rest of the world, had expected a quick and early victory over the Finns. Instead, Finland put up a stiff resistance. The 'democratic government' under the leadership of O.W. Kuusinen, established by the Soviet authorities, was rejected by the Finnish people, who realised that they were fighting for the existence of their country as an independent state. A number of important victories were scored by the Finns over the Red Army, but in the long run they could not hope to match the material resources and unlimited reserves of Moscow. Finland's only hope for survival lay in either obtaining help from abroad or being offered lenient peace terms by the Russians. Yet a quick, negotiated end to the war was not in British interests. By the beginning of February 1940, the Supreme War Council had produced a plan for 'intervention' in the Finno-Soviet war. However, the principal concern of this action would be to seize Norwegian ports and Swedish mineral assets, thus improving the economic and strategic position of the Allies in their war with Germany. The advice proffered to the authorities by Collier and Maclean was much more transparent. While the denial of iron ore and Norwegian ports to Germany was a desirable objective, they felt that aid to Finland was an important goal in its own right. Collier and his First Secretary both understood that a war with the Soviet Union was possible as a result of overt British intervention but believed that this was a risk worth taking.

The arrival of Maclean at the Northern Department marked the occasion of the mutation of Collier's views. It is not clear why this happened, although Maclean's acknowledged expertise on Soviet matters must have given his standing a boost. Unfortunately, neither Collier nor Maclean left any private papers. However, it would be reasonable to infer that personality did have a part to play and individual character has been an important aspect of this work. The leading personalities involved reacted to a set of circumstances over which they had no control but they did make their own choices and decisions within the constraints with which they were faced. The turn of events had obviously conditioned responses to Finnish problems, but even after the Soviet invasion of 30 November, Collier was looking at how the Finnish crisis could be turned to Britain's advantage. From February 1940, he was arguing that British power should be used to secure an advantage for Finland. Maclean's arguments had frequently taken the view that the Soviet Union was a threat to the interests of the British Empire in India and Asia, and that conflict with the USSR might be justified. In the absence of private papers for either Collier or Maclean, it is impossible to assess completely the reasons for the change in Collier's arguments. Doubtless, the turn of events influenced him, but it is equally possible that he could have been swayed by a new set of arguments coming from a new face on the scene.

The outlook of Collier and his First Secretary was, therefore, seemingly different in March 1940 than it had been before the war. This reflects a change from a time when the government had no interest in Finnish matters to a time when Finland formed a topic of vital concern to the Cabinet. In 1938–1939, Collier and his colleagues had control of the day-to-day policy towards Finland. After the outbreak of the Winter War, their control over policy disappeared. Whereas prior to October 1939 they had had an influence over Britain's approach to events in Finland, after the Soviet invasion they were reduced to a position of forwarding recommendations. This was standard procedure for a Foreign Office department, but it was, nonetheless, a position of less involvement and responsibility than they had previously operated under. Before the war, and indeed in its early stages, Collier and his colleagues held a pragmatic outlook which was based on the need to isolate Germany. This was at a time when their influence over decision-making was greater. By March 1940 the tone had become more irrational, based on emotion and the need to do something. This was a time when their influence was of less consequence. This is not to say that they were without influence. This work shows that both Collier and Maclean were capable of arguing positions which found favour with those above them. However, they were not in a position to be the arbiter of events. They were thus in a safer position to recommend extreme action than they, or indeed their colleagues such as Lascelles, Fitzgerald and Hadow, had been a few months previously. It is also possible that they were attempting to make *ex post facto* alibis for the inevitable collapse of Finland rather than endeavouring to influence policy, confident that their suggestions would not be acted on in any case. By the time the mood in the Northern Department had become more hysterical, and divorced from an assessment of Britain's vital interests, decisions were being handled from above. Collier, Maclean and others at the Foreign Office were entitled to their say, but British policy was being conducted without recourse to sentiment or ideology.

NOTES

INTRODUCTION

1 John Charmley, *Churchill, The End of Glory: A Political Biography*, London: Sceptre (1993), pp. 286–287.
2 From Raymond Smith, 'Introduction' John Zametica, *British Officials and British Foreign Policy 1945–50*, Leicester: Leicester University Press (1990), p. 16.
3 'It's the girl that makes the thing that holds the oil that oils the ring that makes the thing-ummy-bob that's going to win the war.' This song was popularised by Arthur Askey and made the point that everybody had an important role to play in wartime.
4 Max Jakobson, *The Diplomacy of the Winter War: An Account of the Russo-Finnish War, 1939–1940*, Cambridge, MA: Harvard University Press (1961).
5 Jukka Nevakivi, *The Appeal that Was Never Made: The Allies, Scandinavia and the Finnish Winter War 1939–1940*, London: C. Hurst & Co (1976).
6 Patrick Salmon, 'Scandinavia in British strategy, September 1939–April 1940', PhD thesis, University of Cambridge (1979).
7 Paul Doerr, 'Caution in the card room: the British Foreign Office Northern Department and the USSR 1932–1940', PhD thesis, University of Waterloo (1993).

1 1938: BRITISH POLICY, THE ÅLAND ISLANDS AND FINNISH REARMAMENT

1 Kari Selen, 'The main lines of Finnish security policy between the world wars', *Revue Internationale d'Histoire Militaire*, 62 (1985), pp. 17–18.
2 Snow to Halifax, 1 October 1938, *British Documents on Foreign Affairs (BDFA)*, Series A, vol. 14, Frederick, MD: University Publications of America, p. 419.
3 Max Jakobson, *The Diplomacy of the Winter War*, Cambridge, MA: Harvard University Press (1961), pp. 20–21.
4 Riita Hjerppe, 'Finland's foreign trade and trade policy in the twentieth century', *Scandinavian Journal of History*, 18 (1993), pp. 60–63.
5 The Lapua movement was a sometimes violent anti-communist organisation which looked as if it might stage a coup against the government in 1930. See Fred Singleton, *A Short History of Finland*, 2nd edn, Cambridge: Cambridge University Press (1998), pp. 117–118.
6 Patrick Salmon, 'Great Britain, the Soviet Union and Finland at the beginning of the Second World War', in J. Hiden and T. Lane (eds) *The Baltic and the*

Outbreak of the Second World War, Cambridge: Cambridge University Press (1992), p. 104.

7 Patrick Salmon, 'British security interests in Scandinavia and the Baltic, 1919–1939', in J. Hiden and A. Loit (eds) *The Baltic in International Relations between the Two World Wars*, Stockholm: Acta Universitatis Stockholmiensis (1988), p. 122.

8 Thomas Munch-Petersen, 'Great Britain and the revision of the Åland Convention', *Scandia*, 41 (1975), p. 68.

9 Ibid., p. 68.

10 Mieczyslaw Nurek, 'Great Britain and the Baltic in the last months of peace, March–August 1939', in J. Hiden and T. Lane, *The Baltic and the Outbreak of the Second World War*, Cambridge: Cambridge University Press (1992), p. 28.

11 The Patriotic People's Party (or IKL) was established in 1932 to continue the work of the Lapua Movement, but differed from Lapua in its respect for legality and constitutional processes. See Osmo Jussilla, *et al.*, *From Grand Duchy to a Modern State: A Political History of Finland since 1809*, London: Hurst & Co. (1999), p. 163.

12 Monson to Collier, 14 January 1938, FO 371/22274/N247; Monson to Collier, 25 January 1938, FO 371/22274/N496.

13 Snow to Collier, 25 January 1938, FO 371/22274/N557.

14 Snow to Collier, 25 January 1938, FO 371/22274/N561.

15 Collier to Snow, 25 January 1938, FO 371/22274/N557.

16 Parliamentary Debates HC, vol. 332, 15 March 1938.

17 Hadow minute in Snow to FO, 16 March 1938, FO 371/22274/N1357.

18 Snow to Collier, 23 March 1938, FO 371/22274/N1574.

19 Collier to Snow, 30 March 1938, FO 371/22274/N1574.

20 Monson to Halifax, 29 March 1938, FO 371/22274/N1619.

21 Snow to Halifax, 4 April 1938, FO 371/22274/N1860.

22 Munch-Petersen, 'Great Britain and the revision of …', pp. 73–74; Collier minute in Snow to FO, 4 April 1938, FO 371/22274/N2086.

23 Northern Department memo, 26 April 1938, FO 371/N22276/N2072.

24 Snow to FO and Northern Department minutes, 27 April 1938, FO 371/22274/N2175.

25 Munch-Petersen, 'Great Britain and the revision of …', p. 74.

26 Translations of *Pravda* and *Moscow News* articles in Chilston to Halifax, 23 June 1938, FO 371/22274/N3176.

27 Collier minute in Chilston to Halifax, 23 June 1938, FO 371/22274/N3176.

28 Munch-Petersen, 'Great Britain and the revision of …', p. 75.

29 John Charmley, *Churchill, the End of Glory: A Political Biography*, London: Sceptre (1993), pp. 326–327.

30 C.G.E. Mannerheim, *The Memoirs of Marshall Mannerheim*, London: Cassell (1953), p. 290.

31 Department of Overseas Trade memo, 3 June 1938, FO 371/22266/N2720.

32 Memo from Board of Trade to Under-Secretary of Foreign Office, June 1938, FO 371/22266/N3115.

33 Snow to Collier, 11 July 1938, FO 371/22266/N3658; Snow to Collier, 18 July 1938, FO 371/22266/N3651.

34 Snow to Halifax, 13 September 1938, FO 371/22266/N4771; Snow to Halifax, 23 September 1938, FO 371/22266/N4696.

35 Snow to Halifax, 19 September 1938, FO 371/22266/N4772.

36 Gage minute in Snow to Halifax, 19 September 1938, FO 371/22266/N4772.

37 Snow to Halifax, 30 September 1938, FO 371/22266/N5118.

38 Snow to Halifax, 26 October 1938, FO 371/22267/N5376.
39 Munch-Petersen, 'Great Britain and the revision of ...', p. 75.
40 Hadow memo, 10 June 1938, FO 371/22274/N2894.
41 Collier to Chilston, 7 July 1938, FO 371/22274/N3176.
42 Collier minute, 15 July 1938, FO 371/22274/N3531; Munch-Petersen, 'Great Britain and the revision of ...', p. 76.
43 Duff Cooper to Halifax and Halifax reply, 25 August 1938, FO 371/22275/N4215.
44 Hadow minute in Monson to FO, 8 September 1938, FO 371/22275/N4418.
45 Monson to FO, 9 September 1938, FO 371/22275/N4483.
46 Hadow to Vansittart, 9 September 1938, FO 371/22275/N4503.
47 Gallienne (Tallinn) to C.W. Order (Riga), 1 September 1938, FO 371/22275/N4535.
48 Hadow memo, 19 September 1938, FO 371/22276/N4601.
49 Brownjohn (WO) to Hadow, 27 September 1938, FO 371/22275/N4774.
50 Hadow minute in Brownjohn to Hadow, 1 October 1938, FO 371/22275/N4774.
51 Snow to FO, 27 September 1938, FO 371/22275/N4776.
52 Butler to FO and Hadow minute, 28 September 1938, FO 371/22275/N4791.
53 Walker to Collier, 16 November 1938, FO 371/22275/N5680.
54 Summary of *Izvestiya* article and Collier minute in Chilston to Halifax, October 1938, FO 371/22275/N4994.
55 Snow to Halifax, 24 October 1938, FO 371/22275/N5192.
56 Munch-Petersen, 'Great Britain and the revision of ...', p. 77.
57 Fitzmaurice minute, 1 November 1938, FO 371/22275/N5243.
58 Ibid.
59 FO minutes, November 1938, FO 371/22275/N5243.
60 Munch-Petersen, 'Great Britain and the revision of ...', pp. 78–79.
61 Snow to FO, 13 May 1938, FO 371/22269/N4205.
62 Royal Institute of International Affairs, *Survey of International Affairs 1936*, London: Oxford University Press (1937), pp. 5–6, 534–536.
63 Snow to FO, September 1938, FO 371/22269/N4498.
64 Snow to Halifax, 13 October 1938, *BDFA*, Series A, vol. 14, pp. 419–420.
65 Collier minute in Snow to FO, October 1938, FO 371/22269/N5818.
66 Väinö Tanner, *The Winter War: Finland against Russia 1939–40*, Stanford, CA: Stanford University Press (1957), p. 4; Snow to Halifax, 26 April 1938, FO 371/22270/N2338.
67 Director of Naval Intelligence to FO, 5 October 1938, FO 371/22269/N3733.
68 Patrick Salmon, 'Perceptions and misperceptions: Great Britain and the Soviet Union in Scandinavia and the Baltic Region 1918–1939', in *Contact or Isolation? Soviet-Western Relations in the Inter-War Period*, Stockholm: Acta Universitatis Stockholmiensis (1991), p. 424; Snow to FO, 7 June 1938, FO 371/22274/N3099.
69 Max Jakobson, *The Diplomacy*, p. 23.

2 1939: ATTEMPTS TO SOLVE THE ÅLAND ISLANDS PROBLEM

1 Donald Lammers, 'From Whitehall after Munich: the Foreign Office and the future course of British policy', *Historical Journal*, XVI, 4 (1973), pp. 831–856.
2 Ibid., pp. 832, 846.
3 Keith Middlemas, *Diplomacy of Illusion*, London: Weidenfeld & Nicolson (1972), p. 430.

4   Lammers, 'From Whitehall after Munich', p. 845.
5   Ibid, pp. 847–848.
6   Ibid., p. 841.
7   Ibid., pp. 841–844.
8   Middlemas, *Diplomacy of Illusion*, p. 430.
9   Lammers, 'From Whitehall after Munich', p. 856.
10 Collier memo, 21 December 1938, FO 371/22277/N6261.
11 Sir E. Monson (Stockholm) to Simon, 9 January 1939, *British Documents on Foreign Affairs (BDFA)*, Series A, vol. 15, p. 1.
12 Collier minute, 9 January 1939, FO 371/23650/N162.
13 Collier to Monson, 9 January 1939, FO 371/23650/N164. It should be noted here that all the signatories plus the Soviet Union were given identical notes by Sweden and Finland; see Thomas Munch-Petersen, 'Great Britain and the revision of the Åland Convention', *Scandia*, 41 (1975), p. 71.
14 Snow to Halifax, 17 January 1939, FO 371/23650/N430.
15 UK delegation (League of Nations) to FO, 18 January 1939, FO 371/23650/N356.
16 Collier to Gripenberg and Prytz, 3 February 1939, FO 371/23650/N412.
17 Halifax conversation with Maisky and FO minutes, 27 January 1939, FO 371/23650/N510. The Northern Department was, in fact, about to receive conflicting reports about the likely attitudes of the Finnish military in a Baltic crisis. Colonel Kempff, Swedish military attaché in Helsinki, informed Britain's air attaché, Wing Commander Johnson, that in his view the outbreak of war would lead to 'the senior Finnish generals [forming] a military dictatorship of pro-German complexion' which could lead to Finland lining up against Britain in a future conflict (see Snow to Halifax, 10 February 1939, *BDFA*, Series F, vol. 67, pp. 25–26). In contrast, the same British official was told by Colonel Melander, the senior Finnish military intelligence officer, that 'the first country to violate Finnish territory would be treated as Finland's enemy', *BDFA*, Series F, vol. 67, pp. 67–68.
18 Snow to Collier, 27 January 1939, FO 371/23650/N554.
19 Parliamentary question, 15 February 1939, FO 371/23650/N866.
20 Gage minute, 24 February 1939, FO 371/23650/N1041.
21 Snow to FO, 25 February 1939, FO 371/23650/N1088.
22 Von Blücher to Foreign Ministry, 21 November 1938, *Documents on German Foreign Policy (DGFP)*, Series D, vol. 5, p. 608.
23 Minute by an official in the Economic Policy Department, 20 January 1939, *DGFP*, Series D, vol. 5, pp. 619–620.
24 Memorandum of Political Division VI, 17 January 1939, *DGFP*, Series D, vol. 5, pp. 610–613.
25 Von Blücher to Foreign Ministry, 3 February 1939, *DGFP*, Series D, vol. 5, p. 625.
26 Snow to FO, 22 March 1939, FO 371/23650/N1580.
27 Snow to FO, 3 April 1939, FO 371/23650/N1758.
28 Seeds (Moscow) to FO, 3 April 1939, FO 371/23650/N1794.
29 Snow to Halifax, 6 April 1939, FO 371/23650/N1838.
30 Gallienne to R.W. Orde, 29 March 1939, FO 371/23650/N1848.
31 Snow to Oliphant, 11 April 1939, FO 371/23650/N1993.
32 Snow to Collier, 3 April 1939, FO 371/23650/N1854.
33 Snow to Oliphant, 11 April 1939, FO 371/23650/N1993.
34 See, for example, A.J.P. Taylor, *The Origins of the Second World War*, London: Hamish Hamilton (1961); Jonathan Haslam, *The Soviet Union and*

the Search for Collective Security in Europe, London: Macmillan (1989); Geoffrey Roberts, *The Soviet Union and the Origins of the Second World War: Russo-German Relations and the Road to War, 1933–1941*, London: Macmillan (1995).

35 Snow to Halifax, 11 April 1939, and Gage minute, 20 April 1939, FO 371/23650/N2003.
36 Snow to FO, 21 April 1939, FO 371/23650/N2055.
37 Snow to FO, 25 April 1939, FO 371/23650/N2107.
38 See Chapter 4 for details.
39 Colonel Barker Benfield (WO) to Roberts, 17 May 1939, FO 371/23651/N2535. For more details on the pact proposals by Germany, see next chapter.
40 Lascelles memo, 20 April 1939 and Lascelles telegram to Seeds, 27 April 1939, FO 371/23650/N2154.
41 Snow to FO, 11 May 1939, FO 371/23650/N2413.
42 Gage memo, 'The position of the League Council in the matter of the remilitarisation of the Aaland Islands and the attitude of His Majesty's Government', 13 May 1939, FO 371/23650/N2429.
43 UK Delegation (Geneva) to FO, 24 May 1939, FO 371/23651/N2641: Munch-Petersen, 'Great Britain and the revision of . . .', p. 83.
44 Munch-Petersen, 'Great Britain and the revision of . . .', p. 83.
45 Snow to Halifax, 24 May 1939, *BDFA*, Series F, vol. 67, p. 122; Snow to FO, 24 May 1939, FO 371/23651/N2644.
46 UK Delegation (Geneva) to FO, 27 May 1939, FO 371/23651/N2666.
47 Munch-Petersen, 'Great Britain and the revision of . . .', p. 83.
48 UK Delegation (Geneva) to FO, 27 May 1939, FO 371/23651/N2655.
49 Snow to FO, 2 June 1939, FO 371/23651/N2765.
50 Snow to FO, 6 June 1939, FO 371/23651/N2870.
51 Snow to FO, 16 June 1939, FO 371/23651/N3148.
52 Snow to Halifax, 19 June 1939, FO 371/23651/N3150.
53 Lascelles and Collier minutes, 30 June 1939, FO 371/23651/N3150.
54 Lascelles minute in Snow to Halifax, 29 August 1939, FO 371/23651/N3944.

3 1939: THE PROBLEMS OF REARMAMENT

1 R.A.C. Parker, 'Economics, rearmament and foreign policy: the United Kingdom before 1939 – a preliminary study', *Journal of Contemporary History*, vol. 12 (1975), p. 643.
2 D.C. Watt, *How War Came: The Immediate Origins of the Second World War 1938–1939*, London: Heinemann (1989), p. 80.
3 Richard Lamb, *The Drift to War, 1922–1939*, London: W.H. Allen (1989), p. 296.
4 Watt, *How War Came*, p. 93.
5 David Kirby, *Finland in the Twentieth Century*, London: C. Hurst & Co. (1979), p. 117.
6 Ibid., p. 117.
7 Winston S. Churchill, *The Second World War*, vol. 1: *The Gathering Storm*, London: Penguin (1985), p. 325.
8 Johnson memo in Gurney to Halifax, 29 December 1938, FO 371/23643/N194.
9 Snow to Halifax, 13 January 1939, FO 371/23643/N427.
10 Johnson memo and Gage minute, 14 January 1939, FO 371/23643/N428.
11 Snow to Halifax, 13 January 1939, FO 371/23643/N426.
12 Snow to Halifax, 14 February 1939, FO 371/23643/N949.

13 War Office to Under-Secretary of State for Foreign Affairs, 23 March 1939, FO 371/23643/1545.
14 Monier-Williams (Department of Overseas Trade) to Collier, 23 March 1939, FO 371/23643/N1590.
15 Lt. Col. A.F. Harding (WO) to Collier, 28 March 1939, FO 371/23643/N1638.
16 Harding to Collier, 3 April 1939, FO 371/23643/N1821.
17 For an excellent appraisal of the conflict between military and diplomatic institutions in the UK, see Glyn Stone, 'The British Government and the sale of arms to the lesser European powers, 1936–39', *Diplomacy and Statecraft*, 14(2) (2003), pp. 237–270.
18 Johnson memo in Snow to Halifax, 5 May 1939, FO 371/23643/N2338.
19 Collier to Wood, 12 May 1939, FO 371/23643/N2338.
20 Collier minute, 12 June 1939, FO 371/23643/N2338.
21 FO minutes on Snow to FO, 5 June 1939, FO 371/23643/N2940.
22 Oliphant to Newall, 28 June 1939, FO 371/23643/N2338.
23 Sir C. Newall (Air Ministry) to Sir L. Oliphant, 7 July 1939, FO 371/23643/N3256.
24 Snow to Halifax, 6 May 1939, FO 371/23643/N2493.
25 Snow to Halifax, FO 371/23643/N2587.
26 Snow to FO, 4 June 1939, FO 371/23643/N2939.
27 Johnson memo in Snow to FO, 17 July 1939, FO 371/23643/N3570.
28 A. Rowlands (Air Ministry) to Cadogan, 2 August 1939, FO 371/23643/N3646.
29 Snow to FO, 16 August 1939, FO 371/23643/N3917.
30 Letter of N.C. Moore and Lascelles minute in Snow to FO, 9 September 1939, FO 371/23643/N4424.
31 Moore minute in Snow to R.H. Cross (Ministry of Economic Warfare), 12 September 1939, FO 371/23643/N4575.
32 Lascelles and Collier minutes, 22 September 1939, FO 371/23643/N4575.

4 BRITAIN, THE USSR AND THE QUESTION OF FINLAND

1 Keith Feiling, *The Life of Neville Chamberlain*, London: Macmillan (1946), p. 403.
2 Paul Doerr, 'Caution in the card room: The British Foreign Office Northern Department and the USSR 1932–1940', thesis, University of Waterloo (1993).
3 These terms have been taken from Henry Kissinger's *Years of Upheaval*, London: Weidenfeld & Nicolson (1982), p. 169. Alluding to the notion that the Second World War could have been averted by French resistance to the 1936 occupation of the Rhineland, he commented that if such action had been taken, then PhD theses would be written to this day debating which of the two categories Hitler fell into. In reality, it soon became clear what Hitler was but the knowledge was expensively purchased. The choice between 'moral certainty coupled with exhorbitant risk and the willingness to act on unprovable assumptions to deal with challenges while they are still manageable' is one relevant to the problems faced by the British (and French) negotiators in Moscow and London when considering Finland. In attempting to respect Finnish sovereignty and argue their case from a moral perspective, they were left facing a far greater moral, political and strategic disaster. The arguments put to the Finns by the Northern Department that there were 'greater issues' at stake than

Finnish matters do, however, suggest that there was support in this area for acting on an 'unprovable assumption'.

4   R.J.Q. Adams, *British Politics and Foreign Policy in the Age of Appeasement*, Basingstoke: Macmillan (1993), pp. 145–146.
5   Simon Newman, *March 1939: The British Guarantee to Poland*, Oxford: Clarendon Press (1976), p. 122.
6   Robert Manne, 'The British decision for alliance with Russia, May 1939', *Journal of Contemporary History*, vol. 9(3) (1974), pp. 8–9.
7   G. Bruce Strang, 'Once more unto the breach: Britain's guarantee to Poland, March 1939', *Journal of Contemporary History*, vol. 31(4) (1996), p. 736; Jack R. Dukes, 'The Soviet Union and Britain: the alliance negotiations of March–August 1939', *East European Quarterly*, vol. 19(3) (1985), p. 310; Newman, *March 1939*.
8   Snow to FO, 22 March 1939, FO 371/23061/3849.
9   Snow to FO, 22 March 1939, FO 371/23061/3849.
10 Lascelles minute in Snow to FO, 22 March 1939, FO 371/23061/3849.
11 Newman, *March 1939*, pp. 140–141.
12 Cadogan to Snow in Snow to FO, 22 March 1939, FO 371/23061/N3849.
13 Collier minute, 30 March 1939, FO 371/23654/N1764.
14 John Harvey (ed.) *The Diplomatic Diaries of Oliver Harvey, 1937–1940*, London: Collins (1976), p. 280. Unfortunately, Harvey did not relate which Foreign Office members attended the meeting.
15 Halifax to Seeds, 14 April 1939, *Documents on British Foreign Policy 1919–1939* Third Series vol. V, pp. 205–206.
16 Manne, 'The British decision for alliance', pp. 18–19.
17 D.C. Watt, *How War Came: The Immediate Origins of the Second World War 1938–1939*, London: Heinemann (1989), pp. 226–227.
18 Ibid., p. 227.
19 Ibid.
20 D.G. Kirby, *Finland in the Twentieth Century*, London: C. Hurst & Co. (1979), pp. 117–118.
21 Georg Gripenberg, *Finland and the Great Powers: Memoirs of a Diplomat*, Lincoln, NE: University of Nebraska Press (1965), p. 12.
22 John Wuorinen (ed.), *Finland and World War II*, New York: Ronald Press (1948), pp. 46–47. See also Chapter 2.
23 Snow to FO, 26 April 1939, FO 371/23064/C5983.
24 Collier conversation with Finnish and Estonian Ministers, 25–26 April 1939, FO 371/23064/C6211.
25 Snow to FO, 26 April 1939, FO 371/23064/C5983.
26 Snow to FO, 26 April 1939, FO 371/23064/C5983.
27 David Dilks (ed.) *The Diaries of Sir Alexander Cadogan, O.M. 1938–1945*, London: Cassell (1971), p. 175.
28 Max Jakobson, *The Diplomacy of the Winter War*, Cambridge, MA: Harvard University Press (1961), p. 71.
29 Watt, *How War Came*, pp. 260–261.
30 Ibid., pp. 260–261. It is worth noting that in this speech Hitler denounced both the Anglo-German Naval Treaty of 1935 and the German-Polish Non-aggression Treaty of 1934, an admission on his part that war with Britain and Poland was a near certainty.
31 Snow to Halifax, 2 May 1939, *British Documents on Foreign Affairs (BDFA)* Series F, Part II, vol. 67, p. 99.
32 Snow to FO, 10 May 1939, FO 371/23654/N2391.

33 Snow to FO and Collier minutes, 10 May 1939, FO 371/23654/N2404.
34 Collier minute in Snow to FO, 12 May 1939, FO 371/23654/N2435.
35 Snow to FO, 17 May 1939, FO 371/23655/N2521.
36 Snow to FO and Collier minute, 19 May 1939, FO 371/23655/N2560.
37 Snow to FO, 19 May 1939, FO 371/23655/N2561.
38 Proponents of the view that Molotov's appointment did not signify a change in Soviet outlook designed to facilitate a deal with Hitler include Jonathan Haslam and Geoffrey Roberts.
39 Snow to FO and Cadogan minute, 12 May 1939, FO 371/23654/N2435.
40 Snow to FO, 13 May 1939, FO 371/23066/C7092.
41 Seeds to FO, 14 May 1939, FO 371/23066/C7065.
42 Cabinet Conclusions 28 (39), 17 May 1939, FO 371/23066/C7400.
43 Gripenberg, *Memoirs*, pp. 22–23.
44 Foreign Policy Committee meeting 16 May 1939, F.P. (36) 47th mtg, FO 371/23066/C7401.
45 Snow to FO and Kirkpatrick minute, 20 May 1939, FO 371/23066/C7407.
46 HC statement, 24 May 1939, FO 511/95/64/87.
47 John Charmley, *Chamberlain and the Lost Peace*, London: Hodder & Stoughton (1989), p. 185.
48 Gripenberg, *Memoirs*, pp. 26–27.
49 Collier minute in Snow to FO, 22 May 1939, FO 371/23655/N2590.
50 Snow to FO, 7 June 1939, FO 371/23067/C8105.
51 David M. Crowe, *The Baltic States and the Great Powers*, Boulder, CO: Westview Press (1993), p. 69.
52 Halifax conversation, 12 June 1939, FO 371/23068/C8537.
53 FPC meeting, 9 June 1939, FO 371/23068/C8534.
54 Patrick Salmon, 'British plans for economic warfare against Germany 1937–1939', *Journal of Contemporary History*, vol. 16(1) (1981), p. 63.
55 Snow to Halifax and Barclay minute, 6 June 1939, FO 371/23068/C8380.
56 Snow to FO, 20 June 1939, FO 371/23069/C9100.
57 Snow to FO, 3 July 1939, *BDFA*, vol. 67, pp. 159–161.
58 Halifax to Seeds, 27 June 1939, *Documents on British Foreign Policy (DBFP) 1919–1939* Third Series, vol. VIII, pp. 171–172.
59 Crowe, *The Baltic States*, p. 75.
60 Collier memo, 19 July 1939, D) 371/23070/C10111.
61 Snow to FO, 8 July 1939, FO 371/23070/C9619.
62 Collier minute in Troutbeck to Snow, 8 July 1939, FO 511/95/64/141.A.
63 Oliphant to Snow, 25 July 1939, FO 371/23070/C9753.
64 Sidney Aster, *1939: The Making of the Second World War*, London: Deutsch (1973), p. 97n.
65 Dilks, *The diaries of Sir Alexander Cadogan*, p. 185.
66 Oliphant to Snow, 25 July 1939, FO 371/23070/C9753.
67 Snow to FO and FO minutes, 3 July 1939, FO 371/23070/C9753.
68 See particularly P. Stafford, 'Political autobiography and the art of the plausible: R.A. Butler at the Foreign Office, 1938–39', *Historical Journal*, vol. 28 (1985).
69 Butler conversation with Finnish Minister, 14 July 1939, FO 371/23070/C10111.
70 Stafford, 'Political autobiography', p. 8.
71 R.A.C. Parker, *Chamberlain and Appeasement: British Policy and the Coming of the Second World War*, Basingstoke: Macmillan (1993), p. 225. To be fair to Cadogan, it should be noted that he wrote in his diary on 16 May 'that we'd better go the whole hog [regarding an alliance] if we're to ensure that Russia

doesn't go in with Germany'. Two days later he composed a minute admitting the offence that a Soviet connection would give to Finland among others but saw a pact as the only way of averting war, see Dilks, *Diaries*, pp. 180–181.

72 Ingeborg Fleischer, 'Soviet foreign policy and the origins of the Hitler-Stalin pact', in Bernd Wegner, *From Peace to War: Germany, Soviet Russia and the World 1939–1941*, Providence, RI: Berghahn (1997), p. 39.

73 Schnurre memo, 27 July 1939, *Nazi-Soviet Relations 1939–1941: Documents from the Archives of the German Foreign Office*, p. 34.

74 Statements in Snow to FO, 28 July 1939, FO 371/23071/C10591.

75 Arnold Toynbee and Veronica M. Toynbee (eds), *Survey of International Affairs, 1939–1946: The Eve of War, 1939*, London: Oxford University Press (1953), p. 468.

76 Sir Norman Vernon to Collier, 31 July 1939, FO 371/23071/C10687.

77 See Chapter 2, note 26.

78 Walter Isaacson, *Kissinger*, London: Faber (1992), p. 766.

79 Richard Lamb, *The Drift to War 1922–1939*, London: W. H. Allen (1989), pp. 309–316.

80 Louise Grace Shaw, *The British Political Elite and the Soviet Union 1937–1939*, London: Frank Cass (2003), p. 162.

81 Any real difference between the Northern Department and the government is really only a matter of a few degrees. Hitler's understanding of Stalin and Stalin's obvious preference for the better of two offers meant that a genuine pact between London and Moscow was impossible at this stage. However, some historians have argued against this in much more forceful terms that Chamberlain allowed the chance of a Soviet alliance to slip away. The best examples of this school of thought would be Michael Jabara Carley, *1939: The Alliance that Never Was and the Coming of World War II*, Chicago: Ivan R. Dee (1999) and Louise Grace Shaw, *The British Political Elite and the Soviet Union 1937–1939*. Shaw treats Collier's efforts to encourage an agreement with the Soviet Union very sympathetically.

5 THE AFTERMATH OF THE NAZI-SOVIET PACT

1 Lascelles minute in Snow to FO, 28 September 1939, FO 371/23692/N4828.

2 Barclay minute in War Office to Halifax, 6 October 1939, FO 371/23644/N5027.

3 Collier conversation with Gripenberg, 2 October 1939, FO 371/23644/N4950.

4 Allied Demands Committee, A.D. (39) 31, 13 October 1939, and Collier minute 16 October, FO 371/23644/N5273. The Allied Demands Committee was a body chaired by Sir Arthur Robinson, and whose terms of reference 'emphasised the committee's role in examining and reporting on demands from allied countries in the light of the ascertained supply position and having regard to all other factors – political, strategic and financial', Glyn Stone, 'The British Government and the sale of arms to the lesser European powers 1936–39', *Diplomacy and Statecraft*, 14(2) (2003), pp. 240–241.

5 Collier memo, 26 October 1939, FO 371/23644/N5631.

6 Collier minute in Snow to FO, 9 October 1939, FO 371/23692/N5093.

7 Snow to FO, 8 October 1939 and Collier minute, 8 October 1939, FO 371/23692/N5093.

8 Halifax conversation with Prytz and Boheman, 10 October 1939, FO 371/23692/N5143.

9 Halifax conversation with Gripenberg, 12 October 1939, FO 371/23692/N5190.

10 Snow to FO and Collier minute, 13 October 1939, FO 371/23692/N5251.

11 Collier minute in Snow to FO, 16 October 1939, FO 371/23692/N5270.
12 Collier minute on Gripenberg conversation with Butler, 13 October 1939, FO 371/23692/N5260.
13 Gripenberg conversation with Halifax, 25 October 1939, FO 371/23644/N5631.
14 Collier minute in Gallienne (Tallinn) to FO, 9 October 1939, FO 371/23689/N5338.
15 Snow to FO and subsequent minutes, 13 October 1939, FO 371/23692/N5263.
16 Snow to FO and Northern Department minutes, 21 October 1939, FO 371/23692/N5522. Frederick R. Dickinson's monograph, *War and National Reinvention: Japan in the Great War, 1914–1919*, Cambridge, MA: Harvard University Press (1999), although concerned with the period of the First World War, demonstrates clearly that a continuation of the Anglo-Japanese alliance held no attractions for the Japanese, even during days of relative political moderation. In the militaristic years of the 1930s, the Japanese leaders had even less incentive for such an arrangement.
17 Cabinet Conclusions, 23 October 1939, 57 (39) in FO 371/23692/N5594.
18 Snow to Northern Department and Northern Department minutes, 24 October 1939, FO 371/23693/N5777.
19 Patrick Salmon, 'Great Britain, the Soviet Union and Finland at the beginning of the Second World War', in J. Hiden and T. Lane (eds) *The Baltic and the Outbreak of the Second World War*, Cambridge: Cambridge University Press (1992), p. 96.
20 War Cabinet conclusions, 27 October 1939, 62 (39) 10, in FO 371/23693/N5782.
21 War Cabinet Conclusions, 1 November 1939, 67 (39) 9 in FO 371/23693/N5908.
22 Chatfield to Halifax, 1 November 1939, FO 371/23644/N5934.
23 Collier minute in Snow to FO, 4 November 1939, FO 371/23693/N5947.
24 Copenhagen Chancery to Northern Department, 31 October 1939, FO 371/23693/N6017.
25 Gripenberg to Finnish Foreign Ministry, 11 November 1939, UA 109/A1.
26 Max Jakobson, *The Diplomacy of the Winter War*, Cambridge, MA: Harvard University Press (1961), p. 131.
27 War Cabinet conclusions, 85 (39), 16 November 1939, FO 371/23683/N6384.
28 War Cabinet Conclusions, 85 (39), 16 November 1939, FO 371/23683/N6384.
29 Johnson memo in Snow to Collier, 22 November 1939, FO 371/23644/N6469.
30 Johnson memo in Snow to Collier, 17 November 1939, FO 371/23644/N6511.
31 Snow to FO, 13 November 1939, FO 371/23693/N6285.
32 Lascelles minute on *Pravda* articles in Seeds to FO, 19 November 1939, FO 371/23693/N6285.
33 Snow to Halifax, 23 November 1939, FO 371/23693/N6537.
34 Snow to FO and Northern Department minutes, 27 November 1939, FO 371/23693/N6623.
35 Maisky conversation with Halifax, 27 November 1939, FO 371/23693/N6717.
36 Halifax to Snow, 24 November 1939, FO 371/23693/N6667.

6 THE LEAGUE OF NATIONS DEBATE IN GENEVA

1 John Colville, *The Fringes of Power: Downing Street Diaries*, vol. 1 *1939–1955*, Sevenoaks: Sceptre (1987), p. 62.
2 Snow to FO and Collier minute, 30 November 1939, FO 371/23694/N6776.
3 Collier minute, ibid.
4 Maclean and Collier minutes in Seeds to FO, 1 December 1939, FO 371/23694/N6863.
5 Seeds to FO, 2 December 1939, FO 371/23694/N6868.

6 Lascelles minute in Seeds to FO, ibid.
7 Seeds to FO, 2 December 1939, FO 371/23694/N6875.
8 Quoted in Robert Dell, *The Geneva Racket 1920–1939*, London: Robert Hale (1940), p. 295.
9 Quoted in James Barros, *Betrayal from Within: Joseph Avenol, Secretary-General of the League of Nations, 1933–1940*, New Haven, CT: Yale University Press (1969), p. 15.
10 Ibid., pp. 198–200.
11 Telegram from M. Avenol (Geneva), 3 December 1939, FO 371/23694/N6886.
12 War Cabinet Conclusions 103 (39), 4 December 1939, FO 371/23694/N7035.
13 A.W.G. Randall minute, 4 December 1939, FO 371/23694/N7111.
14 FO minutes by Randall, Collier and Cadogan, 4 December 1939, FO 371/23695/N7200.
15 Jukka Nevakivi, *The Appeal that Was Never Made,* London: C. Hurst & Co (1976), p. 58.
16 Barros, *Betrayal from Within*, pp. 202–203.
17 Sir R. Campbell to FO, 9 December 1939, FO 371/23695/N7235.
18 Cadogan minute, 11 December 1939, FO 371/23695/N7299.
19 Lascelles minute in Campbell to FO, 10 December 1939, FO 371/23695/N7300.
20 Halifax conversation with Corbin, 11 December 1939, FO 371/23695/N7325.
21 UK Delegation (Geneva) to FO, 11 December 1939, FO 371/23695/N7331.
22 Monson to FO, 12 December 1939, FO 371/23695/N7422.
23 UK Delegation to FO, 15 December 1939, FO 371/23695/7459 and 14 December 1939, FO 371/23695/N7511.
24 Campbell to Butler, 23 December 1939, FO 371/23696/N7904.

7 THE WINTER WAR: THE FIRST MONTH

1 War Cabinet Conclusions, 101(39), 2 December 1939, CAB 65.
2 Halifax conversation with Gripenberg, 1 December 1939, FO 371/23694/N7054.
3 Sir George Mounsey (MEW) to Sir Orme Sergeant, 5 December 1939, FO 371/23644/N7015.
4 Halifax conversation with Gripenberg, 4 December 1939, FO 371/23644/N6967.
5 War Cabinet Conclusions, 103 (39), 4 December 1939, CAB 65.
6 War Cabinet Conclusions, 104 (39), 5 December 1939, FO 371/23644/N7081.
7 Lascelles and Collier minutes, in Monson to FO, 8 and 12 December, FO 371/23645/N7226.
8 FO minute, 8 December 1939, FO 371/23645/N7276.
9 Monson to FO, 12 December 1939, FO 371/23645/N7329.
10 Collier minute, 11 December 1939, FO 371/23686/N7371.
11 V.G. Lawford to Campbell Stuart (Ministry of Information), 12 December 1939, FO 800/310.
12 Snow to FO, 14 December 1939, FO 371/23645/N7442.
13 Monson to FO, 11 December 1939, FO 371/23645/N7326.
14 Lorraine to FO, 12 December 1939, FO 371/23645/N7509.
15 Snow to FO, 13 December 1939, FO 371/23645/N7366.
16 Admiralty memo (J.A. Philips), 20 December 1939, FO 371/32645/N7629.
17 Collier minute in Snow to FO, 14 December 1939, FO 371/23645/N7442.
18 Collier minute in Snow to FO, 14 December 1939, FO 371/23645/N7442. Snow's attempts to encourage the formation of an alliance to take on the 'Nazi-Soviet' bloc is reviewed later in this chapter.
19 WO memo, 16 December 1939, FO 371/23645/N7553.

20 WO memo, 19 December 1939, FO 371/23645/N7602.
21 Snow to FO, 20 December 1939, FO 371/23645/N7719.
22 Barclay minute in Monson to FO, 15 December 1939, FO 371/23645/N7520.
23 MacLean minute in Snow to FO, 21 December 1939, FO 371/23645/N7675.
24 MacLean minute, 22 December 1939, in Snow to FO, FO 371/23645/N7675.
25 Cadogan to Wood (Air Ministry), 22 December 1939, in Snow to FO, FO 371/23645/N7675.
26 Halifax conversation with Gripenberg, 21 December 1939, FO 371/23645/N7740.
27 Major Tuckey (WO) to Barclay, 23 December 1939, FO 371/23645/N7772.
28 Barclay minute on French Ambassador aide-mémoire, 23 December 1939, FO 371/23645/N7773.
29 Report by COS Committee on Assistance to Finland and the Scandinavian countries, 26 December 1939, CAB 66/WP(39)173.
30 Halifax conversation with French Ambassador, 16 December 1939, FO 371/23696/N7568.
31 Snow to FO, 9 December 1939, FO 371/23695/N7233.
32 Lascelles minute and MacLean telegram, 9 December 1939, FO 371/23695/N7233.
33 Snow (Gronkulla) to FO, 14 December 1939, FO 371/23695/N7450.
34 Collier minute in Snow to FO, 16 December 1939, FO 371/23695/N7450.
35 Sargent to Snow in Snow to FO, 16 December 1939, FO 371/23695/N7450.
36 Snow (Gronkulla) to FO, 17 December 1939, FO 371/23696/N7568.
37 Halifax to Snow, 17 December 1939, FO 371/23696/N7568.
38 Snow to FO, 20 December 1939, FO 371/23696/N23696.
39 Labour Party pamphlet, 'Finland: the criminal conspiracy of Stalin and Hitler', 1940, pp. 19–20.
40 Collier conversation with de Castellane, 21 December 1939, FO 371/23696/N7829.
41 See Chapter 5. The COS Report on the matter had been given on 1 November, almost a month before the Soviet invasion.
42 Maclean minute in Lorraine to FO, 31 December 1939, FO 371/23696/N7942.
43 Lorraine to FO, 29 December 1939, FO 371/23696/N7942.
44 FO minutes, 29 December 1939, FO 371/23696/N7942.
45 Collier conversation with M. Charbonnier, 29 December 1939, FO 371/24791/N1.
46 Collier conversation with Gripenberg, 29 December 1939, FO 371/24795/N15.
47 Barclay minute, 27 December 1939, in Monson to FO, FO 371/24796/N224.

8 THE WINTER WAR: THE SECOND AND THIRD MONTHS

1 Jukka Nevakivi, *The Appeal that Was Never Made*, London: C. Hurst & Co, (1976), p. 92.
2 See Chapter 1.
3 War Cabinet Conclusions 3 (40), 4 January 1940, FO 371/24796/N243.
4 Minute by Orme Sargent, 21 January 1940, FO 371/24793/N2306.
5 Minute by Orme Sargent, 21 January 1940, FO 371/24793/N2306.
6 Snow to Halifax, 10 January 1940, FO 371/24791/N712.
7 Halifax conversation with French Ambassador, 5 January 1940, FO 371/24796/N264.

8 War Cabinet Conclusions, WM (4) Confidential Annexe, 19 January 1940, FO 371/24797/N836.

9 War Cabinet Conclusions, WM 22(40), 24 January 1940, FO 371/24798/N1034.

10 COS Report WP (40) 36, 28 January 1940, WO 193/744.

11 Sargent minute, 8 January 1940, FO 371/24796/N481.

12 Barclay minute, 10 January 1940, FO 371/24796/N520.

13 War Cabinet MC (4) 6th Meeting, 6 January 1940, FO 371/24797/N676.

14 Hempel, Minister in Eire to the Foreign Ministry, 23 January 1940, *Documents on German Foreign Policy*, Series D, vol. 8, p. 691.

15 Campbell (Paris) to FO, 1 February 1940, FO 371/24798/N1287.

16 Memo by Sir Kingsley Wood, 17 January 1940, FO 371/24797/N685; 17 February 1940, PREM 1/407/36.

17 Sargent minute, 23 January 1940, FO 371/24798/N1014.

18 *Halsbury's Statutes*, 4th edition, vol. 12, p. 117; Maclean minute, 16 January 1940, FO 371/24797/N802.

19 Brigadier Ling memo, 13 January 1940, FO 371/24796/N606.

20 Nevakivi, *The Appeal that Was Never Made*, Chapter V.

21 Loraine to FO, 13 January 1940, FO 371/24796/N548. Ciano had persuaded Mussolini to allow volunteers to leave for Finland on 1 January, M. Muggeridge, *Ciano's Diary 1939–1943*, London: Heinemann (1950), p. 192.

22 Maclean minute in Peterson (Madrid) to FO, 1 February 1940, FO 371/24799/N1507.

23 Labour Party (1940), *Finland: The Criminal Conspiracy of Stalin and Hitler*.

24 Collier minute in Loraine to Sargent, 13 January 1940, FO 371/24797/N767.

25 Sir E. Bridges to Cadogan, 29 January 1940, FO/371/24798/N1193.

26 Collier memorandum, 29 January 1940, FO 371/24798/N1204.

27 Campbell to FO, 1 February 1940, FO 371/24799/N1342.

28 David Dilks, *The Diaries of Sir Alexander Cadogan*, London: Cassell (1971), p. 253.

29 For further information on the plans for the occupation of Norway and Sweden, see Jukka Nevakivi, *The Appeal that Was Never Made*.

30 Tuomo Polvinen, 'Finland in international politics', *Scandinavian Journal of History*, (2) (1977), p. 118.

31 Halifax and Sargent minutes, 3 February 1940, FO 371/24792/N1439.

32 Collier minute in Mallet to FO, 5 February 1940, FO 371/24792/N1497.

33 Sir M. Palaiset (Athens) to FO, 5 February 1940, FO 371/24792/N1495.

34 Collier was correct in his assessment. Unknown to him, Hitler had reaffirmed his backing for the USSR's action against Finland on 2 February, see *Documents on German Foreign Policy*, Series D, vol. VIII, pp. 733–734.

35 Collier minute in Edwards (WO) to Lawford, 31 January 1940, FO 371/24799/N1324.

36 PS to Eden, 24 January 1940, WO 197/744/9A.

37 Paul Robinson, *The White Russian Army in Exile, 1920–1941*, Oxford: Clarendon Press (2002), p. 226.

38 Mikhail Semiryaga, *The Winter War: Looking Back after Fifty Years*, Moscow: Novosti Press Agency Publishing House (1990), pp. 56–57.

39 Nevakivi, *The Appeal that Was Never Made*, p. 102.

40 Mallet to FO, 10 February 1940, FO 371/24792/N1571.

41 Carl Van Dyke, *The Soviet Invasion of Finland 1939–1940*, London: Frank Cass (1997), p. 161.

42 Dominions Office telegram to High Commissioners, 9 February 1940, FO 371/24800/N1639. For full details of the military force which the Supreme War

Council proposed to send to Finland and Scandinavia, see Nevakivi, *The Appeal that Was Never Made*, pp. 98–99.

43 See Roderick MacLeod and Denis Kelly (eds), *The Ironside Diaries 1937–1940*, London: Constable (1962), pp. 215 and 216 on this point.

44 Mallet to FO, 8 February 1940, FO 371/24800/N1697.

45 Maclean minute, 8 February 1940, FO 371/24800/N1697.

46 Halifax conversation with Gripenberg, 10 February 1940, FO 371/24800/N1705.

47 Halifax conversation with Zaleski, 8 February 1940, FO 371/24801/N1966.

48 War Cabinet Conclusions, 12 February 1940, FO 371/24800/N1753.

49 Director of Military Operations and Plans to FO, 19 February 1940, FO 371/24801/N2068.

50 Mallet to FO, 13 February 1940, FO 371/24800/N1776.

51 Mallet to FO, 14 February 1940, FO 371/24800/N1943.

52 Roland Kenney to FO, 15 February 1940, FO 371/24800/N1873.

53 War Cabinet Conclusions 38(40), 10 February 1940, FO 371/24800/N1714.

54 Butler minute, 16 February 1940, FO 371/24801/N1996.

55 Halifax to Le Rougetel (Moscow), 22 February 1940, FO 37/24792/N2252.

56 Butler conversation with Maisky, 24 February 1940, FO 371/24793/N2329.

57 Snow to FO, 16 February 1940, FO 371/24801/N1995.

58 Maclean minute in Mallet to FO, 16 February 1940, FO 371/24801/N2069.

59 Mallet to FO, 16 February 1940, FO 371/24801/N2183.

60 Mallet to FO, 17 February 1940, FO 371/24802/N2379.

61 Collier minute, 23 February 1940, FO 371/24802/N2379.

62 Snow to FO, 20 February 1940, FO 371/24801/N2231.

63 FO minute, 20 February 1940, FO 371/24801/N2231.

64 Collier minute, 2 March 1940, on Mallet to FO, FO 371/24802/N2435.

65 Gurney to FO, 23 February 1940, FO 371/24802/N2320.

66 Mallet to FO, 24 February 1940, FO 371/24802/N2331.

67 Maclean and Collier minutes, 24 February 1940, FO 371/24802/N2331; emphasis in original.

68 Collier memo, 28 February 1940, FO 371/24802/N2492.

69 Jebb minute, 26 February 1940, FO 371/24803/N2595.

70 Mallet to FO, 26 February 1940, FO 371/24802/N2435.

71 Halifax conversation with Gripenberg, 27 February 1940, FO 371/24802/N2493.

72 Cadogan conversation with French Ambassador, 29 February 1940, FO 371/24802/N2567.

73 Halifax to Campbell, 29 February 1939, FO 371/24803/N2591.

74 Väinö Tanner, *The Winter War*, Stanford, CA: Stanford University Press (1957), pp. 176–177.

75 Lorraine (Rome) to FO, 27 February 1940, FO 371/24793/N2507.

76 Vereker to FO, 29 February 1940, FO 371/24802/N2566.

77 Halifax conversation with Gripenberg, 29 February 1939, FO 371/24803/N2629.

78 Halifax conversation with Gripenberg, 1 March 1940, FO 371/24803/N2618.

79 Collier minute, 1 March 1940, FO 371/24803/N2618.

80 War Office communication, 29 February 1940, FO 371/24803/N2573.

9 THE END OF THE FINNO-SOVIET WAR AND THE FRUSTRATION OF COLLIER'S HOPES

1 Anthony F. Upton, *Finland 1939–40*, London: Davis-Poynter (1974), pp. 130–131.

2 Vereker to FO and Maclean minute, 1 March 1940, FO 371/24803/N2642.

3 Collier minute, 2 March 1940, FO 371/24803/N2645.

4 Winston Churchill had used this expression in a BBC broadcast of 20 January. The tenor of the broadcast had been to emphasise the rightness of Finland's cause in the face of totalitarian aggression. Churchill's motive for encouraging British activity in the area was, in fact, based rather more on his calculation of strategic interests in the war against Germany.

5 Dominions Office memo (Cavendish-Bentinck), 2 March 1940, FO 371/24803/N2661.

6 Mallet to FO, 1 March 1940, FO 371/24803/N2627.

7 Communication by Dominions Office, 2 March 1940, FO 371/24803/N2663; Mallet to FO, 3 March 1940, FO 371/24803/N2667.

8 Campbell (Paris) to FO, 4 March 1940, FO 371/24803/N2726.

9 Cadogan memo in Campbell to FO, 4 March 1940, FO 371/24803/N2728.

10 Mallet to FO, 4 March 1940, FO 371/24803/N2738.

11 Vereker to FO, 4 March 1940, FO 371/24803/N2690.

12 Mallet to FO and Maclean minute, 4 March 1940, FO 371/24803/N2739.

13 Collier minute, 5 March 1940, FO 371/24804/N2815.

14 War Cabinet, Chiefs of Staff Committee Report, 7 March 1940, FO 371/24804/N2981.

15 Vereker to FO, 7 March 1940, FO 371/24804/N2847; Vereker to FO, 7 March 1940, FO 371/24804/N2892.

16 Maclean memo and Sargent comments, 6 March 1940, FO 371/24846/N3285.

17 COS (40) 252 in FO 371/24846/N3313.

18 Collier minute in Vereker to FO, 9 March, FO 371/24804/N2960.

19 Halifax telegram in Vereker to FO, 10 March 1940, FO 371/24804/N2994.

20 Halifax to Vereker, 13 March 1940, FO 371/24805/N3132.

21 Collier comment on Butler minute, 8 March 1940, FO 371/24793/N3130.

22 Martin Kitchen, *British Policy Towards the Soviet Union during the Second World War*, London: Macmillan (1986), p. 20.

23 Max Jakobson, appendix to *The Diplomacy of the Winter War*, Cambridge, MA: Harvard University Press (1961), pp. 261–266.

24 COS memo, 10 March 1940, WO 193/744/27A (WP(40)92).

25 Collier memo, 11 March 1940, FO 371/24805/N3214.

26 Collier minute in Mallet to FO, 14 March 1940, FO 371/24794/N3263.

27 Collier minute in Mallet to FO, 13 March 1940, FO 371/24794/N3184.

28 Collier minute in Dormer to FO, 13 March 1940, FO 371/24805/N3196.

29 David Dilks (ed.), *The Diaries of Sir Alexander Cadogan*, London: Cassell (1971), p. 259.

30 Vereker to FO and Maclean minute, 14 March 1940, FO 371/24794/N3265.

31 War Cabinet COS Committee 'Report on the strategic implications of Russo-Finnish peace treaty', 26 March 1940, WO 193/647/38A COS(40)274.

10 CONCLUSION

1 'We have no eternal allies and we have no perpetual enemies. Our interests are eternal and perpetual and those interests it is our duty to follow.' Quoted in Eric J. Evans, *The Forging of the Modern State: Early Industrial Britain, 1783–1870*, New York: Longman (1983), p. 201.

BIBLIOGRAPHY

Primary sources

Unpublished material

Cabinet Office: CAB 65 War Cabinet and Cabinet Minutes.
    CAB 66 War Cabinet and Cabinet Memoranda.
Foreign Office: FO 371 Political Correspondence.
    FO 800 Halifax Papers.
    FO 511 Consulate and Legation Finland, General Correspondence.
Prime Minister's Office: PREM 1.
Ulkoasiaministerio: UA 109.
War Office: WO 193.

Published material

British Documents on Foreign Affairs: Reports and Papers from the Foreign Office (Frederick, MD: University Publications of America).

The Development of Finnish-Soviet Relations during the Autumn of 1939 including the Official Documents 1940.

Documents on British Foreign Policy, 1919–1939, Series III.

Documents on German Foreign Policy, 1918–1946, Series D.

Halsbury's Statutes, 4th edition, vol. 12.

Labour Party Pamphlet *Finland: The Criminal Conspiracy of Stalin and Hitler* (1940).

Nazi-Soviet Relations 1939–1941: Documents from the Archives of the German Foreign Office (Greenwood, CT: Westwood Press.

Parliamentary Debates HC.

Memoirs and diaries

Churchill, Winston S. *The Second World War* volume 1: *The Gathering Storm* (London: Penguin, 1985).

Colville, John, *The Fringes of Power: Downing Street Diaries 1939–1955* (Sevenoaks: Sceptre, 1987).

Dilks, David (ed.), *The Diaries of Sir Alexander Cadogan O.M. 1938–1945* (London: Cassell, 1971).

Eden, Anthony, *The Eden Memoirs: Facing the Dictators* (London: Cassell, 1962).

Feiling, Keith, *The Life of Neville Chamberlain* (London: Macmillan, 1946).

Gripenberg, Georg, *Finland and the Great Powers: Memoirs of a Diplomat* (Lincoln, NE: University of Nebraska Press, 1965).

Harvey, John (ed.), *The Diplomatic Diaries of Oliver Harvey, 1937–40* (London: Collins, 1970).

Khruschev, Nikita, *Khruschev Remembers* (London: André Deutsch, 1971).

Maclean, Fitzroy, *Eastern Approaches* (London: J. Cape, 1949).

Macleod, Roderick and Kelly, Denis (eds), *The Ironside Diaries 1937–1940* (London: Constable, 1962).

Maisky, Ivan, *Memoirs of a Soviet Ambassador: The War 1939–43* (London: Hutchinson, 1967).

Mannerheim, C.G.E. *The Memoirs of Marshall Mannerheim* (London: Cassell, 1953).

Muggeridge, Malcolm, *Ciano's Diary 1939–1943* (London: Heinemann, 1950).

Pritt, D.N., *Must the War Spread?* (Harmondsworth: Penguin, 1940).

Tanner, Väinö, *The Winter War: Finland against Russia 1939–40* (Stanford, CA: Stanford University Press, 1957).

Wood, E.F.L. 1st Earl of Halifax, *Fulness of Days* (London: Collins, 1957).

Secondary sources

Monographs

Adams, R.J.Q., *British Politics and Foreign Policy in the Age of Appeasement* (Basingstoke: Macmillan, 1993).

Aster, Sidney, *The Making of the Second World War* (London: Deutsch, 1973).

Barros, James, *Betrayal from Within: Joseph Avenol, Secretary-General of the League of Nations, 1933–1940* (New Haven, CT: Yale University Press, 1969).

Bell, P.M.H., *The Origins of the Second World War in Europe* (London: Longman, 1997).

Beloff, Max, *The Foreign Policy of Soviet Russia 1929–1941: Vol.II 1936–1941* (London: Oxford University Press, 1949).

Carley, Michael Jabara *1939: The Alliance that Never Was and the Coming of World War II* (Chicago: Ivan R. Dee, 1999).

Carlgren, W.M., *Swedish Foreign Policy during the Second World War* (London: Ernest Benn, 1977).

Carlton, David, *Churchill and the Soviet Union* (Manchester: Manchester University Press, 2000).

Charmley, John, *Chamberlain and the Lost Peace* (London: Hodder & Stoughton, 1989).

Charmley, John, *Churchill: The End of Glory: A Political Biography* (London: Sceptre, 1993).

Clark, Douglas, *Three Days to Catastrophe* (London: Hammond, 1966).

Collier, Laurence, *Flight from Conflict* 2nd edition (London: C.A. Watts & Co., 1949).

Colvin, Ian, *The Chamberlain Cabinet: How the Meetings in 10 Downing Street 1937–9 Led to the Second World War for the First Time from the Cabinet Papers* (London: Victor Gollancz, 1971).

Connell, John, *The Office: A History of British Foreign Policy and its Makers 1919–1951* (London: Wingate, 1951).

Crowe, David M., *The Baltic States and the Great Powers* (Oxford: Westview Press, 1993).

Dell, Robert, *The Geneva Racket 1920–1939* (London: Hale, 1940).

Dickinson, Frederick R., *War and National Reinvention: Japan in the Great War, 1914–1919* (Cambridge, MA: Harvard University Asia Center, 1999).

Doerr, Paul, *British Foreign Policy 1919–1939* (Manchester: Manchester University Press, 1998).

Douglas, Roy, *The Advent of War 1939–40* (London: Macmillan, 1978).

Evans, Eric J., *The Forging of the Modern State: Early Industrial Britain 1783–1870* (New York: Longman, 1983).

Folly, Martin, *Churchill, Whitehall and the Soviet Union 1940–1945* (Basingstoke: Macmillan, 2000).

Gorodetsky, Gabriel, *Grand Delusion: Stalin and the German Invasion of Russia* (New Haven, CT: Yale University Press, 1999).

Haslam, Jonathan, *The Soviet Union and the Search for Collective Security in Europe 1933–39* (London: Macmillan, 1989).

Hill, Christopher, *Cabinet Decisions on Foreign Policy: The British Experience, October 1938–June 1941* (Cambridge: Cambridge University Press, 1991).

Isaacson, Walter, *Kissinger* (London: Faber, 1992).

Jakobson, Max, *The Diplomacy of the Winter War: An Account of the Russo-Finnish War, 1939–1940* (Cambridge, MA: Harvard University Press, 1961).

Jussilla, Osmo, Hentilä, Seppo and Nevakivi, Jukka, *From Grand Duchy to a Modern State: A Political History of Finland since 1809* (London: Hurst & Company, 1999).

Keeble, Curtis, *Britain and the Soviet Union, 1917–1989* (London: Macmillan, 1990).

Kennedy-Pipe, Caroline, *Stalin's Cold War: Soviet Strategies in Europe 1943–1956* (Manchester: Manchester University Press, 1995).

Kennedy-Pipe, Caroline, *Russia and the World 1917–1991* (London: Arnold, 1998).

Kirby, D.G., *Finland in the Twentieth Century* (London: C. Hurst & Co., 1979).

Kissinger, Henry, *Years of Upheaval* (London: Weidenfeld & Nicolson, 1982).

Kissinger, Henry, *Diplomacy* (New York: Simon and Schuster, 1994).

Kitchen, Martin, *British Policy towards the Soviet Union during the Second World War* (London: Macmillan, 1986).

Lamb, Richard, *The Drift to War 1922–1939* (London: W.H. Allen, 1989).

McLynn, Frank, *Fitzroy Maclean* (London: Murray, 1992).

Michie, Lindsay, *Portrait of an Appeaser: Robert Hadow, First Secretary in the British Foreign Office, 1931–1939* (Westport, CT: Praeger, 1996).

Middlemas, Keith, *Diplomacy of Illusion: The British Government and Germany, 1937–39* (London: Weidenfeld & Nicolson, 1972).

Munch-Petersen, Thomas, *The Strategy of the Phoney War: Britain, Sweden and the Iron Ore Question, 1939–1940* (Stockholm: Militärhistoriska Förlaget, 1981).

Namier, L.B., *Diplomatic Prelude, 1938–1939* (London: Macmillan, 1948).

Namier, L.B., *Europe in Decay: A Study in Disintegration 1936–1940* (London: Macmillan, 1950).

Nevakivi, Jukka, *The Appeal that Was Never Made: The Allies, Scandinavia and the Finnish Winter War 1939–1940* (London: C. Hurst & Co., 1976).

Neville, Peter, *Appeasing Hitler* (London: Macmillan, 2000).

Newman, Simon, *March 1939: The British Guarantee to Poland: A Study in the Continuity of British Foreign Policy* (Oxford: Clarendon Press, 1976).

Northedge, F.S., *The Troubled Giant: Britain among the Great Powers 1936–1939* (London: G. Bell & Sons Ltd, 1966).

Overy, Richard with Wheatcroft, Andrew, *The Road to War* (London: Macmillan, 1989).

Parker, R.A.C., *Chamberlain and Appeasement: British Policy and the Coming of the Second World War* (Basingstoke: Macmillan, 1993).

Parker, R.A.C., *Churchill and Appeasement* (Basingstoke: Macmillan, 2000).

Peters, A.R., *Anthony Eden at the Foreign Office, 1931–1938* (Aldershot: Gower, 1986).

Prazmowska, Anita, *Britain, Poland and the Eastern Front, 1939* (Cambridge: Cambridge University Press, 1987).

Prazmowska, Anita, *Eastern Europe and the Origins of the Second World War* (New York: St. Martin's Press, 2000).

Roberts, Andrew, *"The Holy Fox": A Biography of Lord Halifax* (London: Weidenfeld & Nicolson, 1991).

Roberts, Geoffrey, *The Soviet Union and the Origins of the Second World War: Russo-German Relations and the Road to War, 1933–1941* (London: Macmillan, 1995).

Robinson, Paul, *The White Russian Army in Exile 1920–1941* (Oxford: Clarendon Press, 2002).

Salmon, Patrick, *Scandinavia and the Great Powers 1890–1940* (Cambridge: Cambridge University Press, 1997).

Semiryaga, Mikhail, *The Winter War: Looking Back after Fifty Years* (Moscow: Novosti Press Agency Publishing House, 1990).

Shaw, Louise Grace, *The British Political Elite and the Soviet Union 1937–1939* (London: Frank Cass, 2003).

Singleton, Fred (revised and updated by A.F. Upton) *A Short History of Finland* 2nd edn (Cambridge: Cambridge University Press, 1998).

Steiner, Zara, *The Foreign Office and Foreign Policy 1898–1914* (Cambridge: Cambridge University Press, 1969).

Lord Strang, *The Diplomatic Career* (London: André Deutsch, 1962).

Taylor, A.J.P., *The Origins of the Second World War* (London: Hamish Hamilton, 1961).

Taylor, A.J.P., *English History 1914–1945* (London: Penguin, 1970).

Toynbee, Arnold and Toynbee, Veronica M. (eds), *Survey of International Affairs 1939–1946: The Eve of War 1939* (London: Oxford University Press, 1953).

Upton, Anthony F., *Finland 1939–1940* (London: Davis-Poynter, 1974).

Van Dyke, Carl, *The Soviet Invasion of Finland 1939–40* (London: Frank Cass, 1997).

Vehviläinen, Olli, *Finland in the Second World War: Between Germany and Russia* (Basingstoke: Palgrave, 2002).

Watt, Donald Cameron, *How War Came: The Immediate Origins of the Second World War 1938–1939* (London: Heinemann, 1989).

Wuorinen, John (ed.) *Finland and World War II* (New York: Ronald Press, 1948).

Unpublished theses

Doerr, Paul, 'Caution in the card room: The British foreign Office Northern Department and the USSR 1932–1940', PhD thesis, University of Waterloo, Canada, 1993.

Keene, T., 'The Foreign Office and the making of British foreign policy, 1929–1935', PhD thesis, Emory University, 1974.

Salmon, Patrick, 'Scandinavia in British strategy, September 1939-April 1940', PhD thesis, University of Cambridge, 1979.

Collections of essays

Bourne, K. and Watt, D.C., *Studies in International History* (London: Longmans Green & Co Ltd., 1967).

Bullen, Roger, *The Foreign Office 1782–1982* (Maryland: University Publications of America Inc., 1984).

Dilks, David, *Retreat from Power: Studies in Britain's Foreign Policy of the Twentieth Century*, vol 1: *1936–1939* (London: Macmillan, 1981).

Dockrill, Michael and McKercher, Brian, *Diplomacy and World Power: Studies in British Foreign Policy 1890–1950* (Cambridge: Cambridge University Press, 1996).

Hiden, John and Loit, Aleksander, *The Baltic in International Relations between the Two World Wars* (Stockholm: University of Stockholm, 1988).

Hiden, John and Loit, Aleksander, *Contact or Isolation? Soviet-Western Relations in the Interwar Period* (Stockholm: University of Stockholm, 1991).

Hiden, John and Lane, Thomas, *The Baltic and the Outbreak of the Second World War* (Cambridge: Cambridge University Press, 1992).

Militärgeschichtliches Forschungsamt *Germany and the Second World War*, vol. 1: *The Build-up of German Aggression* (Oxford: Clarendon Press, 1990).

Richardson, Dick and Stone, Glyn, *Decisions and Diplomacy: Essays in Twentieth Century International History: In Memory of Georg Grun and Esmonde Robertson* (London: Routledge, 1995).

Sharp, Alan and Stone, Glyn, *Anglo-French Relations in the Twentieth Century: Rivalry and Co-operation* (London: Routledge, 2000).

Wener, Bernd, *From Peace to War: Germany, Soviet Russia and the World, 1939–1941* (Providence, RI: Berghahn Books, 1997).

Journal articles

Anderson, Edgar, 'Finnish-Baltic relations, 1918–1940: an appraisal', *Scandinavian Studies* 54 (1982).

Aulach, Harinder, 'Britain and the Sudeten issue, 1938: The evolution of a policy', *Journal of Contemporary History* 18 (1993).

Bayer, J.A., 'British policy towards the Russo-Finnish War', *Canadian Journal of History* 16 (1981).

Beck, Peter, 'The Winter War in the international context: Britain and the League of Nations' role in the Russo-Finnish dispute, 1939–1940', *Journal of Baltic Studies* 12 (1981).

Bédarida, François, 'Britain, France and the Nordic countries', *Scandinavian Journal of History* 2 (1977).

Carley, Michael Jabara, 'End of the "low, dishonest decade": failure of the Anglo-Soviet alliance in 1939', *Europe-Asia Studies* 45 (1993).

Carley, Michael Jabara, ' "A situation of delicacy and danger": Anglo-Soviet relations, August 1939-March 1940', *Contemporary European History* 8 (1999).

Dilks, David, 'The Great Powers and the Nordic countries 1939–1940: Great Britain and Scandinavia in the "Phoney War" ', *Scandinavian Journal of History* 2 (1977).

Dukes, Jack R., 'The Soviet Union and Britain: the alliance negotiations of March-August 1939', *East European Quarterly* 19 (1985).

Forster, Kent, 'Finland's foreign policy 1940–1941: an ongoing historiographic controversy', *Scandinavian Studies* 51 (1979).

French, David, 'Perfidious Albion faces the powers', *Canadian Journal of History* 28 (1993).

Haslam, Jonathan, 'The Soviet Union and the Czechoslovakian crisis of 1938', *Journal of Contemporary History* 14 (1979).

Hjerppe, R., 'Finland's foreign trade and trade policy in the twentieth century', *Scandinavian Journal of History*, 18 (1993).

Jokipi, Mauno, 'Finland's entrance into the Continuation War', *Revue Internationale d'Histoire Militaire* 53 (1982).

Kaukiainen, Leena, 'From reluctancy to activity: Finland's way to the Nordic family during the 1920s and 1930s', *Scandinavian Journal of History* 9 (1984).

Lammers, Donald, 'Fascism, Communism and the Foreign Office, 1937–39', *Journal of Contemporary History* 6 (1971).

Lammers, Donald, 'From Whitehall after Munich: the Foreign Office and the future course of British policy', *The Historical Journal* 26 (1973).

Manne, Robert, 'The British decision for alliance with Russia, May 1939', *Journal of Contemporary History* 9 (1974).

Manne, Robert, 'The Foreign Office and the failure of Anglo-Soviet rapprochement', *Journal of Contemporary History* 16 (1981).

Munch-Petersen, Thomas, 'Great Britain and the revision of the Åland Convention, 1938–1939', *Scandia* (1975).

Neilson, Keith, ' "Pursued by a bear": British estimates of Soviet military strength and Anglo-Soviet relations, 1922–1939', *Canadian Journal of History* 28 (1993).

Parker, R.A.C., 'Britain, France and Scandinavia, 1939–40', *History* 61 (1976).

Parker, R.A.C., 'Economics, rearmament and foreign policy: the United Kingdom before 1939 – a preliminary study', *Journal of Contemporary History* 10 (1975).

Parker, R.A.C., 'British rearmament 1936–9: Treasury, trade unions and skilled labour', *English Historical Review* 96 (1981).

Polvinen, Tuomo, 'Finland in international politics', *Scandinavian Journal of History* 2 (1977).

Rich, David, 'Imperialism, reform and strategy: Russian military statistics 1840–1880', *Slavonic and East European Review* 74 (1996).

Roberts, Geoffrey, 'Soviet policy and the Baltic States, 1939–40: a reappraisal', *Diplomacy and Statecraft* 6 (1995).

Rotkirch, Holger, 'The demilitarization and neutralization of the Åland Islands: A regime "in European interests" withstanding changing circumstances', *Journal of Peace Research* 23 (1986).

Salmon, Patrick, 'Churchill, the Admiralty and the Narvik traffic, September–November 1939', *Scandinavian Journal of History* 4 (1980).

Salmon, Patrick, 'British plans for economic warfare against Germany 1937–1939: the problem of Swedish iron ore', *Journal of Contemporary History* 16 (1981).

Selen, K., 'The main lines of Finnish security policy between the world wars', *Revue Internationale d'Histoire Militaire*, 62 (1985).

Spring, D.W., 'The Soviet decision for war against Finland, 30 November 1939', *Soviet Studies* 38 (1986).

Stafford, Paul, 'Political autobiography and the art of the plausible: R.A. Butler at the Foreign Office', *Historical Journal* 28 (1985).

Stone, Glyn, 'The British Government and the sale of arms to the lesser European powers, 1936–39', *Diplomacy and Statecraft* 14 (2003).

Strang, G. Bruce, 'Once more unto the breach: Britain's guarantee to Poland, March 1939', *Journal of Contemporary History* 31 (1996).

Vihavainen, Timo, 'The Soviet decision for war against Finland, November 1939: a comment', *Soviet Studies* 39 (1987).

Walker, Stephen G., 'Solving the appeasement puzzle: contending historical interpretations of British diplomacy during the 1930s', *British Journal of International Studies* 6 (1980).

INDEX

An environmentally friendly book printed and bound in England by www.printondemand-worldwide.com

#0565 - - C0 - 234/156/11 - PB